The Ashes of Us

Ashley Baker

Genius
Book Publishing

Published by:
Genius Book Publishing
PO Box 250380
Milwaukee Wisconsin 53225 USA
GeniusBookPublishing.com

ISBN: 978-1-958727-73-7

250703 Trade

Contents

Dedicated to my uncle, Michael Boswell, and my aunt, Denise Clay, for loving Dad as I did.

"For Texas and Miss Lily!"- Judge Roy Bean

"Will you meet us in the ashes, will you meet us in the ache?"- Jan Richardson, Circle of Grace

Author's Note

If B.F. Skinner is right, and parents can make a child into anything, then my father made me imperturbable to blood, guts, and gore. As an anatomical and clinical pathologist, he brought me to his laboratory often, and set me to work, fetching slides or ferrying messages. His last call every night was to the overnight lab techs, reminding them to check the morgue temperature. This ritual was familiar to me as any bedtime story. I can still hear the timbre of his voice, and the quick click of the dial tone.

When I was old enough, he introduced me to his favorite game. Dabbling in forensics (especially if he needed cash, since private autopsies paid well), Dad would begin hypothesizing about the perfect crime. For him it was all fantasy, with no one specific in mind. To him, it was a riddle with a punchline—macabre and tongue-in-cheek. That was Dad. He'd debate the pros and cons of murder and I'd listen, not one to interject since I lacked the medical knowhow.

I listened to each vignette and judged them on their merits. Perhaps that's why I became a psychologist, since I learned at an early age to hold hard conversations in my mind, not my heart. Morbid material for a child, but I played the part. I was the witness and the co-conspirator, smiling at stories that should've scared me.

He died in 2023. This novel pays homage to the doctor and father he was. I hope with these words he achieves immortality. While the events in this novel never happened, the character of Dr. David McCall is very similar to Dr. John Garland Boswell, MD. May they both find their peace.

—Ashley Baker PsyD

Chapter 1

The Phone Call

The shrill ring of David's house phone jolted him from sleep. He flailed for the bedside table, knocking over a glass of water before managing to grab the receiver with both hands.

"Hello, this is Dr. McCall," he croaked, the taste of Guinness still sour on his tongue. He'd brushed his teeth, but Colgate was no match for malted barley and Fuggle hops.

"Hi, Dr. McCall. We are calling on behalf of Watauga Medical Center with regards to pat—"

"Is this about the... morgue temperature?" He blinked hard, trying to clear the fog. "I asked Sienna... she was supposed to check it before... before I went to bed."

His last call every night wasn't to family or a love interest. It was to the lab. As a clinical and anatomical pathologist, David's beauty sleep came easy, as long as he reminded his staff to complete their midnight task. The dead had to be kept cold. The alternative was putrid.

There was a pause on the line. A long one.

"No, sir. We aren't calling about that. We're calling about Addison McCall."

He shot upright, nearly dropping the receiver. Any remnant of sleep abdicated at her name. He thought back to those old public service announcements from the '90s. *Do you know where your children are?*

It used to be a punchline. Now it hit like a blow to the ribs.

The clock blinked 4:32 a.m. in red. Much too late for a courtesy call. He threaded his fingers through the phone coil, twisting them into knots.

"That's my daughter." His voice stilled, awaiting the worst.

"Can you confirm her date of birth?"

"Yes. February twenty-eighth. Nineteen eighty-five." He didn't hesitate. Best day of his life—still was.

"Sir," the voice softened, cautious now, "we're calling because she's been admitted. But she won't show up in the ICU registry. We've enacted law enforcement exception for her safety."

His stomach turned, his body understanding what his mind couldn't.

"She's been assaulted. The injuries are... significant. The doctors are taking every precaution. You're listed as her emergency contact. We wanted to let you know where she is." A beat. "Room ten."

There was the soft rustle of papers, and laughter flickering in the far background.

"The police are here. We needed to confirm her age. She's... nineteen, then?"

Sometimes she's nineteen, he thought. *Other times, she's five, missing her front teeth with fists full of tooth fairy money.* Time broke in strange ways when parenthood was involved. One look and he'd be transported to Addison at fifteen, wearing a golden homecoming dress and beaming at the camera. To love someone for a lifetime meant you could time travel at will. But this version of her, the one behind room ten's closed door, he'd never choose to revisit. Not in memory. Not in dreams. He already knew this night would change everything, as middle-of-the-night calls always did.

"That's right," he confirmed, already searching for his Levi jeans, spotting them rumpled on the floor. "Tell them I'm on my way."

David sprang from the bed and tripped over his cowboy boots. No time for his ostrich leathers. He yanked on his sandals. Cold or not, they'd have to do. The keys—where the hell were the keys? He was supposed to keep them by the door. Instead, they were God knows where, missing when a real emergency occurred. He dropped to his knees. There—half-buried under the bed. Of course.

David ran to the garage, flung open the Jeep, and scrambled inside. The engine growled to life. He reversed too fast, tires screeching as they revved against the dead grass. The sound tore through the early morning, the pavement screaming in protest.

Motor memory carried him from his Jeep to the hospital. The distance was only three miles from his driveway. He had worked at Watauga Medical Center for twenty years and could make the commute with his eyes closed. He blew past the Blairmont stop sign, foot on the gas, the frame rattling under the strain.

A dull throb bloomed at his temples. A leftover punishment from the four Guinness he'd downed, but he barely registered it.

A growing rumble of panic throbbed in his chest. Addison. Hurt. In the hospital. With police.

Each word brought a new wave of fear.

He screeched into the employee parking lot, yanked out his ID, hardly hearing the beep as he swiped in.

Slamming the brakes, he looked down. Was he wearing a shirt? Yes. Somehow he'd selected a clean long-sleeved polo, good enough for the September chill.

No time to wonder how. He was already moving.

Dr. McCall nearly hit the second-floor button out of habit, then froze. The lab was on level two. The ICU was on four. He stabbed the correct button.

The elevator stalled. He considered bolting for the stairs.

Then it lurched to life. Relief hit so hard, he could've kissed the floor. He swayed with the movement, half in the moment, half in shock.

The elevator doors slid open. David staggered from the elevator, his pace almost a sprint. He scanned the faces at the nursing station. No one he recognized was working, but their eyes held a recognition of grief. It wasn't fear they reflected, but a heaviness, like his sorrow might be contagious. They avoided eye contact, as if to imply that he wasn't just a man in a hurry. He was a dead man walking.

David didn't wait. He skidded down the hall, barreling toward the number ten that held his only daughter.

"Addison!" he called, throwing open the heavy door.

Inside, two Boone police lieutenants sat across from the new ICU doctor, the one fresh out of residency. Dr. McCall had shaken his hand at the hiring party, eaten a piece of stale Ingles cake. But none of that mattered now.

The men? Unimportant.

His gaze locked on a female social worker, her clipboard clutched in her hands. Helpful, sure, but that didn't register.

He didn't wait. He lunged for the bed, his eyes fixed on the IV line like it could tether him to reality.

Addison's hair was pulled back in a low ponytail. Wrong. She always wore it down, curly. Pale, with a red dot of blood across her forehead. This imitation only vaguely resembled the child he knew, the one who never tired, always outdoors with the sun as her solar battery. He scanned the crowd, his throat tight. Only one question mattered: how bad, and where?

He glanced around, disoriented, unsure of what to do next. His eyes locked onto the whiteboard, his heart sinking at the words no father should ever see for his daughter.

`Rape Evidence Collection Kit Obtained`

`HIV and Hepatitis B status and vaccination (STD kit ordered)`

`Recent consensual sexual encounters? Last menstrual cycle?`

Then underneath, words relevant to him.

`CBC, CMP, LFTs, UA, Urine Pregnancy, HIV`

He couldn't turn off his training, his mind working through which of the sexual assault nurses was on call tonight. He might not know her, they tended to circle in and out. The majority of his work, as head of the hospital laboratory, was limited to his bright-field compound microscope and rotating lab technicians. His logical mind flashed to DNA, samples, and ranges on a printout. His body revolted, not caring about data, not with Addison lying broken in the bed. A ribbon of nausea surged in his stomach, a metallic taste wafting in the back of his throat. His eyes drifted to the minuscule bathroom.

He swallowed the bile and clenched his fists, forcing his focus onto finding answers.

A red, swollen mark marred her left cheek. His chest tightened. Addison's eyes were shut, but the monitor tracked a steady heartbeat of 72. A quick scan gave him more. Respiratory rate, 16 breaths per minute. Blood pressure, 118/74. *Normal, that's good,* he reasoned.

A polite cough drew his attention. The flash of a white lab coat, the same standard-issue model hanging in his own closet, entered his peripheral vision.

"Hello, Dr. McCall. So sorry to see you again under these circumstances. I'm Dr. Sloane. I wanted to fill you in on what we know so far. I'm assuming this is your daughter, Addison?"

"Yes," he managed. David was surprised his voice worked at all. She was always Addison. Never Addi. Never Dee. Too headstrong to shorten her name. The only nickname she ever tolerated was Spitfire. It spoke to the mulishness that ran through their family, the instinct to make every disagreement a hill worth dying on. The same girl who used to climb trees just to grab the highest branch was now lying still in a hospital bed.

"Okay," Dr. Sloane began. "Let me summarize. Catch you up to speed. She arrived by ambulance at approximately 0330 hours. On admission, she was only partially responsive and unable to answer basic orientation questions. Physical examination revealed two fractured ribs on the left side, extensive ecchymosis across the chest, upper thighs, and back, a cracked central incisor, and signs of recent vaginal penetration with condom use. A full sexual assault forensic exam was completed on arrival." He stalled, letting his words land.

David's eyes darted, knees splintered. The social worker read the ruin in his face and pointed to the chair beside Addison's bed. He dropped into it, breath boxed in his chest.

"She's currently receiving IV fluids and a scheduled regimen of analgesics, including a loading dose of morphine," Dr. Sloane continued. "We've also administered prophylactic antibiotics and emergency contraception. We're monitoring for signs of internal trauma or delayed hemorrhage. Neurologically, she's stable, but sedated."

It felt more comfortable to label her symptoms with medical jargon, to tuck the raw anguish beneath a shield of clinical terminology. Broken ribs became thoracic fractures. Bruises turned into hematomas. The violation of her body translated into sterile phrases from a forensic report. Emotion was swapped for codes from the ICD-9 to keep everything contained.

"Thank you, Doctor," David said, his voice muted, his gaze

never straying from Addison's face. Her lips quivered. He ached for silence and space, for the private paralysis the news demanded.

"I need to finish my rounds," Dr. Sloane explained. "The officers can walk you through the remaining details. Once she's in the clear, we can talk discharge." He looked down at her chart. "Cases like these, best to recuperate at home."

Cases, rape cases, violent ones. The kind that leave women broken, stunted, alone. How could that include his Spitfire, his soccer star, his straight-A student, the one who never snuck out, always with her head on a swivel? It shattered all logic. He didn't belong here. She never did. A mistake of the highest order claimed the night.

David bowed his head, certain he was asleep, that all this was a fever dream or a nightmare.

Dr. Sloane placed a firm hand on David's shoulder, a gesture of support that was both practiced and genuine. "If you need anything, I'm here. Truly. Just give me a page."

David held back his tears. The kindness wrapped in professionalism almost did him in. It was the kind of grace doctors extended to one another in moments too heavy for words. He was grateful, but the weight on his chest made it impossible to speak. David granted him a small nod. For now, that was enough.

Dr. Sloane shut the door carefully, making sure it wouldn't slam.

The officers didn't waste time.

"Good evening, Dr. McCall," one of the officers said, his voice somber. "I'm Lieutenant Daniel, and this is Lieutenant Drax. We were the first responders to the scene. We followed the ambulance here."

He gave David time to absorb the words before continuing. "Your daughter was found in a field behind an apartment complex off Highway 105. There was a large house party winding down when we arrived. We secured the area immediately, roped off the scene to preserve evidence. Several partygoers were still there, but they were cleared out and interviewed."

He hesitated, shooting an uncertain look toward his partner. "It looks like your daughter made the call herself. Her phone was still in her hand when we found her. We've already started canvassing the area, trying to track down anyone who might have seen or heard something. We're working with the hospital to get her full statement when she's able."

He paused again, meeting David's eyes, his voice gentler. "We're going to do everything we can. In the meantime, we'll leave you with your daughter. Here's our card. Please call us when she's ready to give a full statement. We'll be your point of contact at the station."

Lieutenant Drax jumped in. "We can go at her pace, no need to rush. We will be busy with pulling footage from any nearby gas stations." His expression turned somber. "This won't be quick, Dr. McCall. But we'll help however we can. I, uh, I have a daughter about the same age." He stared at his hands and couldn't continue. It was implied, the shared bond of fatherhood and worst-case scenarios.

David rested his head in his hands, unable to reply.

The police filed out, their work done and dusted. Only the social worker remained. She kept her voice melodic, close to David's right ear. His head remained bowed. He couldn't look at her.

"Hi, Dr. McCall. I'm Cindy, head of Social Work. I'm sorry for what's happened. I just need to go over a couple of things with you."

He straightened, trying to summon what was left of his energy reserves.

She reviewed the paper on her clipboard. "First, I'll need you to sign a release form for any medical or legal inquiries. After that, I'll get you some information on local counseling services and legal aid. If you need anything else, just let me know."

She handed David a stack of resources that he couldn't read. The font looked blurry though his vision had always been 20/20. "I'll leave you with Addison now. If you need me, I'll be at the nurse's station until shift change."

With that, she turned and stepped out, leaving David to his grief.

Chapter 2

The Longest Night

Pensive thoughts swirled as he kept vigil by her hospital bed, drowning out the steady clicks and beeps. It was difficult to concentrate, and he'd worked in hospitals his whole life. All were versions of this one, a mix of badges, scrubs, and closed-toed shoes. David should be accustomed to the symphony of intercoms and IV draining, the bustle of codes and shift changes, but the noises startled him every time.

Skittish as they come, he chided himself, *but for good reason.*

His trap wire nerves were on high alert due to the one lying in the bed, breathing slow and steady, with eyes sometimes fluttering. The staff all knew him as Dr. David McCall, pathologist, head of the lab, but to Addison, he was just Dad.

David toyed with the idea of retiring to the beach, to join the flocks of snowbirds, even though all that heat made him flinch. Addison would be giddy, thinking of vacations at Dad's, filled with sandals and days spent lounging by the surf. They could replace the drip castles of old with salty margaritas, heads turned to watch the sun go down over the water. They could live like Jimmy Buffet, keep life simple with swimsuits and beach expectations. He wouldn't miss the biting Boone winters, or the way the town fell into hibernation until summer kissed the valley. Perhaps a taste of the salt life could offer the reset they both needed. David would endure the soaring home insurance and the quirks of Floridians if it meant seeing his daughter light up again.

He stroked her hand, the creak of the hospital bed bringing out all sorts of promises and bargains. Kübler-Ross called them stages. His came as a flood. A tidal wave of denial, rage, and bargaining tore through in under an hour, leaving wreckage behind. His only prayer whispered like a Rosary on repeat: *Please let her be okay.*

Addison was still, breathing on her own, but wheezing, vastly different from the hyperactive nine-year-old attending her first sleepover at Kylee's house. The 3rd grade Cross Creek crew stayed up too late watching *Goosebumps* on television and she couldn't sleep. Addison twisted in the sleeping bag until the nylon burned her skin. By three a.m., she shoved it aside and slipped downstairs. The call was quick. Kylee's mom squinted against the Cadillac headlights, arms crossed, curlers still in. The scowl was her goodbye. Addison slid into the car. The getaway was clean, but the shame rode shotgun.

The roads were quiet, the only sounds the steady click of turn signals and the low hum of traffic lights. In the dark, Addison blushed, embarrassed by her escape. She wrapped her hand in his and didn't let go until her nerves began to settle.

"It was the episode about the mask that wouldn't come off. It wasn't even that scary, but I just couldn't get it out of my mind." She looked out the window, her eyes pricking with humiliation.

"That's part of the deal, Spitfire," he reassured. "You need me, and I come running. Just say the word and I'm there. Middle of the night included."

They let the road lull them into a satisfied silence and by the time they got home, all that was left was a sleepy smile and heavy eyes. She murmured a thank you as he tucked her in tight, leaving her stuffed bunny to take the night watch.

It was easier to think of those memories than the present, with Addison wincing on her side, looking younger than her years. The vital signs monitor tracked her pulse and heart rate but couldn't assess all the damages done.

He had let go of her hand, but one glance at her long fingers with chipped purple polish made him reconsider. Lacing his fingers through hers felt like a cold handshake, but he held on tight, trying to breathe life into her through his touch. Yet with that contact, another memory arose.

"You should play the piano, Spitfire. You have the appendages for it. Look at these digits! You could reach across the room with these fingers. A keyboard wouldn't be a challenge for you."

"Dad, come on," she twinkled. "I don't have a musical bone in my body. And that includes my phalanges."

Her laugh was one of the greats, with an upturn at the end, but remembering it made more tears threaten to fall. His version of machismo wouldn't allow his daughter to register his tear-stained face, to burden her with his parental heartache. David understood there was no soft way to speak the truth, not with the trauma carved into her skin. Choking through sobs wouldn't help the conversation flow easier. David shut down the memory of her head tilted upward, the bubble of her laugh like sunflowers for the sky.

Don't think of it, he chastised. *Keep it together, you big idiot.*

Watching Addison stir made his body feel like blood was replaced with ice, chilling down his spine, making every warm thought turn frosty.

Cut me open, look at the micro level of my cells and what makes them tick, and you will find her there.

David felt her pain, every bit the same as when she cried as an infant, but now she'd surpassed him in what she'd had to withstand. Her pain would railroad David's once broken collarbone and make short work of his football-induced concussion. All were peanuts compared to Addison's list of woes. Even her double ear infections from living in the pool, and the greenstick fracture from soccer barely registered next to this. This pain had roots, changing her from the inside out.

A nurse came in to check her vitals, a look on her face that she tried to wipe clean. Sympathy flickered in her expression, mixed with a dash of pity, as heavy sentiments clashed with her practiced composure. Hospital staff were supposed to be neutral, calm, and curt, so she busied herself with the chart to regain her professional footing.

Then she cleared her throat.

"I'm so sorry, Dr. McCall. On behalf of all of us at the hospital, this just ... floors us. It didn't feel right not to let you know."

"Thank you," he murmured, uncertain on how to balance politeness with sorrow.

David wished for blindness, so he couldn't see his misery shown in the nurse's eyes. They mirrored it back to him anyway, a visage of sadness, multiplied by despair, the bottom of the barrel sinking further still.

The nurse offered her platitudes, then slipped out, sealing the hurt behind the door. David was thankful for the solitude, for the barrier between dusk and dawn. In the still hours before the town woke, David thought of Addison's soft baby hair that fell out in clumps. Sometimes, while holding her, a piece would drift into his palm, as soft as silk. He wished he had kept it, tucked it away in a baby book, pressed between the pages for safekeeping. He remembered the minute details of his daughter and tried to reconcile them with why he was here, sitting by her side while she lay in the false rest of heavy sedation.

The night before felt eons away, reflected only as a half-dream. He had debated calling Addison on Friday but remembered the boundaries they'd established. When she decided to extend her education from Watauga High School to Appalachian State University, he promised to give her space. Her entire academic career was limited to the 28607 zip code, but David was ecstatic she'd stayed close. He respected her rite of passage and agreed to avoid King Street and its plethora of watering holes. Klondike Café and Macadoos offered a weekend brimming in cheap draft beer and scores of students packed in tight. He left her to the underclassmen, unwilling to intrude.

Instead, David ordered a pizza and let the staleness of the work week drift away. He called Guinness Mammy's Milk and drank enough to prove it went down smoother than truth. It kept him full and satisfied, with just enough good sense to kill the trash TV and let the booze rock him to sleep.

Then he got the call in the night, the one parents dread, two rings and then rushed speech, and the knowledge that split his life into a distinct before and after.

He bowed his head into his hands, elbows resting on her scratchy blanket, and resumed his hushed prayers.

He watched her, still as stone, guilt settling in him like sediment. He felt cowardly, a helpless sad sack. Shame washed through his veins, fed by the blind spots that kept her hurting.

When push came to shove, and the tough got going, he felt frozen. It reminded David of the year he put in the pool, sometime around 1994 when Addison qualified for the 50-meter freestyle state championship. Though the neighbors had judged him for installing a pool in a ski town, he didn't care. Addison was part fish, and she needed a place to swim laps. Blairmont Drive would have to adapt.

The local kids would play Marco Polo for hours to escape the

July heat, a conglomeration of 11- and 12-year-olds running wild. David had been reduced to referee, calling out the occasional "No running!" from the sidelines. House rules meant Addison was "it" more than usual, and he'd watch as she treaded water. A girl down the street, Lacy Stevens, had the lithe body of a swimmer, leaning toward the point of concern. David watched as Lacy sat on the edge of the pool, scooting out of the water to avoid his daughter's careful grasp.

When Addison would question, "Fish out of water?" Lacy always replied "No!" with her hand over her mouth, hiding a Cheshire grin. The other kids would giggle as Addison wavered, carrying a handicap without realizing it. He should've shut that unfairness down, called Lacy a cheater or worse, but he capitulated. He consoled himself with the parental narrative of letting kids be kids, while his daughter dogpaddled in tight circles, never the wiser. Now, the memory felt prophetic, a warning that his logic could slip into pusillanimity.

But that was then. Now the call for courage was immediate. David exhaled, burdened by facts and by failure. Rape kits were on the periphery of his business, not as common as skin cells and carcinomas, more in the category of aborted fetuses and amputated limbs. Sometimes David felt like Victor Frankenstein, each broken piece suspended in formaldehyde, waiting for his verdict. He didn't let his mind drift to Auschwitz, not often. But on the heavy days, the parallels hovered. Limbs. Tissue. Damage. All of it laid bare, waiting to be cataloged. Waiting to be claimed.

Every day he investigated people's discards, a process that Addison nicknamed "grossing." She'd visit him after school and let the lab techs practice blood draws on her. David hadn't pressured her into helping but she obliged anyway, giggling with the would-be needle stickers, and laying her thin arm against the metal lip, bracing herself for the slight pinch. She sat patiently, squeezing the stress ball, as the unlicensed phlebotomists practiced poking her.

"I don't mind, I really don't," she assured them, and maybe she didn't, since they plied her with sweets and orange juice afterwards. She'd earned those rewards for keeping still and satisfying their practice obligations. David hoped that making her familiar with the hospital would draw her into the family business. He always wanted a practice that read like a law attorney: McCall and McCall, Clinical Pathologists, Inc.

Truth was, David just wanted Addison close. Medicine, with its grueling hours, promised extra bonding time. He imagined it, two microscopes side by side, content to pass the slides between them every day till the clock struck five. He'd play his music from the computer, and she'd tease him about Herman's Hermits and The Traveling Wilburys. In his daydream, they were a happy island of two, with matching letters after their name, the best of his DNA beside him.

Addison was more interested in resting her feet on his desk, doubling down on her math homework while he read the day's work, straight from the surgeons and OB-GYNs. After trigonometry was done, and book bag contained, they'd head over to check the biopsies and fine needle aspirations, the last duty of the day. There was only one rule for that second part of the day, and that was the specimen collect room opened only after a snack. Medical school had taught David to always eat before the biopsies were examined. That formalin-laced air could down any doctor in 15 seconds flat if there was no food or quick sugar to buffer it. Addison learned the lesson by proxy when he shared how he had hit the floor hard during his first rotation, a fall that left a small scar on his forehead and a trace of lingering humiliation.

David instructed Addison to don latex gloves and close the cytology boxes while she listened to him rattle off size and shape.

He only made her leave once, when a stillbirth came into the room in a larger than normal white bucket. Addison left without complaint. His job demanded detachment, precision, process. But that time, David cried, hoping the baby knew its mother wasn't mourning alone.

Now it was his baby that needed help. The courage he needed felt miles away, like a wish granted for stronger men.

Chapter 3

The Big Ask

A volcano of rage surged in his throat, bitter as bile. David's mind locked onto the faceless monster who hurt his daughter, the hell-spawned villain who'd ruined everything. The longer he imagined the man, the more his thoughts twisted into something violent and primal. A question mark with fists. A shadow with teeth. He didn't have a name, but David's fury carved space for him anyway, his enemy not yet recognized.

It wasn't the first time David had wished death upon someone. That dishonor belonged to a cretinous sixth grader named Adam. He had opined that Addison wasn't pretty because she didn't have pierced ears. David found her on his front stoop, her sobs raw and unsteady, and it took several minutes before she could find her breath again. That little shit and his stinky shirt would've been long gone if society didn't frown hardest on killing children. A shade of that old anger boiled up in him, quick as heat lightning, threatening to break down the door of his body and come out swinging.

Raising a child brought out a multitude of emotions that didn't seem possible, a cyclothymic rainbow of hurt and happiness that could turn on a dime. But the surest way to make a parental enemy was to make fun of a beloved child, and while Addison laughed it off, David gave that boy the side eye every time he saw him riding his bike. David's thoughts turned dark, and involved swerving to the left, even years after the incident was long forgotten by everyone but him. His vengeance carried a long leash.

So, as he watched Addison, it wasn't the first time he wanted to kill someone, but it was the only time David said it out loud. Trying to maneuver on the outdated cushion-covered chair was a challenge, and he thought of all the other sad sacks that had leaned into its bulk, trying to make sense of things. He talked to himself, a habit of solitary living, and he didn't always realize when his thoughts came up for air, making their way into the world before David had a chance to edit them.

"I think we should just kill the bastard. We could let the law take its turn on the wheel, but we'd be disappointed, Addison. The wheels of justice don't ever run smooth and take too long to come round."

The court was never kind to rape victims, even less so for the college set. The smug attorneys questioned the woman's outfit, alcohol level, and whether she really wanted it even if she said no. But the aggressor never got those questions. No, he'd just dress in his Sunday best with a fresh haircut and a smirk. And now, as much as David hated to admit it, the jury of her peers would see his fiery daughter as damaged. She would have to answer every question, reliving the trauma in the process. Once marked, those judgments didn't scrub off. Just enough would remain to knock her down a few pegs and make her question her worth. A scarlet letter, written in permanent ink.

David had been down the murder road years before in the spring of 1981. His best friend in medical school, Cormac, known for sporting a thick brown ponytail, had agreed to partner with him on the month-long elective at the West Virginia medical examiner's office in South Charleston. It was about a 45-minute drive from Huntington to the old school that housed the medical examiner's office. They had time to kill every morning and evening on that winding commute, the road stretching out before them, their eyes memorizing every switchback turn.

Cormac was a record buff with over 2,000 albums and a carver system from which he made great cassette mix tapes. They listened to Breakfast in America and Tom Waits on repeat, volume up high, taking those turns fast. It's funny how certain times in life have their own soundtrack. They spent their days reviewing dozens of cases and reading *Spitz and Fisher*. Maybe it was the commute, normal human curiosity, or two young would-be pathologists trying to feel important, but they spent the time to and from their post listening to songs and talking about killing.

If there was a way to get away with murder, they talked about it. They never had anyone specific in mind, in a way it was an application of the knowledge they'd learned in the medical examiner's office, a morbid means of decompressing. It was their own music group therapy, population two, listening to Springsteen wail about New Jersey and talking about coroner's reports. They limited that talk to the car, as if the open road let their subconscious free, allowing them to tiptoe to the dark side only while the mile markers kept time. Once their feet hit the pavement, they stuffed it all back in, putting on responsible faces like they did their white lab coats.

One case stuck out for David and Cormac. It was about a young man who was murdered by drug dealers and buried in a field way out in the boonies. He'd been out there for about a year, and there wasn't much left of him, only his skull with a big hole in it and a .45 slug rattling around inside. The guys were caught because one of them got busted down in Tennessee on a lesser charge and tried to get a reduced sentence by giving up where the body was. There's an easy lesson, cradled up in something everyone knows. David and Cormac agreed that it went down in the manual of ways to get away with murder. Don't involve anyone else and don't ever talk.

David added to his list of murder rules over time. He remembered watching that movie *Prince of the City*. There was a scene where the old detective said, "They will get you in a room and tell you I talked. Don't you believe them. I will never, ever, talk." But of course the kid does, and the old man never said a word. David knew how to keep a secret and he betted that Addison did too. The key was keeping it contained and not turning on each other.

The second thing he and Cormac learned from investigating death was no body, no crime. If there was no time of death, there was no rigor mortis or lividity to worry about, no stomach contents that needed examining. If a person made someone disappear, especially if they wouldn't be missed for a few days, were they really dead? They could've just split town. An alibi doesn't even have to be solid because the police won't have a good timeline since they have nothing to stack the deck against.

David thought back to O.J., certain that's what the football star was thinking before Ron Goldman complicated things. He'd go over and take Nicole. He'd kill her and stash her somewhere. Then he'd go home, get a limo, and fly to Chicago. When the kids woke up and realized their mom was gone, it would look like she'd run off. And when the police came knocking, all O.J. had to say was, "Me? No man, I was on a plane to Chi-town." David had it all ironed out while watching the news, certain that Simpson would be convicted till he wasn't. David felt queasy then, knowing exactly what the Juice had been planning all along, since it was what he'd do if the situation was reversed.

It was difficult to contemplate dark deeds while staring at Addison's face. Her freckles mapped out a constellation across her features, with the Big Dipper zooming over her forehead scrunched tight with concern. These treacherous thoughts didn't belong with her, they were reserved for the heaviness of life, and she was all light, touching down and making the world bloom. Until now.

She stirred, her face angling toward him. A ray of sunlight tracked down her cheek, making her eyes flutter. David squeezed her hand, heart lifting at the sign of life. But the relief was brief. The opiate cocktail was wearing off, and pain would follow in its chemical footsteps.

Her eyelids fluttered, and her mouth moved without sound. One hand twitched near the IV, fingers uncurling like she was relearning how to move.

"Hey, Addison," David whispered, unsure how to begin.

She turned her head, slow and uneven. A shallow breath. Her lips parted.

"Dad?" Her voice cracked, her brow furrowed with confusion. "Is that you?"

He grabbed her hand, careful not to startle her.

"I'm here, with you. It's Saturday afternoon."

She winced, eyes widening.

"What's wrong with my mouth?" The words slurred, her tongue fumbling for control. "Feels… wrong."

"You've been hurt. You're safe now."

She stared at him, then shifted. Her muscles twitched. She climbed higher in the bed, trying to gain back ground.

"Hey, hey. It's alright. Easy now, Spitfire."

Addison gasped, a ragged, strangled sound.

"No. I heard you. I wasn't dreaming. You said he should be dead." Her voice cracked. She had caught every word. Her face pressed to the bedrail, eyes flicking back and forth, restless and unreadable.

"Could you kill him and get away with it, Dad?" She inhaled, and winced, the words costing her precious effort.

"Is that what you want from me, Addison?" He didn't know she'd been listening but was glad that she had been, knowing that the darkness kept them covered, a snow globe of two, talking about things daylight shouldn't know.

"You're the smartest person I know." She stopped, breath coming in short. "End this for me. If not, he will get away with it or do it again." She stopped, started, words easing in and out. "I need closure. He can't hurt me or anyone else again." She gazed at him, eyes certain, lips pursed tight. "And I need you to kill him." No hesitation was found in her voice, no hedging of bets, no pauses.

He was a sucker for her. He always had been.

"Whatever you need, Spitfire. If that's what it takes, consider it done."

She turned from him. The gown jerked at the IV line, tugged skin. Her breath slowed. David's mind pulled—heat, then static. A blade of thought sliced through the haze.

His motive for murder was simple, she asked him to do it. If this was the price of her peace, he would pay it, not in prayer, but in deed, with both eyes open.

He'd pay it in blood and live with the echo.

Chapter 4

Mommy Dearest

Addison was ready for discharge. He helped her to her feet, guiding her into the bathroom. Her steps were small, fragile, like each took everything she had. He thought he heard a sob before the shower swallowed the sound. He shifted his weight, uncertain if he or a nurse should intervene. David listened for something more, but only water rushed on. He told himself to move, to speak, but stayed rooted. This was just the beginning, and he was already behind.

He busied himself with reviewing her medications. They'd given her a hefty dose of the high-powered pain pills, a bottle of Norco 10/325s, so the worst of this nightmare might not be over yet. He debated knocking on the closed bathroom door but decided against it. He didn't want to imply she needed help or treat her with kid gloves. He wouldn't rush her, and he'd let her lead the way. The best way to address vulnerability is to give her a long leash and the freedom to make her own choices.

When she came out, David scanned the room for a hospital bag before realizing all her clothes were bagged and sealed as evidence.

He blushed and pivoted to the orderly pushing a wheelchair. Addison was dressed in scrubs, her wet hair hanging down her back. He hadn't thought to bring her new clothes, and a burst of shame coursed through him.

David made a wheel motion with his hands, avoiding her eye contact. He'd bring the car around since she couldn't walk far in her hobbled state. She gave him a nod, ready to get the heck out of Dodge, tired of the stiffness of the hospital bed. The orderly waited, his sturdy hands gripping the back of her chair. She eased into her seat, going slowly, avoiding any sudden movements.

They could've been leaving after an appendectomy or kidney stones. All discharge procedures looked alike. But the tell in this case was that no one said a word. David realized in the elevator that they'd enacted a silent scene and it felt completely appropriate. *Not a word was spoken, the church bells all were broken* spun in his head. He pushed the button for the ground floor, his hunched shoulders almost grazing his ears.

Nothing would be the same again. The elevator walls pulsed around him, the dim lighting flickering in time with the pounding in his chest. Claustrophobia rose, with tiny pinpricks of sweat blooming across his skin. He was trapped, not just in the cramped metal box but in a life that no longer felt like his own. Everything was unfamiliar, a seesaw of vertigo where once logic reigned.

As the elevator hummed downward, the lyrics to *American Pie* looped back in his head, uninvited and insistent. *This will be the day that I die.* The words clung to him like a warning, filled with memories of death, destruction, and the truth that history repeats.

When the doors opened, David stumbled into the hallway. His breath, once controlled, now came in sharp, uneven spurts. He was gasping, not only for air, but for control. A simple elevator ride felt beyond him, his body no longer agreeing to be calm, cool, and collected.

He found his Jeep and sank into the front seat. It took effort to turn on the engine and warm up the car. He grabbed the steering wheel, wishing it would morph into a sturdy life jacket and take him far from here. He shook his head, dispelling his thoughts, just in time for his ex-wife to make her appearance.

David parked in front of the E.R., vying for space with Addison's mother, in her dark SUV outfitted for a celebrity funeral. As the years got longer, Mary's cars did too. This Aspen looked solemn and limousine-long, its windows so darkly tinted it seemed like it was self-driving. The only thing amiss was that the mammoth was parked crooked. Mary barreled out of the car, barely jamming on the brake, heading straight for their daughter, laser eyes initiated. She spied Addison shifting in her wheelchair at the front entrance, and dashed as fast as her five-inch Ferragamo shoes could carry her.

Mary moved to help, but Addison cut her off with a look that snapped *I'll do it myself.* Her mother stepped back, taking in every bruise.

"Oh God. Addison. Baby…" Her voice broke. She reached blindly for the wheelchair, fumbling with the handles like she couldn't remember how it worked. Her hands trembled.

David watched her face crumple. One hand flew to her chest, the other hovered in the air. Her nails, polished and perfect, clawed at nothing.

"Mary," he shouted, moving closer. "Here, I've got you." He steadied her by the arm before she could collapse onto the pavement. For a second, he didn't see designer clothes or foundation caked tight—he saw a mother flailing. Then the mask snapped back in place, and all he saw was fury again.

"David," she swerved, glaring at him through her Cartier shades. She side-stepped out of his grasp, her frown deepening as she stared, entirely unimpressed.

"There you are. Nice of you to call me." she sneered, her voice devoid of anything welcoming.

Whenever Mary looked at him, her eyes lingered a beat too long. His collar. The crease in his slacks. The sheen of oil on his forehead. Her mouth tightened at the soft belly, the weak chin. That stare burned, cold and clinical. She turned away, lip curling, taking stock of every flaw. Her thoughts seethed, a storm held back by nothing more than her skin.

David pictured steam coiling from her scalp, eyes wide and glassy, set to a high boil. Her face flushed. The scowl wasn't a grin or a grimace, just heat. They weren't married anymore, but he could still read her. Like a busted clock, stuck on seething.

"Mary," he began, "I, did, um, mean to call. I really did." She glared at him, urging him to choose his next words carefully. "I guess the hospital beat me to it."

She clenched her keys in her fist, gripping them like a weapon. David stepped back. With Mary, her moods could turn on a dime.

"I just loved learning that my only daughter is at the local hospital hours after she was admitted." Her sarcasm slashed through the air, enough to make Addison recoil.

David ate his words, but his face voiced his reply.

So now she wants to play the role of perfect mother?

His eyebrows rose sky-high. At the end, Mary was the one who stepped out of the marriage. No, stepped is too nice; she barreled out the back door. But David acquiesced easily. No tears, no fights, not even half-hearted ones, which is why her complaints remained current.

David had given up on the marriage like it was already six feet under. He could've tried to change but conceded instead, letting their vows slip through his fingers, free from Mary's heavy expectations.

"I even have this damn flip phone that I carry around with me now," she continued, searching haphazardly into the depths of her Louis Vuitton saddlebag. "Just in case I'm ever needed. In case someone should *need* to reach me." One tear streaked down her painted cheek. The sunglasses hid most of her pain, but not all.

David curbed the urge to placate her tears. Reflex, not affection. The death of their marriage wasn't all her fault. Mary viewed perfection as an attainable goal, with competition found on every corner. Mary's decorations at Christmas rivaled the Ramsey family in the Tour of Homes video, shown over and over to recover the lost child. David was expected to have custom suits, attend dinner parties, and label acquaintances as friends. He yearned for the simple ways of a bachelor—a plastic tree on top of the TV, peanut butter sandwiches, and time after work spent reading secondhand novels. With Mary, they were never allowed to rest. She led a manic life, with no breaks, centered by her core of rigid inflexibility. She was beautiful but got caught up in the spiderweb of comparisons and became the spider herself. When David realized what she'd become, he untangled himself quickly, already feeling like his blood had been drained.

"Don was the one who picked up the phone, so really I was third on the need-to-know list. I've been instructed not to shoot the messenger, but really it's such bad form, David. Even you should have the decency to feel embarrassed." She sniffed, her nostrils flaring slightly, and shifted uncomfortably in her heels.

Oh yes, Don the anesthesiologist, affectionately known as husband number two. Mary had left David for a richer upgrade who promised her a lavish L.A. story in a small-town setting. David knew something was amiss before the final act. She was distant, then cold, until she barely came home at all. She left the rings on the kitchen table, without a note. It was a bleak ending to a marriage that had once been lovely.

The woman before him burned with blame, her eyes flint and

fire. But once, she had hair braided all the way down her back and an easy smile. A sunflower was tucked behind her ear, just recently plucked. Back then, her fanciest shoes were leather thong sandals. When she made eye contact, she leaned forward, close enough to touch the buttons on his shirt.

"I'm Mary, it's nice to meet you," she said, and she meant it. Her eyes raked over David, a smile resting on her puckered mouth. He'd been half-asleep at that residency picnic, dead on his feet, until Mary lit a fire the lukewarm beer couldn't reach.

She'd settled into a part-time job as a paralegal, but she winked as she introduced herself.

"I went to law school just long enough to know I'd rather be wedded and bedded." Her neck tilted, graceful and deliberate.

David smiled. He hadn't expected charm with teeth.

"All I need is a porch, a garden, and a man with a plan."

Right then, David was ready for something home-grown.

Their courtship was impatient, their love a whirlwind that felt just right. David scooped her from her aunt's place and settled her into his rental, a placeholder until they could build her double-decker dream home. Her taste in wallpaper made his eyes ache, but he learned early not to say no. They shared cheap coffee and danced barefoot in the kitchen. His head swam, not from textbooks, but from Mary.

Now she lived in Banner Elk with the wealthy, in a custom brick cabin—three stories, all stainless steel and brand new. David heard she and husband number two grew award winning azaleas, and Don made more money than she could spend. She wore his salary on her shoulders, draped in mink coats and dresses meant for off-Broadway performers. She performed well, but not perfectly, the understudy promoted to the big time, who still fumbled her lines. Underneath the lip liner and blush lay the woman he lost.

"You're right, I should've called," David shook his head. "It was so late and I wasn't in my right mind. But you're right. Bad form."

His admission did little to soothe her haughtiness. Mary scowled at him and swung her purse too close in his direction. She adjusted her sunglasses with two fingers, slow and deliberate, then pulled a compact from her purse and reapplied her Chanel Rouge Noir, checking the corners of her mouth without a word. No shimmy. No glance. Just calculation.

David shook his head.

She used to smear ChapStick across her mouth with the back of her hand, grinning before sliding next to him, closer than close. Used to leave the house in cutoff shorts and his old shirts, hair still wet, singing louder than the stereo to Rick Dees and the Weekly Top 40.

That girl had no time for mirrors. No patience for makeup.

And now she looked at him like a stranger.

"Well, what else do you have to say for yourself? Cat got your damn tongue, David?" Her voice rasped like gravel.

David sighed, resigned. There was only one option.

"I'm sorry, Mary. As always, I'm just sorry."

David's defeat felt real, but it always did. He was set back on his heels when he learned she was gone for good. David could've sought an eager replacement. He was still middle-aged, and made six figures, which could tempt pretty nurses into courtship or more. But he didn't have it in him to remarry. All that pomp and circumstance was a younger man's game. Plus, the best thing he got out of the deal was looking at him now with help-me eyes. It was easier to placate Mary than fight her.

"Addison, honey," her mother turned, her ire momentarily paused. "Let me take you back to my house. I got everything ready, *Us* magazines, Sprite, whatever you need or want. Let's get you settled in, and David can get your medication and spare clothes while you rest up." Mary's voice was sweet but laced with that mother-knows-best tone that made Addison retreat. A scowl settled on his daughter's lips, sharp enough to shoot holes through every gentle suggestion.

Mary's love could be relentless, the kind that smothered even as it tried to soothe. Addison's eyes flicked to him, a silent flare in the aftermath of the battle—*too much, Dad, she's too much.*

"Mary," David said, stepping in with practiced restraint. "Let Addison wait in my car. We'll talk more easily without an audience."

This wasn't the place for a fight, not here under the awning of the ER, with patients milling in and out. The hospital was his ground, but not for this kind of combat. And once Mary's anger took hold, there was no shut off valve.

"You no longer have the ability to tell me what to do. Or have you forgotten that too, David?" Mary countered, though her eyes studied Addison's face. She took stock, noting the bruise on her cheekbone, the way she held herself stiffly, favoring one side. Mary bit her lip hard, the fight leaving her face. She reached for Addison, all mother now, her fingers gentle and tentative.

That moment stirred an image, long buried.

Mary had once been easy to love. Hell, he'd fallen for her two days after the picnic, when he saw she had *The River* album on vinyl. She loved Dan Fogelberg and the Eagles, often shucked off her clothes while still singing the chorus. All that poetry and those music notes swirled above their heads, curating a soundtrack for the young doctor and the girl with the quick smile.

Addison's voice cut in, quiet but firm.

"Dad's right," she said. "Let me rest with him for a bit. He's closer. Then I'll come to your place. I promise."

Mary stamped her foot, debating the terms offered.

"Fine," she acquiesced. "But this isn't over, David. I need to be kept in the loop. It's required! I suggest that you do a better job of remembering our divorce terms, or I'll have Lenny serve you again for a good reminder."

She spun on her heel, storming toward her car without a single look back at her old family, fury trailing in her wake.

"She'll cool off," Addison said, the words worn smooth from a childhood spent running interference. She stood, wobbling. David caught her elbow as they moved toward the car, leaning into the wind.

Addison was used to her mother's mercurial moods. She was in kindergarten when the divorce was finalized, though the seams had split long before the final dissolution.

For Mary, motherhood was a mantle she could put down at will. When David came home from the lab, she grabbed her keys, off to a blowout or to buy Burberry at Libba's in Blowing Rock.

Her brand of love came in fragments. David saw it early, in the way baby Addison tracked her mother to the door. The diaper was clean. The clothes were immaculate. But attachment is hardwired, and the wound tangled, fast as invasive kudzu.

David made up the difference. He sang more nursery rhymes, danced to Paul Simon, and laughed enough to cover the moments of sadness. Parenthood wasn't in the flashy monograms or baby books. It was in the minutia, the tender moments like the scent of Addison's just washed hair or her warmth next to him on the couch. He would've told Mary that if she had stayed, but the only sound was the door slamming and the engine roaring to life.

In the end, David gave Mary what she wanted—the keys to a newer, shinier life.

Addison slouched against the front seat window, her head tipped toward the cool glass, shoulders sagging from the weight of the exchange. David mirrored her posture, his body folding into the quiet. Wrinkle-free and starched, Mary had pulled no punches in their latest dust-up, leaving them both wrung out.

"She loves you, you know," David said, his voice a balance between truth and restraint. "It's just that her love doesn't have boundaries or limits."

He didn't expect it to land, not really. But he needed Addison to believe that, in spite of the co-parenting and the emotional baggage, he wasn't carrying old wounds. For most of her life, their mutual indifference had worked. They'd traded matrimony for monotony and found a suitable consensus. Now the script had flipped. The exes were back in orbit, sorting through trauma they hadn't created.

"Let's just go home," Addison sighed, her face tight with frustration. "We can't keep relitigating your divorce, especially since Mom always wins." She shot him a small grin, and the dash of levity went straight to David's heart. Maybe all was not lost.

"Roger that," David replied, his voice even, his gaze fixed ahead. He pressed the gas, the road stretching ahead, both of them silent, unable to tackle any more heartache.

Chapter 5

We're Only Going to Do This Once

Addison wasn't tired. She rejected all of David's fatherly concern, keeping her eyes on the floor, while she removed her shoes and socks.

"I don't feel anything," she murmured, curling on the living room couch David had inherited from his father, a supple leather that just got prettier as it aged. Like her, David thought but didn't say.

"Don't you want to change?" David suggested, eying the borrowed scrubs that were designed for function, not comfort.

"I do, and I will. But first, I need to get this out." She covered her chest with her arms and shivered. A small ball of a girl, in need of a blanket.

David tossed her a throw cover and poured himself two fingers of Woodford Reserve. He glanced as Addison sank further into the leather. Then she straightened, adopting a posture fit for a therapist.

"It's fresh. Might as well give it a go before I crash."

"Okay, if you're sure." He didn't need to elaborate; the need for a post-mortem chat was understood. It was something he admired about her: the way he could speak plainly and trust she'd pick up on what wasn't said. She tracked his glass and tilted her head. He got the message, and played barkeep, pouring her a generous helping.

Addison downed the bourbon in one shot, shooting it straight but placing the glass down gently. He'd never seen her do that and found himself shell-shocked. It was like watching a pet utter a "how do you do." He wondered if all parents felt that way after they witnessed their kids doing something they didn't teach them. A reprimand sat heavy on his tongue, but his hands betrayed him, reaching for the bottle instead. He was relieved that they didn't tremble as he poured them both a hearty refill.

"We're only going to do this once, Addison. I think that's all you and I have in us, right? Give me the details so I can see it straight. I need all you've got if I'm going to fulfill your request. Start where you want but help me see it." He said it like a detective might, trying to sound certain, but there was a faint crack in his tone. If she noticed, she didn't let on.

David braced against the table, knowing he needed the details, but wishing there was another way. He gripped his glass, ready to buckle down into the horror of it all. They say there's no way but through, but to hear the story in its entirety had the power to break him.

"Let me start with what I remember of him. The boy that... hurt me... he's someone I went to school with, Dad. Someone I sort of know." Her voice was steady, though sorrow wove itself through the edges.

Her rapist was someone she knew. That information set him back on his heels a bit. David pictured her assailant as someone big and burly, an outsider, the type found at the end of long alleyways. The kind of trouble that wandered into town and wreaked havoc, not someone who pumped gas and collected a paycheck. Certainly not someone who worked at a local restaurant or was a former patient's son. He realized he was holding his breath.

"It's Josh, Josh Raynor. We graduated from high school together, at least I'm pretty sure he graduated. He was on the fringe, kind of with the weed smokers and drop-out kids."

The name didn't bring up any faces, no long-ago crushes or politician's sons. David registered that the boy and Addison were likely the same age. Not yet adults. Free-falling on the cusp of life with too much freedom and just a slapdash of responsibility. His stomach turned, thinking of her rapist's youth. Still young enough to carry a fake ID. Wishing him dead felt harsh. Then again, evil didn't have an age limit.

"I didn't mention to anyone that I know who did this. I think even when I wasn't really aware, I wanted to set things right." David observed her, wondering why she was thinking of the long con when her thoughts should be on recovery. By omitting his name, Addison had been thinking of a plan before his bedside question.

"You didn't mention him in the ambulance?" He studied her again, thinking of a girl raised by a black widow, wondering if venom could fill up a vein. It struck David as cold that Addison had known all along she would ask for this outcome and had taken deliberate steps to make it happen. He'd believed her answer was spontaneous, a reaction born in the moment. But now it felt rehearsed, a plan set in motion before he even asked. A subtle chill moved through the room, clinical in its calculation.

"No. This story I am telling now, the truth, is only for you. I was too far gone when the police came to give them anything."

She met his gaze and didn't blink. Not once. David did a double take. The softness was gone. Addison squared her shoulders, spine straight, voice steady. She wasn't a kid anymore.

"You'll have to meet again with the police to do a formal interview."

She grimaced. "It's fine. This is the part I'll leave out."

From what he knew of psychology, David understood this: trauma didn't spill like a story. It came in drips, then floods, jagged and out of sequence. But Addison didn't start in the middle. She went back to when they were kids. David let her words settle, laying the gritty groundwork.

Before she could shave her legs, Josh was a wannabe basketball player rejected from the JV team. He had pre-purchased the school jersey and was wearing it until the moment he was cut, as if his enthusiasm could add bonus points that kept him on the roster. He was amped up on school spirit, but wasn't much of an athlete, despite being taller than the other boys in his grade. After his public rejection, Addison never saw Josh at school functions, nor did he rock any more of the school-sanctioned gear. Instead, he ran a scheme selling pencils to ADHD kids who always forgot their school supplies. He gained weight and wore nicer shoes, a subtle sign that business was booming. Addison kept a wide berth around him; he was one of those kids whose name evoked a reputation as dirty as a curse word.

"I wonder if his life would have been different if he made that team." Her voice caught. David resisted the urge to cradle her in his arms. He knew that once he reached to comfort her, she might not be able to finish.

"Seems to me, Addison, that something was broken long before he got cut from JV basketball."

She shrugged a reply. Josh had a friend named Paulo that he sat with at the back table of the lunchroom. They never ate, just scowled and acted like school was a prison that only let them out for work detail. Josh skipped classes in middle school and Addison would see him on the empty football field, kicking rocks alone. She wondered why he preferred to lounge in the hot sun, alone with his thoughts instead of algebra.

"I felt bad for him, Dad. He seemed lonely. He wasn't teased. In fact, it was worse. I'm not sure anyone paid much attention to him at all."

David pictured Josh as that convenience friend, the one you partnered with in class when no one else was available, the name scribbled last minute on the team list. The boy equivalent of an afterthought. He wondered what that anonymity would do to someone's psyche, and he stifled a shudder.

"Word around the locker room was that Josh had graduated from selling gum and mechanical pencils to dealing low-level drugs. Nothing hard, just enough to give him an edge. It didn't make him popular, but it gave him a kind of… murky relevance. He dated this girl named Mikra whose best quality was an interesting name. They sometimes made out by the lockers, and most people laughed. To me, he was barely a peer."

She inspected her fingernails, a flash of doubt covering her face.

"I wasn't one of the ones who laughed at him. At least, I don't think so."

Quick with reassurance, David murmured, "Don't go blaming yourself, honey. Noting his PDA is the least of our worries here."

"I know, I just, I keep thinking I gave him some sort of reason. A motive for all this hate. But I can't figure it out. If I did something wrong, I don't know what it is."

She swirled the bourbon, her voice stopping and starting, until she cleared it and began again.

"At Watauga, he was in on-level classes, while I was on the AP track. I think our lunches were at the same time."

David pictured a cafeteria, with Addison and the other athletes on one side, separated by a long table. Josh was a towering figure ordering from the cafeteria line, wearing clothes two sizes too big with eyes that never drifted from the tray. David imagined a giant, who preyed on younger children and lived on a five-finger discount.

"My friends said his crew cut class to hit the G Billiard's room, that smoky spot where the loners played pool. It's still open, but I've never stepped inside. Not really my scene."

David pictured Addison during her senior year of high school. She'd traded swimming for soccer and kept her sweeper skills tight during Saturday games. Then he imagined Josh, working the pool table, his presence menacing, fiddling with his pack of Marlboro Reds.

Their trajectories couldn't have been more different. Hers pointed forward, filled with promise, friends, and plans stacked sky-high. His sat still, stalled somewhere back in the blur of middle school. Maybe that kind of contrast was enough to make resentment take root. Maybe watching her move through life with ease made him feel like the universe had miscounted, like he was owed a celestial mulligan. To Josh, it might've seemed fair to take what wasn't his, to reach for the closest piece of Addison's world and claim it out of spite.

She paused, trying to force any other memories to resurface.

"I think he drove a red pick-up truck, something rusty and vintage. Those are all the details I remember." She took another sip, mechanical. Drained, she cupped her chin and set down her glass, her face dim in the low light. Liquor couldn't soothe what came next.

"That's good, honey. That's enough to give me some context. You're doing great. I know this is hard."

She nodded. David didn't know how to nudge Addison into the next part. But if the devil is in the details, then last night's nightmare was the opening act. He needed to know, but he wished he could fast forward through the retelling. It would only hurt them both.

"I was supposed to meet up with Lisa last night. That was the plan." Addison wove the blanket tassels between her fingers, slow and distracted.

David remembered Lisa from Addison's high school days. Her choice in roommates hadn't impressed him. You couldn't pick your kid's friends, but Lisa wouldn't have cracked his top ten. He preferred Katie, the studious one, who harbored pre-med dreams, or Stephanie, the one with enough weight on her to keep her humble. She and Addison played a card game called Rat Slap and Stephanie never let Addison win. David respected that. Girls with gumption were always his preference, and Stephanie made it clear —size be damned, she was no one's sidekick. David had pushed Addison to room with someone resourceful, someone sharp.

But Lisa, with her bright pink lipstick and mind full of fluff, made Addison the logical choice for a roommate. Lisa was cotton candy, drifting through the world, watching it spin. Addison shrank around her, swapping sarcasm for lipstick and dark nail polish. He wanted to warn her about the Barbie types, the ones whose beauty fades and end up settling for less than they'd promised. But before he could voice his complaints in full, the paperwork was signed and dorm rooms arranged for the happy bundle of two. His unspoken wishes remained firmly in the rear-view mirror.

Mary played interior designer, stringing up lavender lights and complimenting their blended wardrobe. She took care of the décor, then vanished before David arrived. He was left with the heavier, harder parts.

He'd carried their boxes up three flights of stairs, every step a swallowed sermon of caution. Jokes, smiles, a well-worn mask of support was all he offered out loud. David remembered Addison walking him back down to the lobby, the weight of goodbye tangible in the moment. He couldn't relinquish his world to a girl more absorbed in command hooks and color palettes than in Addison's best interest. He'd lingered by the stairwell, heart thudding, aching for a reason to stay. But the air turned cold, stealing the moment with its frost. When his fingers touched the door, it felt less like a knob and more like a verdict. With every stride, the knot in his stomach cinched tighter.

Look what happened when he left.

"I was supposed to meet her at this kegger off Highway 105. She said it'd be a chill mix of upperclassmen. I wasn't sold, but I didn't have anything better going on. I'd already blow-dried my hair, and the dorm was buzzing with everyone pregaming."

She stumbled, memories sharp-edged and fast. Her mouth opened, but the words tangled. She regrouped, speaking through clenched teeth.

"Lisa loaned me this one-shouldered top," she said. "I was hoping to see this guy from Calc—he'd mentioned the party." She glanced down. "I wore my Uggs." She shrugged, but the gesture was hollow. Her thoughts were nowhere near crushes. This wasn't a story built on butterflies.

"Lisa bailed last minute, but I went anyway. You know how it is at ASU. I'm not ever lonely, not really." Appalachian State had gotten its nickname "high school with beer" due to the number of Watauga High School graduates who stayed close to home and their favorite snowboarding haunts. While some found it stifling, Addison felt safe, surrounded by yearbook photos, now tinged with liquor-sweet breath. She never worried about getting lost, as she'd been down the same roads at nineteen that she did at twelve. That made her stand up straighter, feeling out her surroundings and calling them known.

"I made it to the party and started looking for someone I knew. It was packed, people everywhere, spilling out onto the lawn. Somebody put on old-school Sublime." She smiled, then it slipped. That was the last moment untouched by sadness.

"I saw Josh by the speakers. He caught me looking and kind of lit up, like he thought I'd come say hey. I didn't. I was just trying to find a place to stash my coat. Plus, we weren't really on small-talk terms."

Living in Boone meant constantly shedding clothes, removing scarves and hats until her real outfit could be displayed, hidden under layers like a corset. With the town sitting 3,300 feet up, the cold rolled in quick. Locals carried jackets, gloves, or an ASU beanie. No one needed reminding. Even spring wore snow tires.

"I worked my way into the kitchen but it was disgusting. Someone had spilled hunch punch all over the floor. I went to the sink to grab a Solo cup, but the one I picked was too sticky to use. I turned to grab a cleaner glass, and that's when Josh handed me a drink."

"It was strange, seeing him up close. I remembered thinking he had long eyelashes for a boy. I hesitated, but I took the cup he offered me. The other ones were so dirty, and it seemed safe enough."

She collapsed onto the couch, her body sagging at last. Her voice sputtered in broken fragments, slow and uncertain. David thought of a toy winding down, drained of all backup reserves.

"I know better, I do. I went to all the D.A.R.E. meetings, and I barely even drink. I just... wasn't thinking, Dad."

Her voice faltered at the end, shame tugging at her posture, trying to pull her under.

"The drink was strong and salty, like a cloudy margarita. He said, 'That one's yours,' and told me the lime vodka was at the bottom, so I should drink it all. It seemed weird, being told how to drink a cocktail, but I went along. I didn't know this would... that it..." Her voice hitched.

David's jaw locked. He gripped the side of the couch, knuckles tight, ready to pounce on an enemy who wasn't there. He'd given her a spiked drink. That alone was reason enough to die.

Her story after that became disjointed. An attorney could trip her, make her slip and stammer. But David just listened, seeing a college tragedy come to life, the star someone his heart recognized.

"I stepped outside. There was a bonfire in the yard, making it hard to see anyone clearly. There was fire that looked too bright, the orange and red flames mixing and the smell of lighter fluid." She shivered, even though she was recalling heat. "I was stumbling around. At one point, I was on my knees in the dirt. I don't even know how I got there."

After that, time was a black curtain, refusing to yield until she woke up two yards from the party house, wet with the early morning dew. Her body had one signal to send, over and over, pain running up and down every vertebrae. She registered the dampness on the ground and her mind couldn't make sense of why she was outside. She couldn't isolate the pain, her heart beating overtime, afraid she was paralyzed then reassuring herself she wouldn't hurt this badly if she were.

"I tried to move, but all the air in my body was just gone. I thought I felt my phone in my hand, but my mind wouldn't connect to my fingers. I was so scared. Even my thoughts weren't working."

Tears tracked down her face, the hurt from both the memory and the present coursing through her.

She found her phone in the grass with a barely held charge and called 911, then waited to hear the sirens.

"If I can just hear those sirens, I'm gonna make it, listen for them, can you hear them?" She whispered it over and over, clinging to the hope that staying conscious would get her saved.

When she got to that part, David broke. He sat beside her on the couch, tears pouring down his face. She'd been tossed aside like trash, left there to decay, staring at the sky for rescue that came too late. David's nails dug into his palm, half-moon indents cutting into his skin with rage. Addison lay next to him, her wails rising to the ceiling. They wept together for a long time, letting the sadness wash over them both until despair had its fill and could find other hearts to break.

She didn't remember how she ended up in the grass. In some ways, that spared her. Having no memory is better than post-traumatic stress disorder and snapshot images that won't fade with time. But she would be forever curious about the most important night she couldn't remember.

This made David think of a study he read long ago about rape victims. It said that prognosis is increased by those that fight. Even if they lose, the idea that they gave it their all protected them against seeing themselves as broken. Addison hadn't been given that chance, and he wondered if that would help or hurt her.

He summarized the second act. The police interviewed the party goers, but details were scant. It was a large party, with moderately intoxicated students, the ground littered with cans and firewood. There were no real leads and her assailant had been careful. David side-stepped using any details, just letting her know the gist of what he was told at the hospital.

The question for Addison wasn't who raped her. She remembered seeing Josh before the night disappeared. The question for Addison was why. Like all victims, she thought if she could understand it, she could release it. She felt like this was someone else's story, that she was the main character picked out of a lineup but didn't belong.

"I don't understand," she whispered. "One minute I was at the party, listening to 'What I Got,' and the next... I was in the grass, trying not to black out."

She shook her head slowly, eyes unfocused. "I don't remember the ambulance ride. But I remember the nurse. She had a comb." Her voice cracked.

"She had to hold me up," she said, staring at the floor. "I couldn't even stand on my own."

She reached the point where words stopped coming. Her voice cracked, then faded into silence, and David knew the rest was something she'd bury deep inside. There was no Band-Aid, this was a deep cut, a hurt that demanded to be felt.

He patted Addison's head because it was the body part that didn't hurt. When they were all cried out, they became two people again, just breath and bone, slumped on a secondhand couch, wondering how the world could be so cruel and still keep moving.

"It's okay, Addison. Now it's time to rest."

David held her until her eyes flickered, the bourbon weaving a sleepy rhythm through her bloodstream. He stroked her back in small circles, until it was time for Mary to take over.

❧

HE WORE THE WEIGHT OF THE DAY ON HIS BODY. IN THE shower, he scrubbed hard, wishing he could remove dead skin and the last 24 hours. He reminisced about the old guard way of doing things. Country folks got used to holding their own court of right and wrong, their sense of cowboy justice secured. That appealed to David, as a fan of classic westerns. As long as there's been violence, there's been vengeance, the yin and yang of life's underbelly.

That kind of eye-for-an-eye died an early death, maybe too early. Judge Roy Bean would've called it justice with a spine. There was a time you could gather the right men, ride out with purpose, and set a thing straight. No questions asked. No permission needed. Just grit, God, and a loaded gun. Or at least, that's how it went west of the Pecos. A shotgun and sidekick were the only prerequisites to death by duel.

Addison had given him the starting point. He already had an

address, a rap sheet, and time after work to explore all he didn't yet know. The best part of his job was the 8-4 work schedule. David had flirted with the idea of going into obstetrics and gynecology in medical school, all drugged up on other people's happiness and rooms full of smiles. Then he realized that would keep him full of other people's families instead of his own. He chose his work for the details but now appreciated the short hours of a pathologist. David would cobble together the story of Josh from small town gossip, as accurate as a digital watch, and use his free time to fill in the blanks.

Lucky for him, his memory was almost photographic, 'cause he sure as shit wouldn't be writing anything down.

Chapter 6

A Man With a Plan

I f there are 50 ways to leave a lover, there are 150 ways to kill a man. The ways aren't complicated, but the not getting caught packs a stiff punch. Dr. McCall gave himself a pep talk, locker room speech heavy, about seeing the case from the top down, without letting anything cloud his thinking.

The morning sun shone tepid. The birds sang, and the sound of a lawn mower echoed in the distance. The day awoke, same as the calendar said, but David felt hollow.

He was surprised that his emotions weren't set to a higher boil after the nitty gritty of Addison's story. David dug around in his brain, but felt calm, a plateau, no spikes, no hills. He evaluated his feelings, leaning into them easily, first like they were made of drywall, and then harder, full strength.

Anger was the first feeling up to bat, itching to tip the scale toward hate. Most men got lost in the weeds when words like rape and violence entered the room. The TV was full of kooks who mistook opinion for fact, all puffed up with their own beliefs and not much else. The enraged father on a moral crusade was a familiar trope—storm in, burn it all down, walk out with hard-earned glory.

And those who went down that road got no judgment from him. It would be easy to get there, thinking about what was taken and who to blame. But anger, he knew, was kerosene. It burned fast, no brakes, no mercy, until everything in its path was reduced to ash. A skyscraper of rage, blazing hot, ready to topple buildings and even the score.

He'd long since said goodbye to anger; it left in a trickle and took with it the idea that life was easy or fair. Once David figured out not to expect life to go his way, the rage highway puttered out without a fight. He didn't want to be angry. He'd need to be calculating, less emotion, more analysis. One chance at Josh was all he'd get, and it wouldn't help Addison if David was rotting away in prison and she was left to process two traumas alone.

He swilled his coffee, a headache pulsing on the horizon. Last night's bourbon had tipped the scales from tipsy into too much. Between the burn of liquor and the weight of Guinness, he needed a day to sweat it out and lie still—what Sundays were made for, if not salvation.

Next came sadness, anger's side-swiping cousin, ready to let loose tears that were brimming with DNA. Melancholy could cover whole lives with a sheet not easily freed.

That's why people can sink into sadness because it's a trap that catches you like quicksand. Before you realize it, you're already sunk. He chuckled, realizing he'd said his thoughts out loud again for the kitchen walls to hear.

He'd always been the type to get all cried out. For David, it felt like there was a set amount of tears he could shed, and he figured the depth of his sorrow had been spent in the hospital, watching Addison's raspy breaths. He saw himself by her bed, head hung low, and the image zoomed in on him without restraint. Sadness wouldn't sneak up on him; that son of a bitch had already worked its way in, draping everything in a blue tinge. It was a staple now, enough to motivate, but not enough to bury him.

Scowling, David placed his mug in the sink, choosing not to wash it out even though he knew he should.

And happiness? There was none of that to be found here; that would be saved for the long road ahead and rainy days. His grandfather was a part-time farmer who told him that most ordinary people are happy for the sunshine, but he felt the most thankful when it rained. That piece of wisdom stayed with David, reminding him through every thunderstorm to be grateful for crops that grew and gutters that overflowed.

Happiness, though, was the worst of all emotions because a taste of it was all you needed to get you going, as addictive as any dopamine spike. It carried people through life's peaks and valleys, always a step ahead but just out of reach. It was the biggest liar of all, feeling so good until it was gone, leaving David twice withered and worn, haunted by the ghost of something that had once made him smile.

Now, he wanted numbness and that's what he'd found, as he set the time and place to conduct his biggest plan. Nothing ventured, nothing gained—and nothing felt.

With his feelings tucked up and put away, safe in their respective corners of his heart, he moved back to the living room, taciturn in the loveseat.

He'd picked up two calls from the hospital and police after dropping Addison off at Mary's McMansion.

The tests came back that Addison wasn't a virgin before the rape, but enough trauma had occurred to call it forced. David wasn't surprised by what he heard, since she'd been serious as a seventeen-year-old could be about her high school boyfriend. His name escaped David now, that's how important her paramour had become in the timeline of her life. While his name couldn't be conjured, David recalled how he'd once shaved a big A for Addison in the back of his head. David saw that tribute and tried to contain his laughter but failed. Acne scarred and skinny, he lasted for about six months before Addison's good sense caught up with her.

As a father, he tried to stay on the periphery of knowing too much. The details blurred by choice, but he remembered her giggle when the boy came round, like sunlight streaming through clouds. There were hundreds of hushed phone calls with her best friend late into the night, a dead giveaway that something was changing and forming before his eyes.

But David knew that whether she was a virgin was something juries focused on, not fathers. He wondered if the trauma would change her romantic trajectory, turning her away from men, marking them all as the enemy due to one man's violence. She'd get no argument from him there. David couldn't name a good man outside of John Wayne or Jimmy Stewart, and they were make believe. In the movies, the heroes were easy to spot. They carried double-barrel shotguns, rode into the sunset, and wore their manhood like lily-white Stetsons, souls clean as the hats on their heads.

In the real world, he believed the Mayor of Margaritaville said it best: *Good times and riches and son of a bitches I've seen more than I can recall.* People underestimated Bubba, pegged him as booze-soaked and beach-bound, but there was wisdom in that songbird sailor—the kind that knew not all men, or their desires, were created equal. More prophet than beach bum, if you asked David.

Addison's love life was never at the forefront of his mind. If pressed, he'd hope for a young, professor type. A man with solitary hobbies like reading and a disinterest in sports. The kind who preferred elbow-patched sweaters and good coffee, content to spend holidays by the fire shooting the shit with her old man.

When you're young in the saddle, you hope your children will lead an adventurous life. For some, that spelled temptation for parents to transfer their desires for fame and fortune onto their progeny.

But David had always yearned for a simple life for Addison; a low mortgage rate, sleeping in, a lazy cocker spaniel lounging by a fire full of wood; all the creature comfort pursuits. A man who came home from work on time, after earning an honest wage, solely focused on keeping her happy. Someone who liked good music and wouldn't mind sharing a bit of her with David, letting him tiptoe around enough to stay relevant in her life. As easy as the image of Addison's future husband was invented, he disappeared, and David wondered if it meant her whole future was a mirage.

His thoughts drifted, as concrete as smoke and twice as fickle. He understood why it all felt so tangled. The high-stakes game of murder had come to play a hand at his table, and he was looking straight down its throat. David could dumb it down, label it homicide, or revenge, all synonyms for something lighter, soaking in vocabulary like premeditation and probable cause. But it was murder in the end, wielding the scythe, dripping in finality, and deserving of its name.

To do the deed demanded that he tap into those old perfectionist tendencies reserved for the time of grade point averages and upper residencies. All doctors liked playing the odds, set on a future geared for the best and the brightest. David was no exception, waltzing into medical school with everything to prove. When he realized he was one of many valedictorians in the room, the embarrassment was hard to shake, as was the gut punch of learning each student was only a placeholder among the greats. That realization took his pride and shifted it a little, made him feel off balance and hungry for approval.

He tried to summon that old hunger now because in this one thing he needed to be better than anyone at any time, a magnum opus, a summa cum laude of a plan. He wished he could call up Cormac, spinning and sinking into their old plans, but this road he had to shoulder alone.

David devoted his whole life to researching slides under a microscope. How different could it be researching a person? He knew all the ways the body could kill an individual, cells magnifying at lightning speed till the future was already written on a headstone. The body always kept the score, and he knew its map by heart, the skin and organs weaving a tale that could keep everyone guessing.

Addison mentioned the possible suspect to no one other than him. At the time, she was dizzy, but when the world snapped her back, she left Josh's name out of her mouth. The rape kit only showed signs of trauma but no semen—he'd worn a prophylactic. David lapsed into medical terms because the word "condom" and "daughter" didn't seem to belong in the same sentence. He refocused on the first clue. Josh Raynor. A basic name, no evil found in the cadence, in the flow. Simple to read on a spreadsheet, or a report card, no mention of the mutation kept inside. A flaw of corruption, causing him to rape and pillage, concealed under a common moniker.

He'd watched enough *Sopranos* to know that the first step in this journey was to know thy enemy. Season four had just begun on HBO and was sure to provide some instructional ideas. David knew from the made-up mobsters that his initial hurdle involved understanding his target and learning his shadows before striking.

David reviewed his first assignment: establish a pattern of Josh's movements, find the consistency, then look for a way in. But first, he'd settle Addison in at home, keeping her safe until the world was empty of any threat. He glanced at the clock. Two and a half hours before pickup, plenty of time to begin. Whether she was nineteen or three, his duty was the same: to fend off every monster, whether they hid under her bed or prowled down the street. All were fair game.

Chapter 7

Repercussions

His neck felt stiff, turned all kinds of wrong on his pillow. The sun announced its appearance, not quite bright, and David felt the schedule of the day melt onto him. The need to shower and shave sat on him like a blanket, a holdover from last night's restless sleep. His tongue felt scratchy, like carpet, his stomach threatening a coup if he didn't rise and shine soon. Reluctantly, David kicked the covers away, sad to say goodbye to his sleep-warmed bed. Monday morning came too soon, though his day job would have to wait. The hospital had granted him a week reprieve. He'd mentioned sick leave, but the HR worker took offense, saying the hospital would sort it out on the spreadsheets.

"Just take time to help your daughter heal, Dr. McCall," she concluded. While her sentiments were kind, having strangers know his daughter's personal details seemed intrusive. His instinct was to keep Addison protected, but her assault was now public knowledge. And gossip, once released, could never be contained again.

David sighed, stretched, and pulled himself up, if not by his bootstraps, then with sheer resolve.

The warm shower lulled him into a daydream, the focus set squarely on his old psychiatric rotations. David had gotten a C in the class, a blemish on his near perfect report card, put there by his father and his old man's opinions. His father spoke in the tone of a lecture, each word a swift verdict, opinions cloaked as undeniable truths. Those colloquialisms seeped into David's worldview, lurking in his subconscious, surfacing only at the most inopportune moments. Maybe if he'd voiced his father's failures more clearly, his grades might've improved. The mental health advocates he knew often traced problems back to early childhood schemas and primal scene trauma. Psychiatry had its own default: when in doubt, blame the parents. Had David known this, maybe he'd have spoken up sooner.

He'd tried to land far from his father's guidebook to raising children. His Dad's playbook was as strict as a military-made bed, letting no one shuck off work or blame good intentions. David and his brother Mitch were raised to respect their elders, with the unvoiced message being that their elders were always right. He voiced as much until his professors silenced him, reprimanding him to listen more and talk less.

But his father *was* the kind of man who kept his emotions buried deep, a fan of hard work and gender stereotypes. No matter what era the timeline showed, for his father the household was firmly set in the 1950s. His mother played her allotted role, her only vice packages of Pall Malls, sucking them down, a restlessness so at odds with her stalwartness. David used to think his mother smoked fast so she wouldn't be tempted to argue with his father, her cigarette a placeholder for words unsaid and blood on a bitten tongue.

His old man dreamed of hot dinners, bouffant hair styles, and a house full of silence until he deemed his family could speak. Always the strong and silent type, his father preferred to let all responsibility fall squarely on his shoulders, allowing the world to weigh him down until he forgot what it was like to rest. He worked longer hours than anyone at the factory, always the last to call it quits.

David flirted with the same desire, to take Addison's pain and make it his. At least that way he could control it. But that was a sure way to get burnt out, and unlike his father, he had no built-in reprieve. His dad's favorite pastime was listening to his Motown records, music all bubble gum easy, a direct contrast to his rigorous approach to life. The Supremes and the Temptations belted out a happiness never felt in their family's three-bedroom ranch. The records made David's head hurt while he struggled to reconcile Marvin and Tammy with his father who rarely smiled.

"Ain't nothing like the real thing baby, Ain't nothing like the realllll thing," his father would hum, and just as quick turn his attention toward a rebuff, all rolled eyes and well-timed huffs.

After watching a man bear storms without a tremble, watching others slip past duty was a betrayal of the highest order. David postulated that the mentally ill clients on his psych rotation just needed structure and consistency, but he learned that clashed with humanistic theory. He withheld his observations, but had difficulty relating to the lost ones, who'd given up on showering, leaving themselves to rot. That lack of empathy might be why he was drawn to pathology: less talking, more doing, and no human contact. Just the puzzle of cells, waiting to tell him all their secrets, speaking to him in terms of A, B, AB, and O.

Toweling off, he realized he had no clue how to face the trauma waiting upstairs. Woefully unqualified and out of lectures, David wished he'd listened instead of dismissing analysts as kooks and quacks, seeing them as little more than charlatans with degrees, just a step above osteopaths. He favored the meatier sciences, ones with compounds and order, not childhood trauma and head nods. With no plan B, David felt the weight of every dismissed alternative pressing down on him.

With middle age comes the knowledge that you don't know shit. He pondered how an English grandparent might cure an illness, something hot and comforting. He curated a vision of Mrs. Doubtfire, a movie he and Addison had watched on repeat in her youth. David dressed in workout gear and bounded down the steps to the kitchen. His pantry held packets of old mint tea, long expired, though it seemed improbable that an herb could go stale. He stirred in the sugar and found a pack of Biscotti. He debated on whether to arrange it on a tray, but that felt like overkill.

He made a cup of strong coffee and brought his newspaper crossword puzzle to the kitchen table, alongside his breakfast offerings. Many mornings had been spent doing crossword puzzles together when they couldn't sleep in. After a quick scan, he was relieved to see Addison's trauma hadn't made the *Mountain Times*—one less thing to worry about. Satisfied with the breakfast, he waited for her review, but she didn't come down, despite her eight-a.m. class.

The school would be lenient once they knew. They probably already did. Still, he'd ask Mary to take the lead. She'd know who to call, whether the dean of students or each of Addison's professors. Her web of connections would make it easier, and he was grateful for the chance to step back. He had other duties that warranted his attention.

But for now, what was the next right step? Should he knock on Addison's door? Let her sleep? In the end, he just sat at the kitchen table, jittery, while the tea cooled beside him.

David couldn't remember the last time he took off work. His boss hadn't called yet, nor would he. If David made his numbers, Dr. Rudger kept their interactions hands off, ever the stoic business-man. David kept the lab in the black with surgical biopsies, attending tumor board, and turning over frozen sections fast. He'd never required sick leave because Addison had always been healthy, a side effect of attending public school where she caught everything there was to catch by the age of eight.

Addison rarely caught so much as a sniffle, even in Boone's harsh winters, which left most folks battling pneumonia, bronchitis, or laid up in the hospital. The town seemed to fall apart when the temperature dropped into the teens, the snow a mountain of tissues from the shared sickness of indoor living. David developed a mild hand sanitizer addiction, stockpiling tiny vials to survive until spring's pardon.

If Addison did catch the winter crud, she refused to be babied, calling herself a lone wolf and watching junk television in an Appalachian State hoodie until it passed. Her mother's attempts at caring for her only drove Addison to David's, where she could recover in peace. He didn't want to hover but couldn't leave her alone with the residual pain and memories that wouldn't quit.

David scanned the downstairs closet, hoping to find a jigsaw puzzle with all the pieces. When Addison turned 13, and drifted inwards in the way pre-teens do, David bought hard-ass jigsaw puzzles, 1000-piece ones with rainbows or flowers that all looked identical. With a mind engaged, she was tempted to spill bits of herself, giving away more than she intended. He always let her put in the last piece and she would smile widely, alight with accomplishment until it was on to the next one. What felt like a trick to get her to talk more became a shared enjoyment, which in the parenting world was a bonus point you could take to the bank.

On the top shelf lay an unopened box of a snow-white tiger, each piece discolored but only slightly. Cream versus beige versus white—this one was a doozy. He poured the puzzle onto the table, finding each of the edge pieces, content to wait her out.

Around noon, he heard the pitter patter of socked feet on the steps. It reminded him of a secret she had kept.

Right after her eighteenth birthday, in the heat of June, David noticed Addison had started wearing socks everywhere. It was out of character. From the time she could walk, she did it barefoot because she loved the feel of dew-laden grass on her toes.

He was the opposite. David hated that feeling, the slime of it, mud creasing against the back of his soles.

But now his nature-loving daughter had taken to wearing socks, all day, every day.

"Why are you wearing socks? Take them off."

A small yellow rose bloomed on her ankle, the ink still slick with Neosporin. David licked his thumb, leaned in, and rubbed at it. Nothing happened. The rose stayed put.

"It's, um... it's real." Addison came clean. She was never one to wiggle out of an untruth. "I'm pleased with it," she stated, daring him to make an alternative observation. "And I waited till I was legal." She poked her chin up in defiance, anticipating a fight.

She found one.

"They say there's a correlation between tattoos and lost IQ points. I'd say that one cost you ten."

Her face looked like he had struck her, and she murmured that for her, a yellow rose meant accomplishment. From her first swim award, through every science fair ribbon or dean's list ceremony, David had given her yellow roses for all.

"Red is for romance, and pink is for princesses. But you, Spitfire, are my yellow rose of Texas. One of a kind." A bouquet of yellow roses awaited her in the soccer championship, with David behind them, showing the many faces of paternal pride. He stood confused, thinking that the tattoo was a tribute but not one he would've picked.

That was a moment he should've done differently. Parenting is a

series of mistakes and missed chances, but nothing stung more than
hurting the one person he vowed to protect. That recollection
wasn't even the worst of his venial sins. Every mistake he made lived
somewhere in him, a running list of where he'd come up short. But
if he twisted himself just right, held the line, stayed present, maybe
there was still time to improve.

Or maybe he was destined for failure. Like when she was four at
the local waterpark. They'd waited an hour in the thick heat for the
tube ride, sweat slicking their skin, boredom gnawing at every edge,
wedged together in a line packed to the gills. Then, at the last
moment, Addison's mouth was full of screeches. David had thought
about grabbing her, hauling her onto the ride with all the force of
his fraying patience. But worse than her screams were the groans
and admonishments from the other tired parents.

Instead, he dragged all thirty-five pounds of her down the line
and hoisted her back to Mary. In a theme park loud voice, he
announced, "Here, take your daughter. I've discovered we are
raising a freaking coward."

Turns out there's no age limit on looking gutted, head down,
eyes awash with tears. The memory still made him cringe, recalling
Addison's face flushed with shame, her unhappiness an anchor on
his heart.

While he tried his best, he knew there were copious moments
like that in the past nineteen years, little injustices that pierced her
soul, that left him achy with regret.

She stood in the kitchen, hair a bird's nest on top of her head,
in an oversized sweatshirt and athletic shorts.

"Got any coffee? "Addison yawned. David looked at the tea but
decided not to mention it.

"Yes, and it's hot. Have a seat, I got brand new creamer."

She eased into the seat, her knuckles white. Every movement
lacked urgency, each shift a reminder of her aches. Conversation

slowed and he nudged her in the direction of the dining room. Addison saw the jigsaw puzzle and her mouth shifted, forming anew. She registered that he connected the edge pieces and got to work organizing the rest by color. They both sat together in silence, not touching but close.

&.

THREE P.M. ALREADY. DAVID HADN'T NOTICED THE TIME SLIP. They'd spent the entirety of the afternoon in quiet companionship, piecing the shapes all together, and it didn't take a shrink to see why that appealed to them both.

Chapter 8

Modus Operandi

They say a new normal expands after trauma descends. It was a shift, like furniture moved overnight. Familiar, but not quite right. A lessening of what was.

After a week of recuperation, boredom crept in like rot, and Addison itched to rejoin her life, to shake off the decay. She stood at the kitchen counter, coffee in hand, her battered backpack slumped by her feet like an old dog. Her hair was damp. She'd showered. That was something. She looked up and gave him a smile, faint and frayed.

David lit up too fast, like he'd heard wedding bells instead of weariness

"I can drive you," he offered.

She turned, already stepping away, the coffee steaming in her hand. "I'm good."

He watched her, wanting to give her a strong send-off. Nothing came

"Bye, Dad. I'll see you later."

The screen door screeched behind her, swallowing the words in his throat. The emptiness of the house reverberated around him. It was time to regain his routine, even if an edge of shell shock remained.

David made it to the lab with time to spare and found his red oak desk buried in slides. A graduation gift from his father, the mammoth was too grand for his cramped office. It was made of solid mahogany and built to outlive him and every patient he would ever diagnose.

The stack waiting for him could fill a sixty-hour work week, more than he had expected after a short absence. He had kept in touch with the lab, mostly to help triage the flood of priority cases from Dr. Stegal.

Stegal didn't wait. He called three times a day, each one louder than the last, his voice a chainsaw of opinions trying to hustle cell division.

As David started sorting through the pile, the lab manager, Craig, stepped into the room, pausing awkwardly in the doorway.

"Uh, hey, Dr. McCall," Craig said, shifting his weight from one foot to the other, clearly unsure of what to say next.

David barely glanced up, already bracing himself. *Oh no, here we go again.* Another round on the let's talk trauma wheel. He didn't want to be the guy who was a walking tragedy, yet here they were, labeling him.

"Hey, Craig," David said flatly, hoping it would end there.

"Everything okay?" Craig asked, his voice uncertain. "With... um, your family?"

David nodded quickly, still focused on the slides. "Yeah, just getting back into the swing of things. Catching up."

Craig hesitated, looking for his window. "Right, right. Well, if you need anything, just let me know."

"Thanks," David replied, his tone clipped. He didn't want to drag this out. There was work to be done.

He dictated his notes rapidly, wondering how the transcription staff managed to keep up. He didn't have time to review his thoughts until he took a break for lunch in the doctor's lounge, surprised to find it empty.

He checked the time. Two. His stomach answered with a low growl. He grabbed an apple and tried to re-center his mind, ready to switch gears for the rest of the day. The lounge had plenty of snacks to keep him going until the end of his shift.

The lounge looked like a library, more suited to long lectures and cigars than doctors popping in for a quick caffeine hit. The room stirred up memories of blurry-eyed nights and underlined text, the grind of residency clinging close. Middle age had stolen the stamina he once poured into caffeine and sleepless nights. But today, it snapped him back to the murder club rules, born in that haze, a sharp puzzle to keep him awake.

He could hear Cormac's deep baritone in his mind, declaring them canon, as if they were talking about the latest Indiana Jones movie instead of something darker. *At all costs, David. Follow them at all costs.* The words floated back, making David straighten, ready to be called upon.

He began sorting through the methods in his mind, just like he would a differential. A pathologist's version of planning a crime.

Lesson One: Give the cops a boring case.

No legwork. No new developments. No cause for coffee-fueled strategy sessions or evidence boards. The moment they sensed something routine, something simple, they would move on. That meant no dramatic flourishes. No open and shut homicide. Everything had to whisper self-inflicted. No suspects, no motive, no reason to linger. If the cause was obvious and the story was dull, there would be nothing left to solve. David would be innocent by default.

He moved to the internal checklist beneath it, organizing methods like case folders.

Poison: elegant, historical, but deeply impractical. He remembered reading once that poison was the murder weapon for white people. Used by kings and queens. Favored in spy novels and period dramas. It had literary flair, *with this kiss I die* lethality. Macbeth turned to Belladonna. Cleopatra, allegedly, chose snake venom. Arsenic had been around since the Middle Ages and likely took out Napoleon.

But Josh? Josh didn't deserve that kind of ending. Poison was too good for him.

And the science didn't lie. David mentally recited the tox mnemonic from med school:

Blind as a bat, blurred vision.

Red as a beet, burnt-looking skin.

Dry as a bone, dry eyes and mouth.

Mad as a hatter, mania and confusion.

Thallium. Succinylcholine. Arsenic. Too many variables. Too traceable. Poison was chaos theory wrapped in chemistry. Digestion stopped at death. And any halfway decent postmortem tox screen would catch it. He scratched it off and moved on.

Knife, a favorite of a woman scorned. Accessible, immediate, easily obtained, and personal. But catharsis was messy, and mess got people caught. Stabbing spelled out one thing: trace deoxyribonucleic acid. Blood was a trail, one that led straight to a suspect. A trail that could end with thirty years to life. Knife wounds were for the quick and dirty, but hand-to-hand combat belonged only in video games.

He pictured a sea of red sinking into cloth and floorboards, blood as the star witness, leaving behind soggy footprints and crimson confessions.

A knife was for someone with younger energy. David was too

old to bring a knife to a gun fight. He crossed it off and kept going, narrowing the field one method at a time.

Speaking of guns, David had his ex-wife to thank for the Beretta 9000S stowed in the safe atop his bedroom closet.

The moment the thought crossed David's mind, Don walked into the lounge, his timing uncanny.

"Hey, David. I'd ask how you've been, but I've heard most of it. Sorry."

David's response was brief, almost automatic. "Thanks, I appreciate it."

Neither man had much use for small talk, but then, they didn't really know each other.

Don poured his coffee, the drip of the machine filling the silence. He held the mug in his hands, considering what to say. Whatever was on his mind stayed there. He set the cup on the counter and added a look, one sharp enough to sting.

David couldn't tell if it was trauma's mark or a leftover wound from Mary. Either way, it felt deserved.

During the divorce, Mary had her focus fixed on Don. She watched his new Lexus glide past her apartment, eyes narrowed, calculating. She swore their relationship hadn't been consummated until the papers were signed, but David could see the speed of their courtship for what it was—a little too convenient. By the time the ink dried, neither of them had illusions about reconciliation. They were tired of paying lawyers to duke it out, so they settled with joint custody, alimony, child support, and signatures that promised civility but nothing more.

David had heard of Don, an anesthesiologist always on call, his pager a staccato of emergency beeps, but knew little about him. David wasn't one for hospital social events, preferring quick appearances to satisfy the board's expectations. Don was hard to ignore, but not the primary target of David's anger. David could've played the cuckold card, but instead, he ceded Mary to Don, betting her histrionics would spook Don into a swift parting.

But Mary surprised him. She slipped into her new life with a smoothness he hadn't expected. She wore St. John knits, her every movement now measured, controlled. She wrapped herself in that life like it was a second skin, hoping a big diamond would erase the first marriage entirely. She preferred to think of David as an annulment, the past wiped clean, despite Addison's existence standing in stark contrast.

Don was high-rung, the kind of man who looked down on things like leftovers and mountain folk. David knew him only by the impressions pieced together from Addison's casual comments and Mary's humble bragging. Don had grown up in Rhode Island yet spent summers not at the Cape, but in Boone, skiing. His father, an App State professor, had insisted he experience the small-town life, while his mother, with her polished accent and taste for boarding schools, had wanted nothing more than to wipe away the mountain air from Don's lungs and return him to sophistication. After med school, Don had shattered his mother's vision. He swapped sailing for skiing, bought a mountain house in Banner Elk, and Mary quickly made it her own, thanks to the blank checkbook from a more successful version of her first husband.

David had peppered Addison with questions. He hated leaving her alone with Don. Success didn't always come with good intentions.

Addison had met him with nonchalance, but it didn't feel rehearsed. More like something she'd grown into.

"He didn't really try," she'd said once, poking at the sleeve of her juice box. "Just bought me stuff I didn't want. Never acted like a dad. He was always working or fussing over Mom."

She looked up. "I already have a father, anyway."

David let out a slow breath, relieved that Addison's heart had always been his. If Don had ever posed a real threat back then, David would've fought harder for her than for Mary, because one was gold, the other just fool's gold.

Mary didn't have to play at being country. She and David were the real deal, born and raised in Appalachia, where the crack of a rifle was as familiar as the hum of a bicycle tire on gravel.

That explained the pistol, a gift from her father. Mary's eyes narrowed when she saw Don's disapproval of anything connected to the NRA, and his talk about alarm systems and police. Mary knew, if she wanted to keep Don, she'd have to shed more than just her accent.

"Get rid of it," she said, her voice almost offhand, but the demand was clear. "I don't care how, just make it go away."

David could hear the finality in her tone. Her past, the grit and the gun, all of it had to disappear. She was reinventing herself for Don, into a life more refined.

But David never discarded the gun. He wasn't a gun nut, nor did he believe he'd ever use it. It stayed dusty, unused in a town that shut down for the winter. He kept it mostly because getting rid of it seemed like a hassle. All the paperwork for family transfers felt tedious. He was already worn down from custody talks, child support, and mountains of legal documents. By the time it was over, the gun was still there, stashed away, unused and mostly forgotten. Now, though, it felt like more than just another leftover from a past life.

But the gun was another version of Russian roulette, safe in the distance between himself and Josh, but loud and prone to gaining the wrong kinds of attention. There was no guarantee the bullet would pass through the skull; it was likely to leave evidence behind for forensic minds to review. Plus, blood spatter patterns, proximity to the victim, and ballistic tracing made it anything but a clean in and out. Guns left behind too many clues like trajectory, fingerprints, and residue. As shiny as it was, it was only a distraction, luring him away from rule number one, a case that produces yawns not convictions.

He was left with a compact list. Something simple, like an overdose. Boone was the type of place that embraced the devil's grass, harkening an attitude more suitable with the 1970s. The professors were the look the other way types, content to give a side eye warning and not much else. Addison said they didn't even ticket the students for lighting up a joint on the way to class, and her friends were known to puff, puff, pass. The cold made room for warmth, a bit of ganja to stave off winter's chill—and cannabis was just the beginning. For Josh, too much of a good thing in a college town fit the bill just right.

Plus, Josh's family had no inheritance, no need to suspect foul play. Addison had described him as being on the lower end of the SES bracket, not much saved and nothing to spare. Autopsies were costly, so the police and family wouldn't request one unless something wicked was afoot.

The docs nicknamed the ones that got cut up as TUSU (trauma, unusual, sudden, unexpected). Mostly the ones that got an autopsy dripped another four-letter word—lots of C-A-S-H. Rich people were historically the most curious, and only money answered wrongful death questions fully, likely to appease names on a will. An overdose on someone with a drug rap wouldn't raise eyebrows, especially in a town that already overlooked minor felonies on game days. David figured an overdose warranted a strong consideration, since having Josh meet his end with a needle stick could fit well into an already established narrative.

Suicide was always one of David's favorites on that long drive with Cormac. They'd talk of self-harm, voices full of high energy, contrasting with the mellow voice of Van Morrison singing "Crazy Love." Neither resident registered the discrepancy between subject and background noise, though Cormac couldn't stand the rest of the *Moondance* album. He was as picky about his songs as he was about suicide, arguing it involved too many details to be taken seriously. David could see Cormac ticking the reasons off on his fingers, but he was always more focused on his friend's driving than his rant.

"One Davie, you gotta know if your target is left-handed or right-handed. Left would be better, then you could corner him on the driver's side of a car, pop him one in the head, and put the gun in his hand. Two, there's the issue of blood spatter and residue, but gun powder residue is only good about 50% of the time anyway, as we well know. Three, a note, the hardest of all to fake. But leave it out and it seems shady."

It spooked his buddy to worry about the ins and outs of suicide, but David thought the devil really was in the details. Besides, David had always liked the rhythm and blues bent that Morrison did on *Moondance*. It was an upgrade, as was anything that would keep the police from picking a suspect. Cormac's tastes were always too simple, but David was convinced, then and now, to give suicide a fair shake.

David smirked to himself. *It's odd to interview ways to murder someone.* His appetite held, despite the topic. He tried not to think about how many shades of messed up it made him to still feel hungry.

The second rule was tell no one. He wondered if Addison could keep a forever secret, a lie that would weave a thread around the two of them, a topic to be met with mandated silence. For most young adults, that would seem farfetched. But Addison was the structured type, always quick with a specific Christmas list and someone who stopped the full three seconds at a stop sign. She was far from her vapid peers, with their heart eyes focused on bad boys with bee-stung lips. She also wasn't the creative type, with eyes toward a gap year and European names bubbling up on maps.

She was built more solid than that, the house built on rock, not sand. Addison had to work not to be a teacher's pet and gobbled down novels at whiplash rates. She was the one who brought spare umbrellas without being asked, who remembered anniversaries that weren't hers, who read the fine print. He knew his daughter could keep the secret safe. She was built for sturdy things. It would be lonely to carry a secret like that, the stink of it weaving inside, pushing the afflicted toward an impulsive reprieve.

Luckily, she'd never have to carry it alone. He'd be there when things got tough, when breaking points neared or when she needed an outlet. David figured that made it more likely they could keep it together, equally yoked as they were.

Lesson three was no body, no crime (if rule one deemed invalid). Without the treasure map of a corpse, the cops automatically received a colder case. No body temperature, no time of death or photos of the crime scene where witty detectives noticed out of place things, like pine needles on the body where no pine trees were found.

If they did find a body off the beaten path, time of death accuracy was compromised if the body was decomposed or if it was recovered from fire, water, or ice. That's why outdoor disposal was better than indoors, because of insects and decay and all the ways they could lead investigators astray. The rule of thumb was one week above ground equals two weeks in water and eight in the ground. Predators and parasites could scatter the bones, messing up cases and injecting doubt, all good things if necessity caused the need for a body dump. David was in decent shape for his age, working out more days than not, but hauling a body around under a starless sky was not his preferred disposal method.

The methods were one thing. It was his life's work that was the worst of his worries. The invention of the microscope set about a death spiral for all career criminals. Blood typing and DNA put the nail in the coffin. Murder was about multi-tasking, an equation never completely balanced. There were hair follicles to consider, clothing fibers, fingerprints, and biological materials (like a sneeze). The Locard Exchange principle (that everyone brings and leaves things from a crime scene) would be the opposite of a to-do list—it was a worry doll for prison time. Trace evidence could be the silent killer, always setting a blink and you'll miss it trap. David's mind was already doing summersaults thinking of how careful he'd have to be to leave everything wiped clean.

"Dr. Morgan to the emergency room, Dr. Morgan to the emergency room." The intercom blared, and David rose, finishing his lunch and heading toward the elevator.

If the other doctors could see his thoughts, they'd turn tail and run. He became the black cloud in the elevator, a presence that made morality recoil, leaving only the unsaid things that fester in dark hearts. The rules and his knowledge would shield him, but only until he was ready to make his move. He pressed the button for the lab, his mind humming with dangerous thoughts.

Chapter 9

Know Thy Enemy

"Dr. McCall, do you have anything to add?"

During the tumor board meeting, Dr. Rudger's voice pulled David from his thoughts, but it was too late. His face warmed as he blurted out a quick 'No' to satisfy the meeting chair. He straightened his tie, hoping the distraction would pass unnoticed. His boss' eyebrow arched, and David shifted, feigning chagrin. He stared at the table, unwilling to meet anyone's gaze.

He'd spent his working hours in the lab and his nights reading old forensic textbooks. He was also working overtime to learn as much as he could stomach about Josh Raynor. That left little brain power, and what remained had drained out during the after-lunch meeting.

"A word, David." The chief medical officer, Dr. Gill, spoke as if it were a direct order instead of a suggestion. While the doctors filed out of the room, David stayed behind, wondering if he was due a verbal lashing or sympathy. He hated the prospect of either, wishing instead to be ignored, so that he could go about his own to-do list. He hoped he kept it brief.

Dr. Gill, head of medicine, balanced the hospital's demands with the community's needs, always steady in the face of the CEO's lofty ambitions. He spoke with purpose, each word carefully chosen, leaving space for thought in a room full of pompous blowhards. His calm, measured tone seemed to settle the air, cutting through the noise of the world. With patients, he listened, never rushing; with colleagues, his attention never wavered. David trusted him, not because of what he said, but because of how he made people feel. But David also realized that kindness could lead to slipups, so he committed to saying less around Dr. Gill than anyone else. If loose lips sink ships, so did empathy, and David couldn't afford to forfeit any information.

"Hey Davie, are you doing okay? I don't want to pry, but she was an admission to our hospital. How is Addison?" He looked at David, eyes crinkling with wrinkles, showing his grandfatherly concern. Dr. Gill's white hair was neatly combed and his shirt pressed, but his expression held only understanding.

David stared at the floor, realizing he would rather face a fight with the man he admired than earn his sympathy.

"Oh, well, I guess as good as can be expected. She's recuperating at my house. Well, between that and her mother's. It's been difficult but we're taking it day by day." He kept his gaze lowered, certain that any more attention would bring the waterworks and then he'd really be ashamed.

David longed for the escape of a closed door, desperate to avoid talking about his daughter's intimacies any further. He felt stiff and knotty, unsure of how to phrase things, with reminders in his head to keep this topic short.

"Is there anything you need?" Dr. Gill queried, his voice a balm, a comfort.

David shook his head, not trusting his voice, and deviated toward shallower waters.

"I won't lose my focus in the meeting again, Sir," he added, gathering up his papers to give his hands something to do. Dr. Gill had more to say, but David forced a smile, the gesture stiff with discomfort. The attention felt suffocating, everyone watching, wondering how he was holding up. Dr. Gill's gaze lingered, and the weight of it made David's skin crawl. He hurried down the hallway, glancing back at his mentor's concerned face, frozen in the doorway, too close, too personal.

🐚

DAVID WAS TIRED AND CONTINUED RUBBING HIS EYES AS HE took the stairs, thankful for the end of the workday. Typically, he was an elevator man, exchanging weary words with the gregarious lab techs as the day wound down. But now, he found solace in the stillness of the stairwell, the only sound his loafers tapping the concrete. He craved sleep, but it was already dusk, the Boone sky deepening into a tired pumpkin hue. Rest would have to wait. He still had more work to complete.

Yesterday, Card reader 3000743672, a forgetful library patron with 22 minutes of internet left on their login, allowed him to access Yahoo without being traced, making effective use of stolen time. His home computer would yield no search results, history clean, with no evidence he knew Josh's name, number, or address.

David learned that Josh Raynor grew up without a strong male influence. It earned him no sympathy, nor did it excuse his actions, but it added a small note of understanding to someone easily cast as a villain. His father was in and out of the prison system while Josh was still in diapers, never knowing the other half of his biological beginnings. His father's rap sheet, a mix of drugs and petty theft, created a cycle of addiction that fed itself. When his father wasn't using, he was looking for his next fix, with jail stints in between and no child support, financial or otherwise. His mother worked two jobs, but they remained stuck in the low-income bracket. Their apartment, leaking and creaking, was less a home than a held breath. Nothing in it left room to grow. Josh's life had been whittled down before he could walk.

Poverty was a path many had walked and too many still did. But hardship alone couldn't be a blank check for all the world's ills. It forged determination in some, bitterness in others. It was never fair, but pain didn't grant permission to cause more pain. Suffering could be a crucible or a curse. Josh, with his excuses and circumstances, had learned to weaponize all the luck he lacked. Addison, who'd never scraped by or gone hungry, was the perfect foil to his poverty. Someone with everything had everything to lose.

David was ready to carve each fact about Josh into his memory, eager to stalk him like it was his birthright. He'd traded arrows for keyboards, a spear for the endless expanse of the web. It felt electric to study this man, to memorize every crack in his armor. He imagined slipping into Josh's skin, staying a while, walking in his shoes, as if his thoughts were his own to transcribe. David would bide his time until he knew every mole on his back, every flick of his thoughts, down to the very last detail.

It was easy to reduce Josh's life to a string of arrests and petty crimes, a trail of nothing until age twelve, when he was caught with marijuana. Before that, he was just another invisible kid, too poor to matter, too overlooked to be anything more than a statistic. His mother had kept them off the social services radar since Josh's address stayed the same, year after year. Either he didn't cause enough trouble to matter, or she'd vanished to the point where his cracks weren't hers to notice.

David knew that kind of life, where birthdays were forgotten, and sympathy was a rare visitor. But America was full of people teetering on the edge of survival who didn't wreck other people's worlds on a whim. No matter what he found, David refused to feel sorry for Josh, as sure of his guilt as he was his own right hand.

The jump into selling drugs was likely one of convenience. Josh had enough capital to buy skunk off the streets, nothing too potent or expensive. He knew who to go to; everyone knew who to go to. Even David, who never dabbled in the world of easy forgetfulness, knew where to find cheap pills and strong bud. The men with no jobs sitting on the crumbling steps of the apartment buildings behind Church street provided those seeking quick amnesia, a buffer from pain and a life that lagged. They had a whistle system for potential buyers. With glazed eyes, they sat in the sun and the cold, smoking cigarettes and waiting for their next buy. Under the guise of giving directions, money was palmed, and product was pushed.

They would've given Josh a bit to start off, then more at wholesale once the same kids started buying. Then, as they say, it was off to the races.

Josh got picked up again at 14 for possession of marijuana, more this time, and a longer reprimand. The lists of arrests told the story of a boy who couldn't find a clear path out of trouble. His mother was always the one to fetch him, waiting longer each time to make it to the courthouse. Maybe she was trying to teach him a lesson, adding minutes with every arrest, threatening to stop coming altogether. By then he'd become a frequent flyer, the cops linking his name and address with delinquent behavior, and eyes that clocked him across a courtroom. He completed his probations, careful not to push the system too far, but still managed a decent rap sheet.

David imagined Ms. Gloria Raynor's thoughts. Maybe his mom blamed herself for raising another of the same, her son the spitting

image of her jailbird husband. She might've wondered why her diligence never took hold, why responsibility was buried under the
need for a good time. On nights when Josh was out instead of in
bed, she must've wondered where her good genes had gone.

David felt sorry for her, knowing a child's fate was more than
just their upbringing, though society was quick to place blame. He
could hang a sliver of judgment on her, but Josh was enough of a
disappointment that any more felt cruel. He excused her, letting the
blame rest with Josh, who had already been written off by the cops.
Truant, deficient, delinquent from the start—rehabilitation wasn't
in the cards, no easy sentence, just the one that ended with a
stopped heart.

Now, Josh lived on the edge of town alone, in a collapsing one-
bedroom house off Oak Street. It sat close to the college, but no
one would believe Josh went to App State. Enrollment got harder
when the football team got good. Smarter crowd these days. ASU
wasn't quite Chapel Hill elite, nor did they drip money like Duke
students, but the university was climbing the competitive college
ladder faster than the town could grow.

As close as Josh was to campus, the square footage alone indi-
cated that his place was rundown, just 500 square feet of nothing
special. David stared at the address, his gaze fixed, willing the screen
to give him more. It was unsettling, how much a person could learn
online in 2004. He committed the address to memory, adding it to
his growing dossier, quickly reminding himself that no matter how
it was dressed up, murder was still murder. A slow sneer twisted his
lips. Knowledge was power, and he was holding all the cards.

Josh's picture told its own story. Brown hair, cut short, and a frame
built like a linebacker, burly and heavy with muscle, but not in a way
that invited admiration. He stood tall at 6'1", his broad forehead and
acne scars giving him a weathered look. His shoulders stretched wide,

almost too much for his body. He looked like a man used to taking what he wanted, no hesitation. Not ugly, but rough, too stocky, too raw. A body built for strength, a mind full of frustration.

DAVID CAUGHT HIMSELF. WOULD IT FEEL DIFFERENT IF JOSH had been smaller? A wiry kid with bad posture and thick glasses, awkward in his own skin. Someone who smiled too much. Someone whose face hadn't already been cast in suspicion. Who'd never seen a mugshot, never caught a side eye.

He was Addison's age. Nineteen, still more boy than man. David wasn't naive about what people do to each other. But doubt and regret hold long wakes.

Maybe their worlds had never touched. Maybe Josh came from the kind of life where everything hurt and nothing came easy. That thought hit harder than he expected. It didn't change anything, but it stayed with him.

And Addison? Addison was soft light and second chances. Glass slippers and heated seats. He could almost imagine it—Josh carrying a torch, one he never spoke of. A longing she never noticed. To her, he wasn't even an option. He was invisible. Not rejected. Just erased. No chance to prove he mattered. That kind of sting could rot a person from the inside out. Turn affection into entitlement. Entitlement into rage.

David knew that trajectory too well. He'd seen men rot from the inside out, blaming every wrong on some woman who'd hurt them. Josh wasn't special. Just another boy turned bitter, using anger like a blueprint. The kind of man who left bruises. The kind who tore lives apart.

Maybe Josh hadn't just wanted her. Maybe he wanted to blow up her life. Add fire. See what she'd do in the rubble. Break the glass. Watch her bleed. Take the fantasy and flip it—leave her in a field, caked in blood, no longer a girl but wreckage.

It was all conjecture, just shadowboxing with morality. In the end, what's one less bad person in the world? Josh had taken Addison's goodness. And sometimes, it takes a father to even the score.

Drained from his sleuthing session, David poured himself a nightly aperitif, limiting it to a one drink maximum. Sorrow has a way of needing alcoholic company, but he knew better than to fall into that trap long term. For now, Knob Creek took the edge off and allowed him to rest and refocus.

He chewed the inside of his cheek, considering how to approach Oak Street under the cover of night. It was time to see Josh up close, to watch the young man who had torn Addison's life apart. Whatever happened next would be well deserved. His mind slithered through darkened streets, windows left ajar, with secrets waiting to be uncovered.

Chapter 10

The Silent Girl

He came bearing gifts from Addison's favorite restaurant, Joe's Italian Kitchen. The door banged a hello, but he added his own for good measure.

"Addison! Dinner's hot and ready to eat," David bellowed, listening for her reply.

He placed the warm to-go boxes onto the kitchen table. Since the hospital, she'd lived on granola bars and little else, dismissing her lack of appetite with shrugs and eye rolls. But this pasta was coated in cream thick enough to clog healthy arteries, giving David's poor heart an arrhythmia just looking at it. Addison loved the white goop, calling it as Italian as Vespas and hand gestures, but David suspected an American twist. He'd read somewhere that real cream sauce didn't even contain cream, just eggs and Parmesan. Still, he was happy to feed her, hoping that her appetite would return for fettucine alfredo and garlic bread.

"Addison! I got Joe's," he tried again but got no response. The echo made him weary, his footsteps sounding like horses' hooves as he bounded up the stairs to check on her. He tried not to feel exasperated, to channel patience, and magnanimity. But the food was hot, ready to eat, and she was nowhere near it.

The house was solemn, the doors shut and still. Her room door was barely open, just enough for David to see. A tangle of unwashed hair clung to her face, sticking to her skin. The sharp stench of body odor hung in the air, mixing with the musty smell of neglected laundry. Across her bed lay twisted sheets and papers scattered around, some torn, most crumpled.

David debated waking her but chose to open the containers instead, hoping the scent of garlic would act as a dinner bell, pulling her up easier than a shake of the shoulder. Even with a plan, uncertainty gnawed at him, his eyes lingering on the mound in the bed that barely resembled his daughter.

He bustled back to the kitchen, choosing the fancy porcelain plates and deliberately making copious noise. He figured he was making enough racket to *wake the dead*, but immediately felt ashamed, like he'd cracked a dirty joke in church. David was too old to believe in jinxes, but his mind raced, linking his daughter to tombstones and final endings. If she wasn't down in ten minutes, he'd check again. The subtle shake of his hands showed a sliver of anxiety, so he busied them with unpacking dinner.

The smell did its job, and sleeping beauty trudged to dinner, her first meal of the day.

"Thanks Dad," she yawned, grabbing the chair beside him, one hand resting in her mussed hair. Her face seemed half its normal size, full of hard angles and whittled cheeks.

"Classes today?" he asked, forcing a nonchalant tone, trying to keep it casual.

"Tomorrow," she answered, twirling the pasta around her fork.

"And today, nothing to do?" he prodded again, keeping his voice even, but was met only with a headshake and a shrug. They ate in silence, the sound of clanking silverware too loud, glasses clinking, and napkins crunching, but little else to fill the supper-time void.

"Do, you, um, wanna watch some bad television?" he asked, starting and stopping, like someone still figuring out the clutch.

"Nah, gonna head back upstairs—," she begged off early, leaving him with clean up duties and a head full of worry. Her tooth was repaired, her bruises faded, but the damage remained.

David once told Addison that she made everything easier just by being around. But in the days following the rape, she nibbled on snacks, her calorie count as low as her weight on the scale. She dressed in oversized clothes, her once styled hair pulled back, out of her face. David wanted her heat. He was used to her Spitfire anger, but the numbness was worse, coma-like and distant. She drifted down the hallway, a shell of the person she used to be, moving down the well-worn path like it was death row. Her life seemed coated with apathy, and the emptiness made David's emotions dial up. The less she felt, the more he spiraled. Her stillness made him frantic, a storm without a center.

He tried to connect, renting Blockbuster movies and popping popcorn on the stove, attempting to rustle up some nostalgia. She'd give him a watery smile and curl her feet under the blanket. Often, she wouldn't make it past the previews before slipping into a restless sleep. She was less than before, an Addison-shaped shadow, the days keeping her grey and contained. She went to class, then back to bed, never bothering to change out of her hoodie. No matter how hard David tried, the chasm between them was wider still.

David didn't approach her feelings on Josh or his comeuppance, afraid to push her into rougher emotional waters. He ached to discuss his findings in detail but couldn't find an opening that felt appropriate.

If her roommate Lisa felt sorry, there were no obvious signs of an apology. He'd even added text messaging to her Nokia, with a warning to watch her word count. Every message cost, but Addison needed an extra lifeline to the outside world. Her phone sat misplaced, face down on a table or under a chair. Muted but loud with calls unreceived.

David bit his lip, thinking of all he could say regarding her roommate's faults, but didn't want to inject Addison with more negativity. Turning on Lisa, one of the only supports she had left, wouldn't help her heal, even if David was tempted to call her every bad name, and the worst ones twice.

Life couldn't continue like it once did. Josh had violated her but that's not all he had stolen. The aftermath and the quicksand that threatened to sink her cropped up and never left. David felt he must watch Addison closely or else she'd disappear under the floor-boards, just a mix of sand and molecules mistaken for dust. He thought of her ground down, like something he could sweep away, and it spooked him into needing a glass of cold water.

Her notebook was scattered across the table, full of scribbles in the margins, a doodler like David. He had favored triangles and squares, but she was more of a flower girl, making the margins a garden of daisies and roses. He'd read once that doodlers were intel-ligent, possessing active minds that raced ahead to the top of the class. But now, her paper wasn't dotted with budding flowers or professor notes. Just one phrase was underlined, boxed in and bold, written repeatedly in messy script.

Why am I here?

David wanted to tear the page out, rip it apart, tear into it with all the rage he couldn't say. Cut it into pieces, smaller than confetti. He wondered if similar messages were scattered across the torn papers upstairs, if all her darkest thoughts were inked out, a map of her sadness in blue and black. Heartbreak was a sneaky assassin, catching him off-guard. He stared at the margins, wishing they could go back to being flower dotted, summertime and shiny, with no hard life questions to be found. Her question sunk into his chest, into his veins, until he could feel the sweat crawling down his back.

Mary had her own methods of trying to heal Addison. She offered new clothes, snow boots, anything that might earn a nod or a thank you. With unlimited funds and mounting helplessness, she tried to buy her back to good health. She mailed a Gladiola Girls gift card, hoping the road and the racks might move Addison.

David heard the conversations from across the room. The questions, the soft replies, the long silences in between. Mary called every night, part ritual, part reach. A reminder that Addison had two parents who loved her, even if neither could pull her back.

"No more clothes, Mom. I have enough to fill both of my closets. Here and there."

Addison sank into her chair. She kept the phone on speaker, hands twisting the edge of the throw pillow.

"Addison, honey, let's get our nails done tomorrow. I'm due for a French manicure and you can pick whatever you want. You liked that deep purple tint last time. Let's get you outta that house and into the sunshine, even if it's as cold as a witch's tit outside."

Mary let out a laugh at her own joke, but it didn't carry. It came through the phone high-pitched and thinned, a cackle stripped of levity.

"Mom, give it a rest, will you?"

Addison's voice cut sharp. She used to fake a smile, play along. Not anymore.

"That's not helping," she said, flat and final.

"Oh, okay. Well, I don't want to pressure you." Mary took the disrespect in stride, still hoping a blank check could cover a deep wound. What she couldn't say on the phone, she sent to David's doorstep. The gifts piled up, forming a crooked tower in the hall-way, boxes unopened and stacked shoulder high. David got sick of his home looking like a hoarder's den and emptied the boxes full of purses and coats, a winter wardrobe fit for a queen who'd abdicated the throne.

"You want any of this?" he asked, directing the question toward Addison's room, but there was no response. He stared at the piles of discarded items, glittered shirts, fur-trimmed boots. She was vanishing by inches. The boots, the jacket, the headband like a limb. David held nothing but air.

David wasn't above bribes, but his came in book form. Maybe a trip into a made-up world could stir something in her blood. Addison was a natural reader, quick to trade the world's hard truths for fantasy ones. A bookmark. A tight plot. She chased stories to far-off shores.

At six, she came home with pockets full of acorns and rocks—bits of the world she didn't want to lose. "I'm gonna build a house for my books," she declared, stomping her snowy boots. "And all my treasures can live there." She stood in the doorway, like someone owed her a hammer.

Rocks took out two washing machines, even with David checking her pockets like a TSA agent. Sometimes she'd come home so weighed down by her collections that she slanted to one side, threatening to tip over, like a pint-sized version of the Leaning Tower of Pisa.

Now, he wished he could build her an acorn house. He imag-ined a safe little corner of the world, a place untouched by the hurt that followed her everywhere, where magic could fix what was broken. He pictured her with her hair bundled in a red handker-chief, cooking over a cast-iron cauldron, tending a fire with wood-land creatures at her feet. No one would find her. No breadcrumbs would lead the way. Safe with books and contained like Rapunzel.

He frowned, discontent with his solution, and that the only way to save her was to place her in a fairy tale.

Barnes and Noble couldn't fix what was broken, though David did charge his card enough to make a dent in his savings. The novels went the way of the clothes, another lonesome stack, no movement or motivation found.

The days blended into a monotonous mix of day and night, marked only by Addison's pale face, etched with the creases of sleep. He had to get to work on his promise faster. David felt time biting at his heels, urging him to hurry. It might not be magic that found her, but something darker. If something wicked this way comes, he wanted to be the one wielding the weapon this time.

He had to act before Addison slipped too far. Before the girl who once built acorn houses was gone for good.

Chapter 11

Mary Mary Quite Contrary

It took two rings of the doorbell for David to surface. He hadn't noticed how far he'd drifted. Addison had left for the night, dragging her bag full of stale clothes, trudging back to her dorm room under duress. He surmised that the chaos of the dorm, the speakers blaring, doors slamming, the relentless buzz of youth, might spark something in her. Anything to lift the fog. David used the extra time to bring out his old forensic books, playing eager student for the evening, content to have the house to himself.

Another ring, this time more insistent. Bristling at the interruption, he opened the door, suspecting a frantic postal worker amid a busy fall season delivering more of Mary's bribes. Instead, he came face to face with a head-tilted five-foot five-inch platinum blonde matador on his front stoop.

His ex-wife scowled, her facial expressions giving him a heads up about her current mood.

"I was just WONDERING what you are going to do about this

situation." She took stock in his rumpled clothes, her eyes a sea of judgment.

He evened out his exasperation, trying for something lighter.

"Do you want to come inside, Mary, or do you want to be mad out there?"

She contemplated it, considering whether her anger was red-hot enough to melt his concrete stoop. Not one to cause a scene, she brushed past him, preferring to implode without an audience.

"Enchante, then, allow me," he trilled, edging her into the kitchen.

David wasn't surprised to see Mary. He'd expected her to show up, though he'd lost track of the days and had long stopped tracking his ex's moods. She bustled into the kitchen, wedging herself onto a barstool, looking both out of place and flustered. Her nose scrunched as she registered the breadcrumbs by the sink. Her lips curled, but she showed restraint, until she spoke.

"I shouldn't have to ask, David. A real conversation. A real reaction. I thought we were past the part where you disappear or go dark."

In her mouth, his name sounded like a student who'd been caught cheating on a test.

He watched her, debating the best way to lie. Ex-wives don't have legal privileges, and even if they did, he wouldn't trust Mary with anything confidential.

"Mary. Can I get you tea or coffee? It's cold out there. Let's start there." He made his voice even, aiming for the collected calm of a hostage negotiator.

"Don't patronize me, David. I don't need to calm down, I need to know what's happening here. With Addison, OUR daughter, in case you've forgotten."

Her eyes found his, and he watched her lower lip tremble. Compassion flooded him before he remembered to suppress it.

"Addison. Well, she's adjusting, Mary. There's no right way to go about it, I guess. I'm at a loss too if that helps any." He sat at the breakfast nook table, looking up to speak to her. He figured that ought to put her at ease, getting the better end of the power differential.

She fiddled with the clasp of her Gucci purse, bobbing it in and out.

"She's not talking to me, not really. Just one-word sentences and not much else. I don't—I can't reach her."

David nodded, content to let her speak. On this subject, he was no expert.

"I'm afraid that I might, well, that we might, be losing her."

She drummed her lacquered nails against her purse, her admission making her restless.

"It's not just about her," Mary continued. "I just—I don't know what to do with all this ANGER." She said it like she could hurl the feeling across the room.

Mary said anger, but she meant grief. A cavernous sadness with no bottom, the loss of all hope. A purgatory for happiness lost, with no escape hatch in sight. He couldn't go there with her, not into the dark place that made him feel as if nothing would ever be all right again. Not after they'd both agreed, in front of a judge, to erase all empathy for each other.

"Well, the way I see it, there's two choices. Hold it in or let it out."

He said there were two choices, but really, there were three. Sometimes, if you're lucky, there's someone who can hold your anger for you until you're strong enough to face it again. They can take the heat without getting burned. David bet that was about as close to true love as a guy like him could understand—trusting someone else to hold your pain until you could handle it. That's the kind of love that lasts.

He couldn't be that person for Mary; he wasn't sure he'd ever been strong enough for her. Don didn't seem to be either since she'd come to him. It saddened him that they couldn't be that person for each other, that history and old grievances kept them from bridging the gap. But what started out as a hairline fracture widened over the years until what was broken between them couldn't be fixed.

She shrugged, content to let his words pass over her, putting them in the unhelpful advice category before she sauntered out the door.

David believed he owed her something more, so he pivoted.

"You let it out... like... AHHHHH!" He didn't belt it but said it loud enough that Mary startled.

"Ha. That's silly."

"No, come on, I feel better. You try it."

She studied him, unsure if she was being set up.

"Go on, you've got to really feel it." He made a motion of encouragement with his hands like a dialect coach.

She swallowed, gearing up, and let out a medium "Ahhh" roar.

"AHH!" David reared back, letting the walls shake with his voice.

Mary's eyes filled with tears and then she let out a wail, "AHH-HHHH!!" loud enough that the next knock on the door could be the police.

They smiled. Bittersweet. Guilt crept in like a shadow between them.

David could've offered a hug. It might have dulled the ache. Might've led to more.

Their history swirled between them, tight and unspoken.

But neither moved. The static lingered. The thread frayed. Still, that old instinct remained—the need to make their shared pain smaller.

There were many ways he used to love her. None were allowed now.

He dialed back his emotions. Brokenness had a way of dressing up need as connection. A kiss felt like relief. An embrace, like buoyancy.

But what passed for comfort was really a snare. His jaw tightened. Eyes softened, then steeled. A war was fought on his features, a mess of grief, want, and restraint. All of it written across his face before he looked away.

Mary didn't speak. Her hand drifted toward him, then stopped short. She folded it into her lap, smoothed the crease in her skirt. It took effort. More than it should've.

"We had some good times, didn't we?" Mary's chin trembled. "It wasn't all bad. Us. The Boss. Our friends. My aunt's place with the broken sink and that tiny kitchen. It used to be easy. Then it all went wrong."

This was the woman who ruined Springsteen for him. David couldn't let her take anything else.

For Mary, the well of love had drained slow, drop by drop. What remained was patched over with a rough kind of self-preservation.

He shouldn't have said it. He knew better. But the memory rose anyway, warm and reckless.

"It makes me think of the night we got engaged," he whispered.

Mary let out a soft laugh. "That old place was freezing."

"It did its job. A roof overhead, one bedroom for us both."

"I was just crashing there. It felt private back then, polished even."

"You treated it like a crash pad," he murmured, smiling. "Clothes by the door, dishes stacked in the sink."

"Don't remind me."

"I thought it was charming," David went on. "Lovably messy. You had ambition. A heart set on my last name."

"You were humming when I walked in," she said with a half-smile. "Always singing Springsteen off-key, with a wooden spoon in your hand."

"I was trying not to look at the mess. Scrubbed the tub. Cleaned the fridge. Even did the dishes."

"You shoved everything into the hall closet," she teased, a small smile tugging at her mouth.

"Well, I had a box," David said. "Black, velvet-lined. Cost me a blood donation and two weeks of peanut butter sandwiches."

Mary looked down, her voice softer now. "It was small," she murmured. "But it was enough. You kept glancing at the box."

"I was certain I'd lose it," David told her. "Every few minutes, I'd check to make sure it was still there. Small and certain. Just sitting on the counter like it knew what it was about to do."

"You wrote me a letter," she said. "Sat at the table with that cheap pen like it was something sacred."

"I paused between every line. Had to shake out my hand," he said. "Tried to keep the letters neat. When the ink smudged, I started over."

"You pressed so hard the paper nearly tore."

"My tongue was stuck to the corner of my mouth," he added. "Like a kid writing his name on a school test."

Mary admitted, "I kept that letter for years. Tucked in my sock drawer."

David's voice lowered. "The dogs on Main Street howl, 'cause they understand…"

She joined in, softer. "If I could take one woman into my hands…"

"Mister I ain't a boy, no I'm a man," he sang. "And I believe in a promised land... with you, Mary."

There was a silence, but it didn't feel empty.

"You didn't even let me finish," he murmured. "You were crying too hard."

"My shoulders were shaking," she whispered. "I couldn't speak."

"Then you shouted it."

"Yes," she breathed, eyes damp now. "Yes, a million times yes."

They both went still for a moment, caught in the memory.

"We put on *Born to Run*," she evoked.

"And danced like lunatics," he added, the edge of a smile flickering.

"Then *Greetings from Asbury Park*," she said. "That night felt endless. Like we'd burn a hole in the linoleum with all that love and dancing."

And with what happened next.

The air shifted.

She'd unbuttoned her shirt, slow, one at a time, making him wait for it.

I can't wait to be your wife, she'd whispered, backing toward the bedroom.

All teeth and promise.

A memory too big to touch without bleeding.

And many more like it, when the years piled up and things broke down. David couldn't listen to The Boss anymore, especially *The River*. Even when Springsteen resurfaced on the *Jerry Maguire* soundtrack and Addison played that song on repeat, he couldn't bear it.

All he could think of was Mary—the woman who'd contaminated the E Street Band and harmonicas and left him with a broken heart.

"That was a lifetime ago," she stammered, the blush on her cheeks already fading.

He nodded, no longer wanting to reminisce. They had morphed

back into two middle-aged co-parents in an ancient kitchen, knee-deep in their strained relationship.

Mary picked up her purse and gave him a brisk nod, dismissing him with a glance.

David debated saying a genuine goodbye but stood still, stoic, watching her blond bob head for the door, repeating history by letting her go.

She turned and paused, considering what quip to send him off with but decided against it.

Mary shut the door, her old fury spent and left behind on his floor.

Maybe she got what she came for after all.

Chapter 12

Stakeout

The house clock chimed, signaling another sleepy Saturday on Blairmont Drive. Winter had yet to make its appearance, but it was close—the cold biting the edges of the afternoon, the bare trees standing like ghosts against a grey sky. The promise of snow meant nothing to Boone locals, who were always awarded with a white Christmas. David had chopped extra firewood, just in case, though it wasn't the cold of winter that had him on edge today.

"Make it stop. Oh my God, please! Make it stop, make it stop!" Addison's voice cracked through the silence of the house, high-pitched, frantic. The sirens blared in the distance, heading toward the hospital, but all she could hear was her own deafening heartbeat.

She wasn't here, not in David's home. She was back in the field, the cold dirt beneath her, struggling to breathe. She crumpled to the floor, crawling on her hands and knees, a feral thing.

"Help me, help me!" she wailed. "I can't take it anymore!"

The cold dirt beneath her hands, the sharpness of it scraping against her palms, the pressure of the weight on her chest, the fear of never making it out. Her body shook with the memory, her limbs betraying her, movements jerky and uncoordinated.

"It's okay. It's okay. It'll be over soon." David's voice was soothing, but distant, in a language she no longer understood.

His arms wrapped around her, trying to hold her steady. He rocked her, back and forth, like an infant. She was nineteen, but the world she knew was spinning, and no matter how tightly he held her, he couldn't ease her flashback. He matched her breath for breath, his own chest tight. Addison accidentally clawed him, the scratch of her nails dragging across his bicep. He winced but ignored it, focusing on her, on keeping her tethered. The shaking began to subside, though the triggers kept coming, relentless, paired with her unpredictable moods.

"I can't be here near the hospital, Dad," she murmured, her voice hoarse. "I'll go stay at Mom's." She let out a long, shaky exhale, a shattered sound. "If you really want to help me, do what I asked."

"I'm working on it, Addison. I promise."

Her haunted eyes locked onto his, piercing with a hint of accusation. "I don't even recognize myself anymore. Who I am is so far from who I was."

She was right. His daughter, almost unrecognizable. It was time to do something. A reconnoiter was in store, but that presented its own set of problems.

On the drive back from Banner Elk, after dropping Addison at her third-floor suite, Boone's beauty unfolded through David's windshield.

He passed students in cashmere coats and black toboggans, incense curling from open doorways, and dreadlocked locals waving at college kids hauling bags of produce from the farmers market. A teenager in ski goggles pedaled past on a mountain bike, a knit peace-sign jacket slouched over his shoulders.

David's cracked window caught a guitar riff outside a coffee shop, where the smell of patchouli tangled with roasting espresso. A billboard near the bypass advertised luxury cabins with "double stacked fireplaces" and "uninterrupted mountain views." Around the next bend, iron gates rose behind spruce trees, guarding houses with more windows than walls.

Two women stepped out of Mast General—one in a boutique-tagged puffer, the other stuffing a cheap fleece cap into a shopping bag. Up ahead, a girl in a sequined dress shivered outside a bar, a North Face coat over bare legs. Addison's friends had said the weather ruined party outfits, but they dressed up anyway.

Even in October, the town breathed deep. Signs in shop windows asked patrons to recycle. Bumper stickers urged kindness. A café flyer listed potlucks and yoga in the park. Boone didn't preach. It didn't need to. It just rolled by, slow and steady, like snow collecting on a porch whose patron believed in peace but paid in cash.

David loved mountain life, even when winter turned people into Popsicles. Beanies iced over, beards froze mid-conversation. Some mornings, the frost made him feel like an old-world settler with a fire roaring at his back, staking out survival like his life depended on it. He tried growing a beard each year, aiming for burly, landing somewhere between patchy and tragic. Addison called it his "baby beard." He didn't laugh. He never wore flannel either, worried he'd look like a knockoff lumberjack.

The winters gave way to perfect summers, cool enough that his house didn't need air conditioning. He'd picked the place on Blair-mont Drive for the drop-dead view, watching the sun touch every building from his porch—a high-country wake-up call.

Boone was the antithesis of evil. It was built on small-town hellos and easy mornings, joggers bustling down the greenway and neighbors waiting to mow grass at a respectable hour. David saw it all and called it home. Boone was authentic in its mission statement, declaring itself open and welcome to all.

"Come and stay for a while," it preached. "The mountains are calling you back."

David slowed at the stop sign by the greenway. A kid zipped past on a scooter, trailing a backpack with patches stitched into the seams. Someone had tied a scarf around a lamppost with a handwritten note: *Free if you're cold.* A neighbor waved as he pulled onto Blairmont, the same neighbor who once helped dig his car out of the snow.

He should've felt comforted.

Instead, everything looked off-kilter. The town hadn't changed. Addison had.

He parked in his driveway but didn't get out. He watched as a jogger passed, headphones in, nodding along to some invisible beat. Life kept going in Boone. It was still good, still gentle. But worry pressed hard against his ribs. His home, no longer safe. His daughter, no longer okay.

His weekend was free. It was time to begin.

DAVID DECIDED TO START BY WATCHING JOSH'S RENTAL. HE needed to get a sense of his schedule.

The Oak Street playground served as a good scouting spot, long deserted of children's laughter. The cold kept the kids away, as did the slanted equipment, making the merry-go-round look like a suspicious death trap. Oak Street itself dead ended at the Horn in the West parking lot, and David knew it was busy enough that he could blend in. On Saturdays, the farmers market drew in the locals, their bags heavy with lavender kombucha and fresh produce. Tourists came for the Old West play during the summer, and college students parked here in the fall and spring. It was a bustling spot, and David could walk around unnoticed. No one would pay attention to him, and the crisp mountain air gave him the excuse to stroll without raising suspicion.

He could go down to the bottom of the hill on Blairmont and catch the Applecart bus. The bus was a free service, frequented by hunched-over senior citizens who drove the elderly around town on frozen roads. The drivers got special training to drive on ice, heads full of caution and brakes trained on slippery surfaces. He'd scope it out, but David bet there were cameras aboard the bus. If he went more than twice, the driver might remember him, and he couldn't risk being picked out of a lineup.

The best bet was on foot, low temperatures be damned. He wouldn't drive. The less attention he drew, the better.

David pulled on an old leather bomber jacket and gloves, knowing he'd need to keep moving to stay warm. He cut through the greenway, walking quickly toward Oak Street. He crossed the street, moving toward the vacant park behind the IHOP, blending in with the shadows of the autumn evening. His black beanie and Ray-Bans shielded his face, leaving only his ruddy cheeks exposed. He kept moving, the cold biting at his skin. He reached the park, scanning the area. No cameras.

David approached the picnic tables at the edge of the park. From here, he could see Josh's listed address through the trees. He checked the binoculars in his pocket, then took a quick peek through them, his eyes sharp and focused on the house. His pulse quickened. This was it.

Josh's one-bedroom house was a ramshackle abode, the roof sloped and close to needing replacement. A rusted red pickup with a dent by the taillight sat in the driveway, its license plate ATG-

4987. David memorized it, watching for movement. Next time, he'd bring food and a water bottle that could serve the dual purpose of something to drink and something to pee in. He didn't want to leave any unnecessary DNA around. He might also bring a crossword puzzle, under the guise of a man waiting for a granddaughter to swing in the park.

The house seemed empty. The dingy front door was shut, and the lights were off. For a college kid, that seemed suspicious. David imagined Josh as the type to blare music, not care about his neighbors. The house was smaller than expected, barely big enough for a twin bed and a pull-out couch. The creeping paranoia made David twist his neck, a nervous barnyard owl. But the street remained still, everyone indoors as winter settled in.

David yawned. It was true what they said, stakeouts gave room to think. Most people didn't slow down enough during the day to process their thoughts. The air was colder now, his breath hanging in white wisps, drifting toward the sky. The clouds above were thick, heavy with the promise of snow. His mind wandered back to a time after medical school, when he thought he was destined to live by the beach, where it was never cold enough for a sweatshirt.

He and Mary had rented a cheap condo, the kind with an ant-sized balcony. They had to stretch every dollar then, living on his work-study salary. Mary made more as a paralegal, but David began to wonder if her salary was worth the constant complaining about her bosses. She wasn't the working girl type. Her list of regrets piled up faster than her paperwork, draining his patience. He couldn't wait until he made enough money to let her quit.

They could afford the vacation because Dr. Roque, his old mentor, paid to get his lab in shape. David suspected the old doc suffered from depression, though he knew better than to ask. Instead, his mentor wore it in the shuffle of his movements and the disarray that overtook his lab.

David would arrive, and Dr. Roque wouldn't have signed out anything for weeks. He hadn't dictated any of his reports, just looked at the slides and called the docs about the serious ones. David knew the drill, head to the beach but not for the sand, a solo clean-up mission to smooth over Dr. Roque's mental health. Suit up in latex gloves, keep his mouth shut, and get to work, all at a road-runner's pace.

It wasn't a vacation for David. He spent the first few days at warp speed, signing out cases and catching Dr. Roque up. The doctor would then show him a morgue freezer full of six or seven legs he'd put off for two or three months. Each visit seemed worse, the work piling up, turning David's week into a 60-hour job while Mary enjoyed her solo vacation. But he liked Dr. Roque, who'd come from Cuba in the '50s and trained in Boston with the greats. He loved Travis McGee books and always paid David overtime, though David tried not to see it as hush money for a job Dr. Roque could no longer handle. He was glad to help but knew it wouldn't be long before his mentor couldn't keep up with the deluge.

David remembered that call from December, sooner than expected. Dr. Roque had taken a hard hit—a heart attack, followed by bypass surgery. David took the week off and headed straight to the beach, Mary riding shotgun, happy for the unexpected break. The lab, however, looked worse than ever—months of backlog that ten-hour days couldn't cure. Still, he made the time to visit the old doc in rehab, told him to keep his spirits up. It was easier to do the work without Dr. Roque there, producing excuse after excuse when they both could see the rotted fruits of his labor.

Dr. Roque had said, "You are too good to me, David. When you finish residency in June, come work for me for a year or two, and then it's all yours."

David blinked, trying to process it. "You want me to have your practice?" It seemed impossible—an opportunity too good to be true, no buy-in required.

Dr. Roque had smiled, weak but sincere. "Hell, son, you've helped save it over the years. I don't think I'd still be around if it weren't for you. You deserve it, Doc."

David dreamed of palm trees and beach living. Mary curated a list of realtors, focused on finding a place with a backyard pool and a wide deck.

"Don't forget, we have a budget. That's as important out here as sunscreen," he warned.

She stuck out her tongue. "Well, pass the baby oil, because I'm gonna be as brown as a biscuit. And you're gonna be rolling in dough."

They laughed, and he swung her around, Mary's hair tangling in his hands. She kissed his neck, arching into him. "I'm ready to set down roots."

Around the first of February, two things happened. The first was a call from Ricky, David's old med school roommate.

"What are you doing with your life, Davie?"

David grinned. "Me and Mary are headed to the beach to be fat and happy, live out our days like a Bob Marley song."

"You ever think about coming back to the mountains?" Ricky suggested. "Mountain air and mountain paychecks do a doctor good."

"You know I grew up in the hills of Tennessee. All my night-mares live in high altitude," David replied. "Why freeze in the hills when my toes could be in the sand?"

He and Mary had made a blood pact never to go back to the mountains their extended families still called home. That life, to them, was a string of dead ends. They believed there was more to life than familiar faces at the grocery store. Mary wanted bigger and better, and David followed suit, eager to give her something new, something theirs.

"Well, that's too bad," Ricky said. "There's a hospital in Boone handing out big buckets of money for a young pathologist. You could shine the powers that be on Friday. We can get drunk and tell lies on Saturday. And you can go home Sunday with the job in hand."

David laughed. "I'll think about it, Ricky," he lied.

The second call came from Dr. Roque. His voice, an enthusiastic baritone, pulsed with new energy. Rehab and surgery had worked wonders. He felt fifty-nine years young and had given up on retiring. David was crushed. Mary cried, leaving her beach-sized dreams behind. They moved. They had Addison. And life started getting drawn in permanent ink.

It had been an hour with no movement inside the house. David shook off the cold, taking the long way home. The beach dreams belonged to another life, back when he and Mary thought they could outpace gravity. The world, once wide open and weightless, had been flushed with opportunity, as simple as saying yes to a job.

The wind clawed at his coat, and he pulled it tighter, quickening his steps until the porch light flickered into view. Home. His shoulders relaxed, releasing a tension he didn't know he was carrying.

The neon visions of youth had dispersed, traded for larger worries. All that David had taken for granted, the safety of Boone, the kindness of strangers, the health of his daughter, felt paper thin. Danger didn't always announce itself. Sometimes it sat still. Sometimes it waited.

David had been burned too many times by unreliable mentors and greed. Now, he trusted only deadbolts, his steady hand, and the belief that if the world wouldn't bend to his will, he could force it to.

Faith and trust were just pixie dust; he'd bet on the black of his work ethic every time.

Chapter 13

Better Make Sure

The crockpot stew smelled better than it tasted. The air in David's home was thick with broth and bread, welcoming two snow-covered figures in with promises of a full belly and enough salt to cause blood pressure problems. Addison, a leftover from the custody agreement days, was over for Wednesday dinner.

Afterward, they stood side by side at the sink, watching the water rise. David had a dishwasher but preferred hand washing with water as hot as he could stand. Addison, always up for the challenge, didn't mind the food particles that floated to the top.

Mary never liked washing dishes, disgusted by the leftover bites on plates. "All those chewed particles, swirling around my fingertips. It's gross. It's disgusting!" Her complaints still rang in David's ears. He reached for a joke, then let it go. Wrong moment.

Addison had the stomach to be a doctor, unfazed by soggy food or worse. They traded washing and drying, their routine as regular as an alarm clock.

Addison dried a plate, uttering, "I haven't changed my mind."

David felt a wave of relief. He'd stepped up his spying sessions but needed to be sure she was all in.

"I'm glad you told me," he said, eyes on the plate, hands busy with the rag. "I've been working on it, but wasn't sure it was still the way to go." He didn't ask the question in between their conversation, that she had been doped up on morphine and still in shock. He didn't want to imply she wasn't fully cognizant at the hospital. Any hint at questioning her judgment would only have her coming out swinging. He wasn't expecting a reprieve, but he wouldn't have been surprised if it came. With time, her conviction might dull, and he'd be off the hook. That would be preferable, but he was committed now, ready to go either way. It was Addison's choice.

"You sure that's how you want to play it?" His voice was even, but he wasn't sold.

"I do, I am." She nodded, biting her bottom lip. "I know it's what I need. What has to happen to make things better."

Cryptic, but effective. There were questions to pose, but David found he couldn't voice any. They washed the rest of the dishes in silence, each contemplating what those words meant and why.

"What if you change your mind?" he queried, setting a bowl into the stack, its heat still lingering.

Her movements froze, then she turned to face him.

"That's offensive, Dad. Like really fucking offensive."

Her eyes narrowed. She shoved the plate she was drying into the water with a splash, the water sloshing over the sink.

"Inexcusable."

She scrubbed harder than necessary, like she was trying to drown the dish. Each movement grew more aggressive, punishing the water for what her father asked.

David took a step closer, about to speak, but she whipped around, the plate in her hand cracking against the edge of the sink. The broken piece of porcelain rested in her palm, her face flushed, jaw tight. David wondered if she'd throw the whole thing at him. In that moment, she looked like Mary, a shade of her mother's rage on her freckled face.

"Addison," he began, his eyes locked onto her hand. A dribble of blood turned the water a shade of pink. "You're bleeding." All thoughts of addressing the disrespect vanished.

He grabbed a hand towel, moving her over to the bar stool. She acquiesced, letting him bandage her up.

"Look, Addison, I didn't mean to offend you. I just wonder how sure you'll be in ten years, in twenty. I'm in, but I keep thinking you can't promise how you'll react in a situation you've never been in."

David kept his tone even, not acknowledging the anger that washed over him. He felt her stiffen beside him. Her face, a mess of red, held back squinting eyes.

"I live this life every day," Addison fumed. "I carry the reminders of what was done to me on my skin, in my body. I feel it, even when no one else can see it. How dare you ask me if I'm sure? *It's all I can see!*"

Her voice cracked, and David fought the urge to hug her. She was broken, and he wanted to comfort her without pushing her further away. But she wore her anger like a shield, making David uncertain of his next best move.

"I just... I need it," she croaked, still vehement, arms crossed tight, lips pulled into a grimace, her mother's miniature.

David lowered his voice, like he was talking to a spooked horse, just enough to be heard and not a note more.

"I'm sorry. I'm so sorry, Addison. That's all I've got to say, but I'll keep saying it if it helps." He touched her arm. "And know that I'll stay the course. Whatever you need, I promise." He knew she wanted reassurance, and so he gave her that too. "I'll do it. I'm sorry. I'll do it for you."

David wasn't a natural apologizer. With bosses, he swallowed his mea culpas, stood silent, took it on the chin. He owed Mary a few I'm Sorry's, his brother even more, but he'd never looked too deep, never cared enough to fix things. But with Addison, the regrets spilled out easily—they were true, and they sandpapered her rough edges.

"Thanks, Dad," she said, turning to face him, leaning against his chest, letting him wrap his arms around her and pretend they weren't talking about murder.

That night, he sang to her like he did when she was little. Every night back then, he would tuck her in just right, buried under a mound of blankets, only her head peeking out like the Princess and the Pea. He curated his greatest hits, full of Waylon, Willie, and the boys. Cat Stevens, too, with sad songs about better days and men who couldn't be good. Those songs taught her about faraway places and broken promises. The hurt so good music that left them both a little achy. She could've used more princess stories, but instead he gave her music, his kind of love passed down one song at a time.

He took it upon himself to give her life a good soundtrack. David preached Stones over Beatles, except when comparing albums. Then *Sgt. Pepper's Lonely Hearts Club Band* took home best of all time. He'd be miffed if she failed a college course but proud she'd grown up on a steady diet of Blondie and Junior Brown, enough to cover the obscure bases. Her brain held what she'd learned in class. Her heart held all his favorite songs.

He threw in the bubblegum tunes of his youth—Lesley Gore, the Supremes—as a nod to his father, who only smiled when something bright was playing. From the '80s, he gave her less Guns N' Roses, more Smiths and Queen. David couldn't control every narrative, but he could give her a great playlist.

Around adolescence, Addison tried to assert her music authority, but her deep cuts and indie obsessions just bounced off David's temples. She'd tried to convert him with bass-heavy tracks, like Jurassic Five, but that rap only gave him a migraine. He warned her —old dogs, new tricks—but she kept at it and queued another. Outkast almost gave him a conniption. He gave her points for effort but told the truth. His taste tapped out in '89. Even Tom Petty had taken time to appreciate.

Her tunes were too slick, too polished, too easy to fast forward on the heartache. She kept her tunes confined to her pink iPod mini, no longer wanting to share.

Still, they found some common ground. The real lesson was never to settle for the top 40. Always listen to the B-sides first. Let him serenade her with the soundtrack that came before the singer stepped on stage. He called it his dowry, lyrics that hit where it hurt and healed something hidden.

Tonight, he settled on something sad, not wanting to white-wash her pain. "Red River Valley" was the pick of the night, the lyric, "Do not hasten to bid me adieu," hitting just right. Comfort wrapped in sorrow. Can't go wrong. He stayed after the last note, watching her body rise and fall before slipping out like he used to when she was little, cracking the door rather than closing it all the way. She slept, yet he remained unsettled.

He probably should've picked something happier. Maybe her melancholy moods were fed by all the sad bastard music, never a happy ending in the bunch. But it was too late to change the story, too late to write it all in pink ink. The sad songs were the best ones anyway. He hoped he'd trained her well enough to know that too.

Arches, loops, whorls—black-and-white Rorschach prints twisted around him. David was back in Cleveland, Tennessee. The air thick with the weight of memory, but it felt wrong. He was trapped inside a dream.

Johnny Red, still too big for his age, loomed in front of David. It was all there, like it was in the 5th grade. Johnny's smirk, the discarded dirt bike, the scent of cheap nicotine. Johnny Red laughed, mocking David's boots, calling him short. David's boots weren't just boots—they were ass-kicking boots. A defense, and a prophecy, because boots like his made a statement.

Johnny knocked him down, rough and relentless. Days of getting pummeled, with nosebleeds he blamed on allergies. The dream felt too real, like blood was back in his mouth. David called in reinforcements. Mitch, his older brother, football strong, was ready to fix things. Mitch shoved Johnny Red against the lockers, hitting him with a punch to the gut. Johnny crumpled, the wind knocked out of him. David watched, feeling grimy. Johnny slid down the lockers, but David felt no satisfaction.

Mitch wasn't affected by the beating. He sauntered down the hallway and winked at David.

"If you can learn to do that, you should. That's your one freebie for family. The next one's all yours."

David awoke with a start. He rushed to the bathroom, dropped to his knees, and grabbed the toilet seat. He spewed, the bile rising, the same gut-wrenching reaction he'd had when he was younger. Both real David and dream David reacted to violence with vomit. It took a dream to remind him that it was Mitch, not David, who was unaffected by aggression. Maybe he wasn't meant for killing after all.

Chapter 14

A Hole in the Soul

After his nightmare and midnight sickness, David spent the next several Sundays exploring different churches, each stirring his soul in unexpected ways. Seeing Josh's home up close had made his future feel too real, his upcoming sins scraping at his conscience. So he rustled up some religion, seeking both conviction and clarity.

Ever the scientist, David feared what might slither out if he pulled back the cover of belief. His mind was honed by facts, but the faith of his youth remained. Doctors were trained to strip the world bare, dissect the bones, and make sense of a body. Faith had to twist to fit in that equation. He'd watched healings unfold in clinical settings, cures no one could explain. But to use the word "miracle" was something else. Instead, they labeled it *spontaneous remission* and moved on. Somewhere between the sterile smell of antiseptic and the hum of fluorescent lights, something bigger waited to be known. David hadn't been able to define what he believed, which made him uneasy. As a pathologist, he wasn't used to uncertainty. It was time to see if the pulpit clarified his questions or deepened them.

The Methodist church on the corner was first, his choice dictated by proximity. A square, gray stone building with narrow windows and a steep roof, solid in the way old things were—steadfast and unmoving. The wooden doors creaked to let him pass. He had to put some oomph into it to get them rolling onward.

Inside, the air was cool and faintly metallic. Like the inside of a toolbox left out in the rain. Light filtered through colored panes of glass, fractured and soft. The sanctuary was plain, but a bundle of fresh-cut holly sat at the pulpit, red berries nestled like small wounds among the leaves.

Rows of dark pews shined, polished by hands that had held questions like his. People who needed answers.

The service was gentle. The words forgiving. The minister's voice was warm and steady. The kind that didn't rise much but somehow filled the room.

"We all come here searching for forgiveness," the minister intoned. "Scripture tells us in First John, 'If we confess our sins, he is faithful and just to forgive us, and to cleanse us from all unrighteousness.'"

David sat back in the pew, arms folded. The cushions were thin. Someone had carved initials into the hymnal rack years ago, and he traced them absently, wondering about their origin. A kid, probably. Or someone old enough to know better. He pressed a fingertip into the groove, feeling the edge where the wood had splintered.

Forgiveness sounded clean in the minister's voice. Too clean. David wasn't sure his sins could be scrubbed out.

He bowed his head, but he wasn't listening anymore. His mind drifted to the list. The names came easy. They should. It was part of his routine.

Simon, the know-it-all from medical school. Top of the class and an asshat.

David darted his eyes toward the pulpit, as if the minister might have heard his thoughts.

Mrs. Malcom, the woman who'd filed a complaint about the textbook-perfect fine needle aspiration that led to an inquiry that went nowhere.

Even his current boss, Dr. Rudger. More bite than venom but still made the list.

He prayed for them every Wednesday. This rundown of venial enemies. Not for fire or fury. Just a prayer for their well-being. Their success, even. Addison had caught him once, hands folded tight, voice low.

"You know," she stated, "if you really forgave them, you'd stop saying their names."

He hadn't answered. Just closed the Bible and went back to folding laundry like she hadn't spoken.

But he kept the list. Tucked into the same rhythm. Every Wednesday.

He told himself it was grace. The mature kind. But really, it was memory. A set of scratched-in wrongs he refused to let go of.

The minister's voice rose again, calling the congregation into the final hymn.

David stayed seated.

He wasn't ready to stand with the saved.

He waited until the last of the congregation had filed out, until the sanctuary echoed with nothing but air and old wood. Then he stood, his cowboy boots clicking across the just-mopped floor, forgiveness still caught somewhere between habit and belief. The list of enemies stayed current. So did the questions, worn smooth from handling.

Two blocks away, the Presbyterian church glowed, a tall sentinel with stained glass windows. He changed into his three-piece suit, the one he kept pressed for weddings and funerals. The building was grander than the Methodist church, with arched doorways and a bell tower that pointed to the sky. Inside, everything was deliberate. Vaulted ceilings stretched toward heaven, their thick beams standing the test of time. The stained glass did not just color the light. It commanded it, pouring deep jewel tones across the marble aisle.

David smoothed his lapel and grabbed a seat in the back. The pews were packed. He'd chosen the 11 o'clock service, the one where everyone wore their Sunday best. Pearls and pressed collars. Matching handbags and dress shoes that had never touched gravel.

The crowd was mixed. Young families tried to corral their wayward children, wedged between elderly couples with clasped hands and quiet nods. Beside him sat a man ten years his senior, wearing an expensive watch and polished cufflinks. David felt bare next to him.

He wasn't meant for lapels and handkerchiefs. Suits never suited him.

At his day job as a pathologist, he could wear what he wanted. Usually khakis and a polo. There was little patient interaction, so he kept his creature comforts. On Fridays, he swapped his boots for Crocs. Craig would shoot him a side-eye, but they were closed-toed, so technically up to code.

The collar tugged at him. Too tight. The fabric scratched at his neck, the starch stiff enough to sand a floor. He shifted in his seat, tried to loosen it with a finger, then gave up and pulled at the back instead.

The man beside him didn't speak. Just turned his head slightly. A flick of the eyes. The slow inhale of someone registering a disruption. He didn't frown, but he didn't have to. The look said enough.

David straightened, like a child caught wiggling during the

benediction. Nothing stopped the itch. Maybe his suit knew he was an imposter, assumed his costume was meant for someone holier.

The preacher hastened to the pulpit, making his stage entrance. He cleared his throat, and the crowd stilled. His robe was spotless, gleaming against his bald head.

This one's a showboat, David surmised, then felt a wave of guilt over the judgment. He couldn't go a moment without sinning, even while at church.

"Mercy," the minister began, letting the word hang in the air. "Mercy is not approval. Mercy is not passivity. Mercy is what God shows us when we don't deserve to breathe another minute."

He paced once, slow and deliberate. A quick jaunt to the side. The crowd held its collective breath.

"Micah 6:8. What does the Lord require of you but to do justice, love mercy, and walk humbly with your God? Not when it's easy. Not when it suits your pride. Always."

David sat still. The collar still itched. His soul sent up a warning flare. This sermon might hit home, and not in a good way.

The minister paused at the edge of the platform, his hand mangling the side of the pulpit.

Oh gosh. Time to hit them with the hard punch, David thought.

He strained not to roll his eyes. He was already on thin ice with his pew-neighbor.

"Mercy," the minister repeated, louder this time. "Is not weakness. It is not rolling over. It is strength. It is Joseph feeding the brothers who sold him into slavery. It is Jesus saying, 'Father, forgive them,' while the nails were still fresh in his wrists."

A few heads nodded. Someone near the front peppered an "Amen!"

The minister's eyes scanned the crowd like he was hunting for someone in particular. Then he smiled. Just a flicker. The kind of grin that knew it had the room.

"Mercy isn't about keeping score. Mercy means you stop measuring who hurt who worse. Mercy is what you do instead of vengeance."

He stepped back toward the center of the pulpit, voice rising, rhythm sharpening.

"And don't pretend you haven't thought about vengeance," he preached. "Don't act like you haven't pictured it. Because I have. We all have. But mercy says not today. Not this time. Not in my name."

David swallowed. The fire crawled from his neck to his gut, blooming into the shape of a sin not yet committed. One that understood everything about vengeance.

David shifted. Then stood too fast, knee knocking the pew in front of him with a dull thud. He muttered, "Bathroom," just loud enough for his fellow parishioner to hear.

The man raised an eyebrow but didn't stop him.

David moved sideways, excusing himself in a whisper as he squeezed past coats and elbows. His boot caught the edge of a purse, nearly sent it toppling, but he caught it just in time and kept going.

He didn't look back. He hurried into the hall, like his sins were following him. Like they already knew his name.

He turned on the air in the Jeep. It took two services before he was ready to drive.

That one was the hardest. Because Addison's plea left no room for mercy. Not a drop. It was eye-for-an-eye justice, straight from the old law. Solomon's wisdom. King David's sword.

What she asked of him didn't call for grace. It called for blood.

Last on the list, the Boone Baptist church, a true holy roller. This one was smaller, rough around the edges. A squat brick building with peeling paint and a hand-painted sign that leaned a little to the left. The front steps groaned under his shoes. Inside, folding chairs replaced pews, and the pulpit looked like it had been built in someone's garage. A single fan buzzed in the corner, pushing warm air in lazy circles.

The loud preacher dominated with fire-and-brimstone certainty, his words thick with drawl and sweat. The syllables bled together, almost slurred.

"I, uh, thank you, very much for a' coming here today," he said, wiping his face with the back of his sleeve. "We've got offering plates on standby, awaiting your donations. As you know, our chapel is in need of repairs, so anything and everything is appreciated."

David glanced around. The pulpit wobbled every time the minister pounded it. One of the folding chairs near the aisle had a bent leg. The ceiling tiles were stained in the corners, watermarks blooming in slow rust-colored circles. A chunk of plaster near the fan had flaked off entirely, revealing exposed wood beneath.

The offering plate came down his row. A battered metal tray, edges dulled and dented from years of passing hands. David fished into his wallet, thumbed past the larger bills, and pulled out two crumpled ones. He smoothed them awkwardly and dropped them in, careful not to meet the deacon's eyes.

The bills clung together from the humidity. They hit the metal with a soft hiss.

David blushed. Embarrassed at the sound. Embarrassed at the sum.

The preacher slapped the pulpit again. The whole thing shuddered. It might be reduced to toothpicks if he kept hitting it with such force. The wooden joints rattled a protest.

But the Reverend was just winding up.

"You think God don't see what you do in the dark?" the preacher shouted, voice rising to a roar. "You think He don't hear your thoughts, don't smell the rot under your good deeds?"

The fan buzzed louder, like it was trying to drown him out. It failed.

"I'm talkin' to the one who walks in with clean shoes and a dirty heart. I'm talkin' to the man who plans his sin in silence and thinks he's safe 'cause he ain't done it yet."

David froze.

"You think Hell waits politely?" the preacher screeched. "You think the flames take attendance after you act?"

He leaned forward, knuckles white on the pulpit.

"No, sir. That damnation is already circling. Already licking at your heels. You are known. You are marked. And unless you repent, you are damned."

Someone shouted, "Yes, Lord!" Another clapped, caught in the rhythm of fear.

David sat motionless, sweat beading at his temples. His hands rested on his knees, fingers twitching with restraint.

There it was, laid out plain. Murder. The top dog on the Ten Commandments.

The preacher hit his stride, rolling toward fire and thunder.

"You think the Devil waits for blood?" he shouted. "He don't. He slips in quiet. He don't need your sin to be finished, only started. Just the thought is enough to give him ground."

The congregation murmured. A few heads bowed. A woman near the front rocked in her seat, whispering something under her breath.

"The Devil don't knock. He don't ask permission. He walks in when the door's cracked. And some of y'all been standin' there holdin' it open. Welcoming him right in. Pull up a chair, Satan, and have at it!"

David blinked. His vision blurred for a second, sweat creeping into the corners of his eyes. He knew the door. Had felt the weight of it in his hand. He hadn't opened it yet. Not fully. But the knob had turned. The hinges had groaned. David had let the devil in, had felt the sting of his options. He looked down at his boots. Scuffed, dusty, soaked in the words he'd just heard.

His thoughts thudded loud in his skull.

Eternal damnation, indeed.

He slipped out during the closing hymn, before the line formed to shake the preacher's hand. At this church, that was the way of things. Just like the church of his youth. Sealing the sermon with sweaty palms and forced smiles.

It felt false, too clean for what he carried. David worried the touch might burn, that skin to skin would expose him. That somehow, the preacher would know. Would feel the weight of what he was planning.

Better to vanish before the benediction. Before grace got too close.

&.

AFTER DAYS OF CHURCH HOPPING, DAVID FOUND A SMALL corner coffee shop and began nursing his thoughts and his cappuccino. The hum of conversation around him faded into a low murmur as he stared into the cup, watching the white froth dissolve into the rich espresso beneath. The bitterness, the sweetness, the contrast—it reminded him of the sermons he'd heard. It mirrored what churned inside him, that noxious mix of guilt and justification.

He'd hoped the buzz of the shop would drown out the noise in his head, but it only intensified it. He set the cup down, the porcelain rim clicking softly against the saucer, and leaned back in his chair. Redemption felt distant, too good for the likes of him. Doing bad things for good reasons didn't make them any less wrong

Each church had offered something. Grace. Forgiveness. The law. Sin. But nothing had clicked. His own plans were already in motion, the weight of his decision pressing down on him, a celestial trap.

The barista moved in and out of view, hands steady, face unreadable. David envied his ease, wished he could compartmentalize his thoughts with the same detachment, push morality aside for a while. The balance between good and evil, good intentions and bad actions, all of it churned inside him, a dark undercurrent overwhelming whatever good he possessed.

He didn't confide any of this to Addison. Her recent flash fire anger made him hedge all his bets, not wanting to trigger another meltdown. For her, the solution was emotional, built on the removal of sadness, the absence of sorrow. But she left no room to ask what it might take from them both. When she spoke about it, there was no wavering in her voice, just that hollow certainty. No emotion, no cracks, just steel.

David wasn't built out of stone.

The plan lodged itself deeper every day, the weight settling onto his chest, spreading out like roots. He tried to stay logical, to think like a man who knew the world, who had handled blood and life and endings before. But this wasn't medicine. This wasn't science. This was sacrifice—the kind that burned down everything around it.

Doubt coiled in his gut. He was the adult, not Addison. He needed to be mature, to think through all the strategies. Still, it gnawed at him. What was the price of a soul?

He paced the sidewalk outside the coffee shop, the cold cup still in his hand. His fingers twitched against the paper. With a sigh, he stood and tossed it into the trash, the sound too small for the weight of the choice that followed.

Well. The burden was his. He'd carry it, even if it cost him everything. To the bitter end, and beyond. God was also a father, so may he'd understand.

The sound of distant church bells rang in the distance, which David took as celestial agreement.

Chapter 15

Demarcation Line

David imagined the McCall family tree cracked, a distinct before and after in September 2004. The shift wasn't subtle. In both his and Addison's lives, the divide was permanent. David no longer recognized his face in the bathroom mirror. While shaving, he glimpsed his gaunt reflection—cheekbones too sharp, skin stretched thin over bone.

Addison, too, had changed. He would find her on the edge of the couch, eyes distant and glassy, staring at nothing. Her shoulders would shake, and from across the room, he couldn't tell if she was laughing or crying. But these days, she no longer laughed. Only the occasional, broken sobs. Their present felt Polaroid fragile, life's colors dimming, edges curled and fading fast.

David gave Addison's door a gentle rat-a-tat-tat, tiptoe soft. Before, he would've knocked once, quick and almost unnoticed, before turning the knob. Now, he waited in the hallway, asking to be let in to a room in the house he had bought. Standing statue still, it reminded him of how vampires must be invited in, granted permission before they could wreak havoc. A polite killer, asking first before devouring. If given the choice, David would do the same, take a life with dignity, injecting a bit of noble gentleman into a story built for a carnivore, except when it came to Josh.

Addison cracked the door open just a sliver, never wide. Like everything else, it stayed partway shut.

"Yes?" she asked, her voice thick with sleep, eyes adjusting to the light. Her sleep-mussed hair tangled wildly, and her slow movements were evidence that the night still clung to her.

"You want some breakfast before class?"

"No, Dad. I'm fine." She kicked the door closed with her toe, leaving David to frown at the door. His unsaid words hovered, as did the uncertainty of how to bridge the distance between them.

Yesterday after work, David found her dribbling her soccer ball outside in the drizzle, letting the rain wet her face. Maybe she practiced outside on purpose, so her tears could be mixed with everything else until it was all a wash anyway. She wouldn't look at him, just kept kicking the ball into the net that had seen better days. He'd installed it when she first started club soccer, playing on the Bluebirds team, excited to gear up at only five years old. She took to the ins and outs of the game fast, never grumbling about the tight socks or cleats, and lining up her shin guards precisely.

David was out of his league. His sport of choice had been wrestling, all testosterone-laced and buckets of sweat. He didn't even watch soccer during the World Cup or Olympics, his mind labeling it as British football, letting those across the pond keep it.

But in Boone, soccer was a girl's game, the female set ran circles around the boys, until everyone was breathing hard. With less rules than football, and more engaging than baseball, both David and his daughter were hooked. Weekends became a mishmash of games and practices, Gatorade by the gallon and practice shoes, and never-ending piles of grass-stained uniforms. He never missed a practice, watching her take the ball up the field, pass, wind in her hair and a smile on her face. He called her a soccer star and installed a net, always ready to pinch hit as goalie. Their team in high school had made the playoffs her senior year, and he lost his voice yelling, unable to sound anything but hoarse for a week. David wasn't knowledgeable enough to be a coach, and all the better for it. Instead, he got to play the role of her biggest fan, and both were happy to admire winning scoreboards and rack up trophies.

Soccer was one of the few things that still tied David and Mary together. They sat on opposite ends of the bleachers, eyes meeting only when Addison scored, a quiet pride flowing between them. Mary always looked away first.

But co-parenting meant sharing soccer duties. The same talks about turf burns and cleats, the same walks down the field at homecoming games. Addison's talent made for plenty of overlap, especially with award season in full swing.

Mary dove into her role as soccer mom, all in with flashy enthusiasm. She painted Addison's car windows before big games and stocked up on top-tier snacks—no cheap Doritos for the Watauga Pioneers. Always first to grab the sign-up sheet, she made life easier for coaches with donations off the wish list. She and Don hosted sleepovers, their basement a crash pad with enough big screens to keep the girls entertained. Soccer gave Addison's parents a reprieve, a fleeting escape from the mess of their divorce.

It was funny that when Mary was pregnant, David had wished for a boy—a chip off the old block, someone he could bless with Roman numerals after his name. He'd be built like a linebacker, but taller, ready to tackle and punch, leading with his fists and quick feet. His son, Matthew Laredo, would already hold a cowboy's name, ready to honor his family with respect and healthy living.

Back then, they didn't have gender-reveal ultrasounds, so David was as surprised as anyone to learn Mary was carrying not blue, but pink. Barbie pink, he imagined, full of wet fingernail polish and hairbows, tea in fragile flowered cups, and mountains of frilly dresses.

He smiled at how wrong he'd been. Addison had missed the Y chromosome, but she was every bit as sure-footed as his fantasy son. She was a natural on the field, her strides powerful and graceful as she sprinted down the pitch. Ever the striker, she'd wait until the last possible moment to unleash a perfectly timed shot on goal. She was more than he deserved.

David had watched her in the rain, sure she could see him, eager to know if company was wanted. She fixated on the goal, kicking shot after shot, even though the muck coated her bare legs. He gave her a little wave, an invitation on his lips, but she ignored him, kicking the ball repeatedly until she was drenched in mud.

He'd assumed that because the future was set in concrete, Addison would feel better, less weighed down by her past, and ready to inch forward into a happier winter season. Her grades were still good, and her attendance, too. On paper, she seemed fine.

But as he watched her pound the soccer ball, he realized she wasn't getting better. She leaned over, hands on her knees, palms slick with blades of grass and dirt. His mind and heart struggled to understand her setbacks. It was possible she didn't trust him to complete the task. She could be lost, trapped in a purgatory that never quit. His breath caught in his throat as a question he wasn't ready to answer surfaced.

What if she never got better at all?

Addison came inside, and David was ready with a towel. He picked the plushest one and wrapped her in a soft white cocoon. She was soaked through, more dirt than girl, her clothes clinging tightly to her withered body as the rain dripped from her. Addison let him hold her, and he knew then that there was more desolation to come. He held her while she sobbed out all the unfairness onto his shirt. He hugged her as she shivered, waiting for her to speak if she needed to, to simply bear witness to the weight of it all.

She pulled back just slightly, eyes rimmed red.

"You used to say I was your favorite lab tech," she whispered. "And your favorite emergency contact."

She gave a small, hollow laugh. "I don't think I'll need either much longer. Not if this keeps feeling the way it does."

It's a hard thing to ask of a person, to see anguish so exposed and not want to cover it. To not want to shame it back into its secret place.

"Addison," he started, but the words dried up. Nothing could soothe what she had just said.

So he let her cry. Let the tears drain into exhaustion.

Then he picked up her ball and bounced it toward the garage.

She dragged herself up the stairs, shoulders slumped, feet barely lifting. Her body surrendered, giving into autopilot, heading back to her bedroom cave. David watched her ascent, but no fatherly platitudes rose to his lips. His world, laid bare. Addison, a different girl.

He stayed there, speechless with a tear-stained shirt, holding the damp towel, wishing it was an escape hatch. Because while Addison might have been wrung out, emptied for now, David's nerve endings were lit up with helplessness, screaming for a release that wouldn't come.

He couldn't sleep that night, replaying their exchange in his mind and thinking that people only cry like that when someone dies. He pushed that thought to the very back of his brain into his version of Pandora's box. There was no corpse to be found here, he told his mind, warning all hearses to keep on trucking. Nothing to see here, no accident to rubberneck. Nothing but a boatload of tears with a dash of what ails ya.

Still, the scene on loop. Maybe she was saying goodbye, laying herself to rest before the formal burial.

The next morning, Addison shot him a tentative smile with clearer eyes, reminders that she was still alive and kicking, no matter how bruised she might be. But David felt that the sands of the hourglass were poised, set to run out if he didn't start making moves, pace set to double time. It was time to pay Josh another visit.

Chapter 16

Sun Salutations

The home phone rang early on Sunday, each shrill signaling a bill collector, a collect call, or something worse than those two combined. David rolled over, not even bothering to glance at the clock, knowing it was early because the sun had yet to rise in the valley. His bedroom was all black, not even a hint of the day waking up peeking through the grey curtains. He worried the inconsiderate caller would wake Addison, until his brain caught up and reminded him that she wasn't there. She returned from the dorms with dirty laundry and a trace of company. She was a nomad now, scattered across borrowed spaces. But any journey into the land of the living counted as progress. He'd gone to bed late, sucked into a movie that ended up predictable, allowing himself a later curfew since it was the weekend.

The home phone continued to barrage near his head, and he picked up the receiver, his voice full of irritation.

"Can I HELP you?" He hoped his voice sounded papa bear grumpy, awoken from hibernation and ready to pounce.

"Oh good, you're up." His ex-wife's voice was chipper, irritating him even more with her friendliness. When they were married, Mary was the early riser, quick to remind her starter family about the advantages of catching early worms and daily doses of Vitamin D. With her yoga-toned body, she never looked her driver's license age and used her physicality as proof that everyone should greet the sun with salutations and downward dogs.

"Mary. It's early. You have someone else to torture with all this now, remember?" He refused to open his eyes, hoping this would be quick and he could snuggle back down and redeem the morning.

"Oh David, please, I'm doing you a favor," she said, her voice already barbed. "Up and at 'em, am I right? Seize the day? I could go on but that's not the reason for my call." She laughed too loudly into the receiver. "The thing is, Addison didn't come here last night. I wanted to see if she was with you."

"Are we keeping tabs on her now, Mary? She's a college student, so she went back to the dorms last night, as is her right, since she does, you know, live there?" He enunciated his words, wanting to get off the phone quick, but also convey his anger at the interruption.

A silence descended on the phone.

"She. Did. What?" Her words trilled, making the line cut in and out.

"She went back, with other people her age. I assume she's there now. Why don't you call her, wake her up, and check? If you are so concerned with her whereabouts, why bother me?" He stared up at the ceiling, feeling his body waking up, knowing the last of sleep residue was shaken off and hating Mary for it. His neurons had already started spinning, the last remnant of sleep discarded, all on his one day to relax.

"Now, why on earth would you let her go back? When there's a madman still on the loose? Have you lost your ever-loving mind, David?" She was now amping up toward shrill, her voice increasing in decibels at an alarming rate.

"Mary, locking her up won't help. Now that you've roused me, if you want to continue this conversation, the least you could do is buy me a cup of expensive coffee. If I must lecture you about parenting skills, you're buying."

She huffed, "Boone Bagelry. Ten minutes. And I do NOT need assistance from you on the parenting front, thank you very much, though I do wish we'd come to a consensus on this."

"Fine, Mary. Whatever you say." He hung up first, a small consolation for a ruined morning.

He pulled on the closest jeans he could find, skipping a shave knowing that Mary would notice. As detailed as they come, she could spot grey hairs and lint like a hawk, making everyone feel dressed down. That was part of the way she maintained her power, noticing the flaws of others first. The whole plank in her own eye thing was a foreign concept to her, Mary being more the if I see it, I say it type. What she labeled assertive often teetered into the know-it-all category, especially when it came to David and his faults. That was her favorite dissertation subject, and he wasn't in the mood to spend an hour listening to her list of disappointments.

He grumbled his way to the Jeep, noting that even NPR couldn't salvage this early morning. A Terri Gross rerun, typically something he would thank the airwaves for, got turned off prematurely, since David's sour temperament wasn't easily cured.

He had to circle King Street twice to find parking. The bagel shop bustled with patrons. It was a popular weekend spot, feeding carbohydrate-loaded grease to hungover fraternity brothers and their brethren. He spotted Mary at a table, poised and waiting like a designer-clothed viper. She'd secured two cups of coffee and his favorite bagel, whole wheat with extra cream cheese, but he knew better to consider that a peace offering.

She stared him down, waiting for him to sit.

"Nice of you to dress up for the outing," she smirked. She had on her full face of makeup and a bright pink sweatsuit, paired with diamond earrings the size of cherries on her earlobes.

"Not all of us wake with the sun, for good reason. Anyone who is chipper this early is suspicious. Makes one think they might not be quite human. But for you, everyone already suspects that." He aimed the barb at her, pulling out his seat at the same time.

She smiled at him, shoving the bagel forward.

"I don't have to have a rebuttal when my ex-husband looks homeless." She smiled at him, but it didn't meet her eyes.

David took a sip of coffee like it was a shot, hoping it could fortify him against her future barbs. But it was futile and only burned his tongue.

"It's been a while since we've had a meeting of the minds. Since you possess all this infinite wisdom on how to keep our daughter safe, I'll cede the floor to you." She clicked her acrylic nails on the counter, the sarcasm sweeping over her words, while she tapped out an uncoordinated rhythm on the cheap veneer.

David saw two options; remain petulant or try something different. In dealing with Mary over the years, he'd let her goad him far too often, trading little insults until they both forgot what they were fighting about. He mustered up what little affection he could find and aimed for something real.

"Okay. Let's call it what it is. We're both scared." He exhaled hard through his nose. "You're scared, I'm scared—hell, I'm terrified. Of whoever did this. Of what it's doing to Addison. Of how far this mess might reach."

He let that hang there. No sugarcoating, no fixing.

"But something like this... it can shrink a person's world. And Addison's world is already small. It's my house. Your house. Not much else. That's what I meant."

He looked up at her, jaw set.

"I don't want it getting smaller."

Mary frowned then conceded a small nod. It was a microscopic concession, something David would've missed if he hadn't been looking right at her.

"I just want to watch her all the time, like she's little again. I know that doesn't do a bit of good. But it makes me feel better, to keep a close eye on her, like maybe if I do then..."

"Then it won't happen again. I get that, Mary. But this didn't happen because we took our eyes off the ball. That's not why."

"Are you sure?" Her voice cracked slightly before she caught it. "Because it feels that way sometimes. This mistake or that one, and we've ruined it all for her."

She refused to look at him, studying the exterior of her bagel, examining each poppyseed. Her blond bangs fell in her face, shielding her. She pushed them back behind her ears. Her eyes were wet now.

Her hand rose to her chin. Her lips trembled. She pressed them together and kept still, holding herself in place.

David forced himself not to reach for her hand. She sniffled, keeping her chin tucked in tight. Shit, he still hated to see her cry. Not when her pupils had the same gold ring as Addison's, not when she was already beaten down, clinging to a fragile filament of hope.

He wanted Mary back in the ring, ready to throw punches. In a way, that was his gift to her. Keeping her braced for the next sneak attack. David couldn't love her anymore, and he sure as hell couldn't save her, but he could remind her there was still something worth fighting for.

She was always at her best when she was all round-house kicks and flash-fire anger. She held off the sadness with a samurai sword of cynicism. Less princess. More warrior. That was Mary.

His job was to keep her on her toes. A trainer in easy irritation. It was the role he knew best and the only gift he had left to offer.

For Mary, anger had always been easier than sadness.

Now he just had to remind her.

"Well, Mary," he started, his voice already cross, "I'd appreciate next time that you don't rouse me with the damn birds. You know better, there's someone in your home who does your bidding for free. No bagel necessary, though maybe he should keep an eye on his waistline." David said it to make it hurt, and made a gesture to hit it home, miming a beer belly on steroids.

She glared at him, her wet eyes rounding into an eye roll.

"Oh, you're one to talk. Look at you, all slovenly, barely held together with Walmart pants and a decades-old belt. There's so much I could say…"

Her agitation returned just in time for David to lob a quick smile her way before tossing his bagel in the trash. He came back to the table and let her blow off steam, her words washing over him. He didn't mind. It was a relief to see her recalibrated, back in her naturally indignant state.

He stopped listening somewhere around minute five. Eventually, Mary ran out of words, leaned back in her chair, and he realized he was being dismissed.

She looked pleased with herself, her manicured hands laced together in a winner's pose.

"Always a pleasure, Mary," he concluded, adding a wink for good measure.

That should wind her up, he thought, smirking.

"I wish I could say the same," she shot back, slamming her chair against the table.

The movement knocked her Fendi scarf to the floor.

David bent to pick it up, but as his fingers brushed the fabric, he paused. It was damp. Not from a spill. And it hadn't been raining.

He turned it slightly in his hands, confused at first, then looked at her.

Mary reached for it, fast. "Give it here."

But he'd already seen it. The truth soaked into silk. Tears. The kind she hadn't let him see.

"I mean it," she said, snatching it from his hands. "It's not your style."

She huffed, cramming it into her purse like it never existed. Like it wasn't proof of vulnerability.

"Mary," he began, but she was already barreling toward the door, pushing past a server with a tray and nearly knocking into a couple on their way in.

"Hey, watch it!" floated past David's ear.

She didn't look back. She just kept moving, like she could outrun the moment if she moved fast enough.

He braced for the cold, walking quickly to the car and farther from his bossy, complicated ex-wife. But distance didn't mute what was left unsaid.

On the drive home, the weight of her worry settled in. Not just the sadness, but the fear beneath it. There was still someone out there. Someone who could hurt Addison again. Someone who might be wondering what she remembered.

David gripped the wheel tighter. He knew the man's name. His address. His license plate. The make and model of his car. And he knew there were more details waiting, buried in records and routine, just begging to be uncovered.

He turned up the Stones' *"Sympathy for the Devil,"* letting it punch through the silence. He knew the weight of decisions made when the streetlights were the only witnesses.

And he hoped Josh would never guess his name.

Thoughts drummed in time with the beat as he pulled onto the road, headed for the Oak Street playground.

There was still work to be done.

Chapter 17

Time is On My Side

Another cold park stakeout. The kind of day that made people ache for a fireplace and a thick paperback. David had neither. He needed clear eyes, trained on his enemy's front door. This time, the house stirred. Lights on. Movement. A pulse. Time to make his move.

He leaned in. Binoculars up. Hood tight against the bitter mountain air. Josh trudged inside without looking back. David followed his shape through the windows—kitchen light flicked on, fridge opened, a long pull of orange juice straight from the carton. Josh stood in his living room like he'd lost something. He wandered back outside, climbed into his truck, too big for his frame, and turned on the dome light. He searched the seats, front to back, like a kid scrambling for a lost glove. Then the engine growled, and the truck jerked backward, fast and clumsy.

David shifted lower behind a gnarled oak, knees flaring in protest. He watched him go, the truck spitting exhaust into the cold air.

Studying Josh, memorizing his every move, felt clinical, unnatural. Like watching streptococcus grow in a petri dish. Necessary, but strange. All motion, no meaning. Like a zookeeper, studying the animals, his morality tugged by their sadness, fueled by the need to keep going.

Josh resembled every other university student. A hint of a mustache grazed his upper lip. He tossed his keys into the passenger seat, already fishing for his sunglasses. More man than monster. Just a boy chasing something he forgot. He even wiped his shoes on the doormat before stepping inside, the kind of small habit that made him seem almost... ordinary.

David edged closer. With Josh gone, the house stood exposed, all angles and shadows. He crossed the street low, body tight to the ground, boots landing soft in the gravel. No lights on in the neighboring homes. No dogs barking. No movement behind curtains. His small abode was far from neighbors' wandering eyes.

The porch sagged on one side, enough to catch a toe if you weren't careful. He scanned for cameras: none by the door, none in the corners of the windows. He noted the muddy boot tracks leading up the steps. Fresh. Still wet. Tread matched the tires he'd seen earlier.

No deadbolt on the front door. Just a standard knob lock—cheap and easily forced. He filed it away.

To the side, a trash can overflowed with fast food wrappers. Mostly burger joints, two pizza boxes, a crumpled bag from the gas station up the road. No recycling bin. No attempt at order.

The curtains in the back room were open an inch too wide—enough to see the blue glow of a screen left running. Probably a TV. Possibly a computer.

David clocked it all. Lighting, entry points, line of sight. He wasn't just watching now. He was laying ground.

David retreated behind the oak, knees tight, breath slow. The air had thinned again, and a fresh gust stirred gravel across the pavement.

A few minutes passed before the truck returned, headlights sweeping over the yard like searchlights. Josh parked crooked, wheels still turned from the rush. He climbed out holding a hoodie —just a ratty old thing, balled up in his hand—and paused to sniff the sleeve. Then he pulled it over his head in one motion, arms tangled for a second like a kid dressing in the dark.

That was all it took.

David blinked, and for a moment, he wasn't watching the boy. He was the boy. Nineteen years old. A freshman at Marshall. That awkward mix of cocky and clueless, trying to impress girls and professors with the same half-smile.

When David was a young adult, most of his thoughts revolved around yelling "Go Bisons" at football games or cracking jokes with his buddies between classes. He weighed a solid 185, pure muscle back then, and led the university's forestry club with pride. Those days were stitched together with casual responsibility. Drink beer. Pass classes. Throw axes at trees. It was the good life, the ease of which only noticed in retrospect.

He'd been dating Lynda Byrne at the time, a girl who laughed easy and kissed hard. He stayed at her place more often than not. Her apartment was cleaner than his trailer, and she made him eggs before class, still wearing his T-shirt and smelling like sleep. She had a glass eye, though you wouldn't notice unless you were looking. She didn't ask for much. Didn't need much. Lynda took life as it came and expected David to do the same.

That version of David lived simple. Classes were his only real worry. Good grades, his only real goal.

At nineteen, the world was at his feet. The nights ran together, priority time spent necking in the back of movie theaters and dragging his ass to class. But it wasn't the specifics he remembered—it was the feeling. The way life felt generous. The way it felt to skip along, when nothing had gone sour, and wounds healed fast. When the biggest decisions revolved around electives and exam schedules.

David stayed low, watching Josh from behind the oak, the cold creeping through his clothes. Josh had reached the porch now, the light glinting off his brown hair. The sharp meow of a cat, paired with scurrying paws, circled through Josh's legs. It darted from the steps, its black fur gleaming in the porch light. Josh didn't even flinch. Instead, he took a slow, deliberate step forward. The cat froze, spotlighted in the streetlight. Then Josh stomped hard, his boot coming down with a sharp crack on the wood. The cat yowled in panic, a streak of fur shooting across the yard, vanishing into the dark. David blinked, his throat tight. The mirage was broken. His youthful recklessness had been the kind born of innocence, a wild sense of freedom, when being young and dumb was just careless fun. Josh, however, held something else, a meanness that was deliberate.

David stayed hidden behind the oak for a while longer, eyes locked on Josh's house, the cold creeping deeper into his bones. Josh wasn't what David had expected. Not the innocent, reckless youth he'd once been. He wasn't just a kid stumbling through life, caught in the rush of youthful mistakes. David's mind spun, weaving the pieces together. He'd been watching, waiting for an opening, and now he had one.

He understood Josh in a way he hadn't before. The house was a mess, a reflection of the boy who lived there. It wasn't just about the physical vulnerabilities; it was the cracks in Josh himself, the arrogance that bled through every careless gesture. There was nothing fragile here. No innocence to preserve. David saw him now for what he was—an abuser, a perpetrator. Someone who had already crossed lines, who wouldn't hesitate to do so again. All pity fled.

Josh had already chosen his path. And David would be the one to end it.

He jogged down the hill toward the Jeep where he'd parked on the street. Seeing Josh in the flesh made it harder—extinguishing a light before it had a chance to shine brightest.

"Too late for second thoughts," he muttered, picking up his pace to keep warm. He told himself age didn't matter. If Josh was concerned about living a long life, he should have kept his distance from Addison, miles, worlds, light years away. Instead, Josh had chosen his future, etched it in stone with every loop he unbuttoned on his belt, with every impure thought he had about a girl who couldn't move. David burned that image into his mind, forcing away any lingering discomfort.

A man is made by his choices, he told himself, each repetition a step closer to believing it.

Chapter 18

Hourly Rates

David tried to see the waiting room with new eyes, though that was tough with the shabby couch on display, its fabric frayed and faded from years of use. The magazines scattered on the coffee table were two years old, their pages curling at the edges, a mix of old celebrity gossip and outdated health tips. The soft hum of the fluorescent light overhead mocked the space, flickering just enough to do their duty.

He told himself that psychotherapy was not medicine, more of an art than a science. There was no need for squeaky clean surgical supplies or glistening lab countertops. Here, smudges were acceptable. Still, he found it hard to view the dusty room with kind eyes. The beige carpet was threadbare, patches of it worn down to the rough matting beneath. The walls, once a soft shade of cream, had yellowed in places, and the clock on the wall was stuck a few minutes behind. A few mismatched chairs were scattered around the space, none of them particularly inviting. One had a broken leg, propped up with a folded napkin. A cheap potted plant sat in the corner, its leaves browning at the edges, too neglected to thrive. David held back the critique but judged anyway, clocking the dry soil, the indifference, and everything it implied.

He and Addison had entered the waiting room together before she was ferreted off and he was left to twiddle his thumbs. They were brought here partly because they'd run out of choices, and because of Mary's need to always call the shots. David wondered how much of his life had been shaped by her need to control, and why in her presence all free will was lost. Likely, he'd lost a couple of years off his life to Mary's relentless drive. She was content to burn bridges just to watch the chaos unfold, constantly picking and nagging, full of righteous indignation. He was used to being on the receiving end of her fury, even more so when she felt unmoored. An ex-husband, it turns out, was a perfect stand-in for a punching bag.

In the weeks since their bagel fiasco, Addison's gloomy mood only seemed to stoke the fire in her mother. Mary couldn't direct her ire onto Addison, who had become more withdrawn and thinner than a broomstick. With limited options, Mary turned her sights on David, her phone now the weapon of choice. He regretted letting Mary be more angry than sad, her fury now aimed squarely at him. As they say, no good deed goes unpunished.

In the last week alone, she'd called him a son of a bitch and a poor excuse for a father, her anger spilling over in a way it hadn't since the divorce. Sure, Mary could always be snarky, her words often laced with venom, but she usually kept it within the bounds of propriety. Recently, though, she had torn down any sense of restraint, casting all the blame onto David as if he'd willingly offered Addison up as some kind of sacrifice, like he was the root of every wrongdoing in their daughter's life.

David couldn't shake the latest conversation, its sting still fresh in his mind.

"DAVID, I know that you devoted so much of your life to

higher education. But how can you be so dumb that you don't see what's going on here?"

He told himself to stay calm, to summon patience.

"Mary, I'm not doing anything wrong. She says she doesn't want to come over there tonight. She's an adult. I can't force her into compliance. It's her choice."

"But don't you see the part you play? She has two parents, David. Two! I'm her mother, for God's sake, and I need her here so I can help her. She needs me, I know she does. I'll do anything, but somehow, someway, she wants to be with you, which can't be right. Because you—you're historically an asshole!"

She screeched the last of it, so loud that Addison overheard. Tears pooled in her eyes, adding contentious divorced parents to the list of injustices done to her. David didn't fight back, choosing instead to give up and ask for help. In the past, he would have countered with his own brand of aggression, firing back with bad names and SAT-level insults. He would've tried to trap Mary, to make her say things she didn't mean, all so he could feel justified in winning an argument he hadn't even started.

Instead, he hung up the phone and reached for a business card he'd been carrying around since the hospital. It had lived in the back of his wallet all semester, creased and forgotten, part of the packet given by the social worker.

He hadn't wanted to use it. He had lied to himself since September that breakfast, puzzles, and sarcasm could heal what was broken here. But Mary wouldn't quit, and Addison wasn't getting any better. He scanned the card again. End of the line. No more pancakes. No more pretending.

He pressed the number with a trembling thumb. The line clicked. "Freshman. Struggling. Not eating." Just enough for an outline. The receptionist filled in the rest. Dr. Kim McKinney. 4 p.m. He scrawled it on a crumpled receipt, squinting at his chicken scratch. He didn't ask the cost. "We'll take it. The fee is fine."

When he set the phone back in its cradle, he noticed Addison watching him, her eyes peeking just over his shoulder. Wide but unreadable. He turned toward her, slowly, unsure whether she'd say thank you or bring her own anger down on his head.

"Spitfire, we've done all we can. The hospital said the college center's tops for therapy. Maybe it's time to let someone else take a crack at it."

He showed her the Post-it note with a follow-up phone number.

"You're of age so you got to call to confirm but here's what they had available next week."

Addison studied the information like she would be tested on it later. A slow nod surfaced, then another, conceding to his logic.

"Tell her what you need to," David said, his voice low but firm. "But keep what's between us, between us." He hesitated, then added, "Yeah, there's privilege between a therapist and client, but don't count on it. No psychologist is going to take your side if it's between you, confidentiality, and jail time." He looked her in the eye. "I'm serious, Addison. Say enough to get help. But not all of it."

"Come with me?" she'd asked. And that's how David ended up in Dr. Coben's waiting room, surrounded by her numerous credentials. The college counseling center had accidentally double-booked her, but they offered a referral to a nearby private practice, not far from campus.

With no receptionist in sight, it was just David and the wall of diplomas. He stood to study them. Back in school, they used to call this décor the hall of accolades, every certificate framed and mounted, a show of competence before a word was ever spoken.

Dr. Coben must've received the same memo, her wall lined with heavy frames. Dialectical Behavior Therapy certified, complex trauma trained, PhD in Clinical Psychology, and ABPP board certified—each diploma a mile marker in a life spent chasing the complexities of human behavior. David eyed the titles, scanning for something amiss, still half-convinced mental health was the laxest of all the sciences. But everything seemed legitimate. No flashing signs branding her a charlatan, no snake oil tucked on a shelf, no crystals promising to cure what reason could not.

In this room, the couch squeaked, and the books, with broken spines, weren't even worth a casual thumb-through. It set an expectation, aiming for homey, but missing by a notch and landing squarely in drab. The room lacked in reading material but made up for it with the heavy rhythm of clock ticks. At the 50-minute mark, a bell rang throughout the office, signaling that time was up.

From the waiting room, he heard the uptick of Addison's voice, followed by a deep chuckle. He strained, wanting more, then caught himself. He was as bad as Mary, hovering and trying to control what wasn't his to overhear.

Dr. Coben emerged, hand out for her billable hour. David peeled off $110 in cash and passed it over. He continued to sit, waiting to see if he'd be called inside, but Dr. Coben turned away, their transaction satisfied.

David dutifully waited for Addison each week, mentally calculating what the money could be used for to make the place feel less dingy. Dr. Coben, PhD, wore casual dress slacks and a simple blouse, her frizzy hair loosely tied back. Her bespectacled eyes were paired with a warm smile. She was punctual and bland, which David thought was intentional.

He hadn't interviewed her, not wanting to seem more involved than he already was and unsure of the consent that therapists required. Instead, he paid for each session and kept his mouth shut. The doctor accepted the money without a hint of awkwardness, always offering a cheerful "See you next week" as if he were just another nameless payer. She never asked for collateral, never really acknowledged he was there. That suited him fine since the goal was to give Addison space to speak with someone other than her quarrelsome parents. It was clear they were out of their depth, which led to the reluctant intake session, and all the appointments since.

Addison clunked in and out of the office door, each movement like the pacing of someone trapped on a widow's walk, each step heavy with grief. David remembered when Addison was eight, when she and her friends would practice jump rope rhymes, skipping in time and waiting for the moment they'd all jump in together. Addison had laughed when her friend Katie couldn't get the timing down. "GO! Now, Katie, now!" she'd shout, her voice full of energy. But Katie would hesitate, and the rope would fall.

He could hardly square it. That same girl, once all blur and breathless motion. Addison's current pace now felt like someone heading toward the gallows. A vibrant young adult, now replaced by a slow-moving, hesitant box turtle.

If he looked closely, which he tried not to do, David saw the shell of his spunky daughter, withered and worn, all her broken bits showing. She looked thin enough to sink into the earth, dust curling around her bones. He imagined her skeleton—vintage, fragile—all vertebrae and sadness. An archeological find of a college student, meant to be studied and pitied. The urge to save her rose up hard, just as strong as the temptation to look away. Her ribcage poked through the see-through shirt, ready to jump out of her too taut skin. Disgust, sharp and shameful, flared through him before he forced his face into a mask of fatherly concern.

David didn't ask how the therapeutic work was going, nor was he tempted to play a game of telephone with his ear pressed against the closed door. He lied to himself, repeating all those reassuring phrases about therapeutic rapport, trusting the process, as though doing so would make them true. Really, he didn't want to hear that it wasn't working, or worse, that Addison was beyond saving. So, he paid the $110 in silence, convincing himself that the therapist had found a lifeline into his daughter's pain. He paid because he needed to believe there was someone who could reach her, even if he had to bury his doubts beneath layers of optimism.

For him, the verdict was out on whether words could heal but with every session, he found himself wanting to be convinced of the talking cure. He hoped for Addison's sake that Dr. Coben's degrees taught her how to hold that agony, to encourage his daughter to continue fighting, that when the last battalion is outnumbered and it looks like reinforcements are few, that's when she had to dig in her heels and ring out a rebel yell. That was the cowboy way, the rules of the old guard, never give up or surrender, and he hoped that the therapist was more Churchill than Freud.

In the waiting room again, alone with his thoughts, David's gaze wandered to the shelf in front of him. He picked out a developmental textbook about toddlers, its soft yellow cover drawing him in. It reminded him of a time when he'd pored over books like that, trying to decode the mystery of childhood growth, the first steps toward independence.

It was no surprise his thoughts drifted back to Addison. Every parent reminisces about the younger years fondly, the sappy sweetness of interlocked hands, one large and one small. Those times were candy cane sweet, sticky and messy, always busy with never enough sleep. Blurry and nostalgia tinged, parents rest easy in those memories, thinking of first words and bumbling steps, Santa pictures, and mornings that came too soon. He and Mary were lucky to sidestep through the terrible twos and go headfirst into the curious threes, a question always dangling from Addison's lips. "Story about it" became a common refrain, her asking to have anything and everything explained to her. Parks and swings kept her happy until the sun threatened to close shop on another idyllic day.

But those weren't the times he catapulted back to, even as innocent as they could be. In the timeline of being a parent, the toddler years weren't his favorite, not even earning a third-place ribbon. Instead, David remembered when Addison learned to read.

He expected elementary school to be a blur of bus rides and braids. But Addison's insatiable curiosity had no limits; she would learn about something and expect to see it immediately. In her childlike mind, she didn't understand why they couldn't fly to Paris and see the Eiffel Tower. She'd learned about Queen Nefertiti and couldn't wait to see the Egyptian pyramids, eager to catch a glimpse of the mummies, her tiny suitcase half packed in her mind. Her face fell with devastation when she learned they couldn't just up and go.

For a second, David wanted to live life that way, impulsive and sporadic, the opposite of the structure a child needs. To live like that though, to even dream of it, felt reckless and wonderful, all Indiana Jones and dark caverns, seeing the sights with their very own eyes. He was tempted to grab whatever they could carry, speed to Charlotte, catch a redeye, Mary be damned, and live life on their own terms. But the world crashed down, echoing words like kidnapping and truancy, vocabulary that kills a life lived for fun and fantasy.

Instead, they hunted for answers in the pages of library books. David favored mysteries, the kind with blood on the carpet and secrets buried beneath gardenias. A good whodunit always made his list. Addison tore through anything: memoirs, thrillers, even old instruction manuals. Her mind never lingered. She was already halfway into the next story before the last one cooled. They spent weekends surrounded by dog-eared spines and cracked covers. David found comfort in that kind of silence, the kind reserved for libraries or churches. Two separate worlds, side by side, tethered by presence. As long as there were books, this side of the McCall family stayed fed.

David's eyes wandered to a title he recognized: *Reviving Ophelia*. The cover rose up, sharp as a snake's bite. The puberty book. The origin story of parental nightmares and eating disorders. He'd read it when Addison entered a world he didn't understand. The one with bras and blood. Where they carved into their own skin. Where hunger became currency.

He remembered the softening of hips and bellies, the moods that threw a sheet over the sun. He'd expected the acne and the tears. What surprised him was the way girlhood closed like a trapdoor.

He flipped through the paperback, remembering the withdrawal. Addison had shut him out, choosing instead to pore over glitter eye makeup like scripture, a secluded Avril Lavigne in the making. He burned daylight chasing ways to matter, eventually settling on a weekly dinner date, even when she rolled her eyes so hard it looked painful. David figured if he could convince himself he was still relevant, maybe he could convince her too. It worked well enough. She dipped a toe back into life with her old man, teenage shame and all.

He slid *Reviving Ophelia* back onto the shelf, letting his fingers linger on the spine. Just beside it sat a slim booklet—*An Introduction to Couples Counseling*, an afterthought wedged between thicker psychology tomes. He studied the image of the glowing couple, all bright white teeth and curated affection. He'd never been tempted to remarry. Having Addison had been enough.

With her, he was never lonely. Whatever primal instincts he'd once had had long since gone quiet. He'd eased into middle age with the comforts of a simple life: Mammy's Milk, a wood-burning fire, and great shows on HBO.

His mind wandered often to fictional detectives like Harry Bosch, men who met the world with a bitter laugh and a loaded gun. Sure, he ate lunch with a few doctors, but those conversations only made him grateful for the silence waiting back home. Most days, he was just playing out the clock.

Without realizing it, David had built his life around Addison's footsteps. Without them, his world lost its tether.

He knew it wasn't healthy. He also knew it was true.

The bell rang, another session over. He knew Addison would never risk discussing their most private joint venture. David got out his wallet, ready to pay whatever price to bring her back, knowing full well that the answer wasn't found in dollars or cents. The cure was of the killing kind, his decision the only thing that could stitch her back together, back into the late-night reader he'd raised. Once healed, a plane ticket and a suitcase held an answer for them both, changes in latitudes making a weary girl rejoice.

"Same time, next week," he heard Dr. Coben say, but all David saw was Addison's smile.

Chapter 19

Lucky Ducky

David slogged through another workday, bargaining with himself to stay awake. He'd already bitten the inside of his cheek and downed more coffee than advisable, but still, his eyes were hound dog heavy, with hours of work left to do. The night before had been spent in the park again, temperatures just above freezing, edging closer to the tree line to peek in the windows. If he had any good sense, he would have worried about pneumonia or worse. But instead, every synapse was focused on the dark house.

David scouted the windows, looking for a way in. He knew this wasn't a knock-on-the-door, let-me-in kind of situation. Whatever deeds lay ahead, surprise would be his only ally. The window over the kitchen sink was just his size, and it could be accessed with one good pull-up. He was thankful he still fit into his 33 x 34 pants, never one to age into higher waistlines. Traffic on the road picked up, and David scooted back to safety, head whirring with half-formed plans.

David had studied the place for weeks, taking note of the

patterns. The lights in the living room flickered on at 7 p.m., casting long shadows through the windows, but the kitchen remained dark until much later. Around 8 p.m., Josh came home, drank his Sunny D, and heated up a microwave dinner. A late-night shower followed, a few brief moments of water running, then a stretch of silence as Josh retreated upstairs. The kind of dull repetition that made a person easy to track, easy to predict. The question now wasn't what David could see, but what he was missing.

The stakeouts created a shaky truce. His body ran on caffeine. His conscience ran on fumes. Exhaustion sanded down his last reserves. But the mountain of slides waiting on his desk reminded him there was no room for rest. He gave up and headed toward the doctor's lounge for his fourth cup of coffee. A quick hit, then back to the breast biopsy slide with the jagged margins and angry cells.

Then luck, plain and stupid. The kind that hits with a gale-force wind.

An absent-minded doctor had left the shared computer logged in, the screen still open to a patient chart. David blinked. From the lab, he'd never have this kind of access. His workstation was connected to the hospital server, sure, but without clearance for inpatient files.

Some gifts, you just take.

He glanced over his shoulder.

Pathologists were an afterthought. No narcotics like the anesthesiologists. No glory like the surgeons. Most doctors barely noticed him until a result came back late or sepsis tripped a red flag. Then he became the white knight, summoned with charts and printouts, expected to speak the language of certainty.

They called him a lab rat. David had learned to shrug it off. He always remembered the old joke: What do you call a med student with a 2.5 GPA?

Doctor.

David scooted into the seat, still warm, and grabbed the mouse. His fingers moved to the keys, typing in Josh's name. Having lived in Boone his whole life, Josh likely had some medical history at the local hospital, where all records, including those of contracted professionals, were stored. The pediatricians on the first floor might've seen him as a child.

Watauga Medical had better electronic records than the VA. The system had been upgraded a few years back, partly in response to the college town's quiet drug problem. Everyone knew the red dots in cold medicine could be cooked into meth with nothing more than a bottle of drain cleaner and a YouTube video.

David hit enter.

As the files loaded, his mind drifted to the Bosch novel he'd been reading all week. In it, a character had a fatal allergy. A convenient death wrapped up in a peanut shell.

David wondered what weaknesses Josh might have. Diagnoses. Old injuries. The facts of his enemy were at his fingertips.

A profile emerged, but as David opened the file and skimmed through it, he saw that Josh's check-ins were sporadic. He was the son of a working mom who couldn't afford to take time off unless Josh was on death's door. Half of his yearly physicals had been skipped, and his entire medical record barely spanned 15 pages.

David's eyes scanned the file, hoping for something with teeth. A hidden cardiac condition would have been ideal, something like arrhythmia that could give out under the right pressure. An MAOI antidepressant would've been a goldmine—lethal if paired with the wrong foods. Even a history of blood clots could've opened a door. But there was nothing. No hint of an underlying vulnerability. Just old dental records, a couple flu screenings, and one visit for mononucleosis that wasn't. The SOAP notes offered no clues, no leverage. He leaned back, irritated. It wasn't enough.

He logged off the computer. The other doctor would never be

wiser to the opportunity he'd afforded. Not wanting to leave completely empty handed, David stole gloves from underneath the sink, a lackluster consolation prize but a handy one. He spent the rest of the day in poor spirits, only later realizing he was mourning an effortless way to kill someone. He could ache for the person he'd become but chose instead to pick up his briefcase, stifle a yawn, and head for home.

It crossed his mind to ask Addison. She held the greater stake in this. Vengeance had become her currency. It was a partnership, though he was doing the majority of the background work. It shouldn't be hard to ask for her advice, but his pride lectured him on working alone.

She'd always been sharp, testing into the gifted program by third grade, gliding through it with the eager ease of someone built for brilliance. Now she overloaded semesters, chasing early graduation at App with fervor. School was the only thing she still got right.

What unsettled him wasn't her drive. It was the realization that she might be smarter than he'd ever been. David had grown up as the family brain, earning his place with flashcards, Latin roots, and sleepless nights. He'd worn his MD like proof he belonged in the rooms where intellect ruled.

But Addison made it look effortless. And in her glow, he felt something he hadn't expected. Dimmed.

Mastery lit something in David. Knowing the nuance of every slide, every cell, set his pulse racing. He loved solving the secrets written in tissue, lived for the charged thrill of disease revealed beneath the microscope's glare. This was his craft. The slides spoke in riddles, and he, fluent in their language, translated each into answers. Diagnoses became his signature. The hero in a lab coat. But Addison was different. From the moment she strung her first sentence together, the sharpness was undeniable. At four, she tackled puzzles meant for adults, and by five, she was designing her own logic games. The word prodigy entered the room, and David felt his stomach turn.

Once Dr. Carhartt, the hospital surgeon, stopped David in the hallway, noting Addison was calculating fractions of his daughter's birthday cake at six, even reducing denominators.

"She's smarter than my own, and hell, I was impressed, Davie. That one's going places." He patted David's back, all chummy buddy, and David resisted the urge to shake it off. The surgeon's hand felt like dead weight, his praise of Addison every bit a trap. What should have been parental pride shifted into something resembling rivalry. The moment was awkward, and David knew he was expected to beam with family pride, but all he could manage was a quick exit. There were no replies for Dr. Carhartt. He turned away, boots clicking against the freshly mopped floors. The shame burned in his gut, his ego sickened by the unspoken competition.

In the stillness of the night, as the day's weight slipped away, David confronted the truth he'd been avoiding. His search through the computer had yielded no answers, hadn't provided him a great idea tied in a macabre black bow. But that wasn't why he lay simmering, his mood foul and perturbed. He hadn't asked Addison's advice about Josh because he needed a win. He wasn't trying to solve the problem of murder. He wanted to be the best. To elevate himself above, to take hard things and make them look easy. That hunger, to remain the brightest star, kept him from being a partner.

Instead, he made it into a competition. Remorse reverberated from his brain to his heart. This silent rivalry wasn't foolish, it was cruel. She was his daughter, not his adversary. He vowed to abandon his ego and include her in his deliberations, especially with time slipping away and no clear path ahead.

Chapter 20

Fear the Reaper

Addison's startle reflex was sharp, akin to a wild animal who jumped at every creak of the door or scattered book on the floor. A clank here, a squeak there, and her body morphed into a coiled spring, eyes darting, never fully settled. Even in the safety of David's home, she could never quite let her guard down.

"It's like you've done a tour in 'Nam," Mary deadpanned on the phone.

No one laughed. The air stayed thick with awkwardness long after the call ended. David knew Mary's reflex was always to deflect. She'd slap on a laugh or sweep pain under the rug, but the unease lingered, unaddressed. This was something Mary couldn't fix with retail therapy and a credit card.

Addison's nightmares hadn't loosened their grip, even with the therapy sessions. The screams still echoed through the house, lingering from her room, seeping down the stairs, and curling into the kitchen, a chilling reminder. She woke to damp pillows, her body trembling from the fright that visited her in the dark. There were no words to untangle the fear that found her when dusk turned to night.

The sudden skittishness in Addison was a stark contrast to the girl she used to be. He remembered her as the first to scale the highest branches of every tree, the first to dive headfirst into the creek, her laughter echoing as she splashed through every puddle, her grin always the answer to every challenge. Born half-billy goat, she spent her summers at the creek, boasting to the daredevil boys in the neighborhood. Always ahead, always first. If that hadn't been her motto, it should've been. Now, that fearless girl had been replaced with a shadow, one who ran from things she only saw in her nightmares.

Her willfulness and David's invisible leash clashed like storm fronts. He had banned her from going on her 8th grade Savannah overnight trip, certain that the low number of chaperones spelled out danger. The teachers promised to lock the kids in at night, taping the doors to keep them inside, but David knew there was no such thing as a perfect plan. Security seemed scant, and David was surprised that those with childcare degrees could be so naive. Addison's tears hadn't budged him. She sulked, but he stayed firm.

"Safety is every parent's trump card," he'd told her, the words sharp, no negotiations found.

Her obstinacy created rivers of worry for David that he'd spent the last decade trying to soothe. But when there were no crises, and no close calls, he put his anxieties away. He lay down the rest of his caution, content to just ride the wave of parenthood into calmer seas. Then, evil came for Addison, in a field at a college party, and he could no longer look the other way.

Addison's depression was an iron cuff, clamping her to the couch, refusing to let her move. It had dug into her, even with the therapy. Every attempt to break free left her weaker. Her limbs were waterlogged. Her thoughts, dull knives. David sat beside her on the couch though she barely recognized his presence. The blanket swallowed her shape. Her shoulders sagged. Her hands trembled at the edges. Addison looked hollow, like someone had carved out the spark and left her shell behind.

He remembered the girl who ran barefoot through mud. The girl who climbed trees too thin to hold her. The one who laughed when she fell and dared the boys to follow. That girl had guts. That girl never looked over her shoulder.

She was buried now. But maybe not gone.

"You're a Lozen, Addison. You just need reminding." She blinked, barely turning her head.

"What?"

"You don't remember?" He leaned closer. "When you went into high school, all gun-shy, scared of everything? I told you about Lozen. The Apache warrior who didn't take shit from anyone. She was the leader. Fierce. Smart. The world couldn't break her. I told you—" He paused, waiting for the flicker of recognition.

It didn't come.

Then, "I remember," she said. Her voice was flat, her face blank. "You can be weird sometimes."

David almost laughed. Almost. "Yeah, well, I'm here to remind you. You were born to be a Lozen. The world can take a lot from you, but don't let it take that. Don't let it take the fight."

Her face didn't shift. The walls were up. Nothing. David was a mosquito, not a dad, a barely registered annoyance.

"You were the first to climb every tree. Race every boy to the creek. You went higher, ran faster, jumped further. No one had your fire."

Her eyes dropped. Her head bowed. She shook it once. "I don't know if I'm her anymore."

"But you can be."

She didn't lift her head.

"I need your help," he said. "With Josh. I can't do it alone."

She didn't move.

"I have ideas. But I want yours."

She didn't answer. Her head remained tucked, out of reach, like everything else about her.

"Come on, we are in this together. Remember?"

Addison's mouth twitched. Not a smile. Not a frown. Just movement. Then stillness again.

"I don't have ideas," she remarked. "Not anymore."

"You do, that's not true. Don't sell yourself short." He wanted to shake her, to make her remember every good thing about her, to waylay her with all her wonderful attributes.

She shook her head. "They're gone."

David reached for her hand. It stayed limp in his palm.

"I used to think I could do anything," she whispered. "Now I can't even get off this couch."

He gripped her hand tighter. She didn't squeeze back.

"I feel like a ghost. Like I'm wearing someone else's name."

David didn't speak. He couldn't. Addison's spine bowed, her face turned towards the cushions. The blanket rose higher, covering her chin. The room went still. She was right there, inches from him, but already so far away. The stillness was toxic, like mustard gas, squeezing out the last of the good air.

With his home no longer safe, and his daughter a stranger, David recalibrated toward the one thing that made sense. Josh, his enemy, his constant. A pattern he could follow, a face he understood. David had his habits on lockdown, the turns he took, the places he parked. It was a twisted comfort, to recognize that his enemy was easier than grief. There was something steady in that.

He called out a quick goodbye, light and rehearsed, then slipped into his car. The rusted red pickup was still there, parked in the same spot at the end of Josh's block, just like before. David passed it once, made a slow U-turn a block away, then eased back down the street. He parked three houses up, close enough to see the truck's bumper through the windshield. Two cars buffered him.

It was a tight fit, close enough that a door swinging open would've made him flinch. He grabbed the newspaper from the passenger seat, folding it up and holding it in front of his face in case of a passerby. His eyes never left the truck. Tracking Josh wasn't easy. But it had turned from a task into instinct, his movements mapped in David's private geography.

He settled in for the long wait. The solitude was interrupted by the *brrring* of his phone. It was cold against his palm.

"Dad?" Addison's voice floated out, thin, uncertain.

"Addison? You okay?" His whole body tensed. His mind flipped through a reel of worst-case endings. Ten minutes gone, and already it felt like too long.

"I love you, Dad. I'm sorry I was short with you, or whatever. I didn't mean it like that. I know you're always trying. I'm trying too. And I love you."

The tenderness in her words broke him, like residual shrapnel. He deflected with a laugh, and said, "I know, Spitfire."

He hung up before his throat could give him away. The sob hit fast, violent, catching him in the crosshairs. His hands shook on the wheel, his cries swallowed by cars zipping past. He stayed parked until the sun dipped low and the sky went pink. Josh never came. David drove off, wrung dry.

Later, he passed the two-story Wendy's. Crowds lined the windows, traffic moved like clockwork. His breath evened out, but his eyes remained raw. By the time he got home, Addison was asleep. She hadn't meant to gut him. Hadn't even seen it land. Still, he was glad he could break in private, not wanting to add his burdens to hers.

David undressed in the dark, the pillow soft on his cheek. Sleep pulled him under, with no resistance left. The wounds would wait. His daughter might heal. Tomorrow always came.

His last thought before sleep was black fog creeping in, swallowing everything he touched. He shivered, shifted, but the fog had already settled in.

Chapter 21

Proof Long Discovered

Josh's truck was distinctive, not in a flashy way, but worn. The bumper sagged. The paint had peeled to primer. It was in obvious need of TLC, but the way Josh lived showed that funds were limited.

David had graduated from watching him at home to following him around town. He learned his schedule, made it his own. Today, Josh parked near the stairwell at the end of King Street, skipping his usual drive out to the complexes along the highway. He smoked before getting out, grinding out the end of his cigarette in the dirt.

David took note. It was important to clock each address and every habit. He'd gotten better at mirroring Josh's movements. If the pickup pulled a U turn, David matched it. If Josh sped up, he gave space. If he paused too long, he looped the block. He kept his eyes down, his mind sharp. David felt less like a doctor and more like a detective, fed by cable reruns and browed rules.

Josh stalled in the parking lot, amid beer cans and crooked bikes. The apartments sat too close together, all cluttered neglect and peeling edges, the kind of mess ignored by people in search of a good time. By sophomore year, App State let students move off campus, and if this was what was offered, David was glad Addison had stayed in the dorms.

Josh had entered apartment 2B after banging on the door. A peer in a sweatshirt and backwards hat high-fived him, gesturing inside. Twenty minutes passed. David stayed parked, his heart hammering. A sheen of sweat glistened across his forehead. He wasn't just watching Josh now. There were friends, or dealers. The kind who knew what to slip in Addison's drink. His jaw clenched. He saw Addison, eyes glazed, blinking back confusion. Josh might not have acted alone.

David popped the door and stepped out, ready for a dose of fresh air. November cut through him, sharp and instant, as if icicles could form in the time it took to breathe. He shuffled to the back of the car, pretending to check the tires, just to get his stiff joints moving. Hours spent sitting took their toll. His knees creaked when he bent down, the crack of old leather snapping under pressure.

His nerves boxed in his chest. Watching Josh with others raised the stakes, heightened every risk factor. David wasn't meant to be here, had never visited this place before.

But he was Josh's shadow now. And he would follow him to the end.

David wasn't used to feeling scared. After years of autopsies, corpses, and medical school bone boxes, he was accustomed to seeing the parts of a person laid bare. Anatomy had taught him how to handle the grisly. But tracking Josh and his comrades set David's nerves alight.

The last time he'd felt this kind of gut-punching fear, it had hit just as hard. Sirens in the rearview. Blue and red lights slicing through the night. He'd had a brain in the back of his cherry red Cadillac.

Not a metaphor. An actual brain. Floating in formaldehyde.

He'd panicked. Hands slimy on the wheel. Heart thudding fast enough to spill a confession right then and there. Body parts in a trunk—*that* wasn't something you talked your way out of.

The cop had stepped out slow. Aviators. Wide stance. The kind of man who didn't need to raise his voice to ruin your life.

"You know how fast you were going?" the cop had asked, voice a dry scrape.

David had nodded. He hadn't trusted himself to speak. His tongue had felt like Velcro stuck to the roof of his mouth.

Don't act suspicious.

There had been a reasonable explanation. He'd just given his yearly talk at Addison's school. He always saved the brain for last, the coup de grâce of his anatomy lecture. Addison had been mortified, eyes fixed on her shoes, just waiting for David to get gone. He wasn't some assassin. Just a scientist trying to teach young minds about cognition.

Still, he'd hesitated, unsure whether to confess or keep quiet.

"I didn't realize I was speeding, officer."

He hadn't. He'd been thinking about Addison. The way she flushed when he walked in, how she barely looked at him. How *Dad* had turned into *DADDDDDDD*, all teeth and groan.

He handed over his license with trembling fingers.

Please don't ask me to pop the trunk.

"Forty-five in a school zone is not nothing." The cop gave him a squint.

David pictured the headline. *Local Doctor Caught With Human Remains.*

The terror was pure. He was sure the cop was reaching for handcuffs while running his info. He debated making a run for it but stayed still. His fate was sealed, whichever way it went.

"Drive slower next time, Doc." The cop gave him a grin.

"You helped my mom out with her breast mass workup last year. Called her yourself with the results."

He tipped his chin in thanks.

"Appreciated that. But next time keep an eye on the speed limit."

He'd waited until the cop pulled away, his palms still wet on the wheel. That night, he returned the borrowed brain and whispered a thousand celestial thank you's for getting out clean.

This was worse.

Not a brain in a bucket. A dead body. A crime scene.

His medical license would be gone. His name stripped from hospital rosters. Mary and Addison pulled into the fallout, their lives cracked open by the press.

He knew exactly what was at stake.

And still, David shifted in his seat, the leather creaking beneath him. The dashboard clock read 6:30 p.m., the soft orange sun reflecting off the windshield. His stomach growled, a hollow reminder of another missed dinner.

His eyes stayed locked on apartment 2B. A figure moved in the doorway, Josh, with his scruffy companion. David's gaze tightened, catching the outline of the vial stuffed into Josh's pocket, the motion deliberate but unhurried. The practiced patience of someone trying to go unnoticed. From a distance, he couldn't see the cash exchange, but the slight shift in posture, the way Josh's hand briefly dropped out of view, told him payment was secured.

David assumed it was GHB. Gamma-hydroxybutyrate. A central nervous system depressant, fast-acting and notoriously hard to trace. It metabolized quickly, often vanishing from the bloodstream within hours. That was the danger. That was the design.

It wasn't tasteless. The sodium content had to be high for absorption. Addison's memory of salt, the grime of the margarita, the bitterness. It all fit.

It likely started as gamma-butyrolactone, a common solvent. Once ingested, the body converted it to GHB through basic metabolic pathways.

Simple chemistry, with devastating impact. Too much sodium, and the balance tipped into seizures, respiratory arrest, or death.

Josh tucked the vial deeper into his pocket, a furtive look to his left and right.

Fear made the boomerang doubts conscious and clear, spinning through his frontal lobe.

Addison, intoxicated. Beaten. Her story blurred. The timeline murky. The plot full of holes. She said it was just the one drink. But college kids drank. They blacked out. They forgot.

He'd told himself all of it, had debated her story from every angle. But what he'd seen wasn't theory anymore. It was evidence.

Josh had done it. And he had enough to do it again.

The fear stayed, but it no longer begged him to run. It settled into a cold, clear thought. This time it wasn't paralyzing. It prepared him for the only thing left to do.

Chapter 22

Lessons in Parenthood

Two more stakeouts left David nodding off over his slides. He no longer had the stamina for late nights. He wasn't a resident anymore, running on Redman and vending-machine Coke. He didn't even remember when he drifted. One minute he was staring at squamous cell carcinoma, zoomed all the way in. The next, a black curtain. When he came to, his chair was tipped back and a thin line of drool sat on his lip. He wiped it quickly and blinked the haze away.

No one had knocked. The door was closed. The lab techs were still busy with intake and orders. He smacked his cheek, hard enough to sting, and sat up straight. David recovered his attention but not his nerves, feeling shaky over his midday doze.

His scope still sat open, the slide unchanged. He reached for the fine focus, but his hand hesitated. Just the thought of getting through the backlog made his eyes ache.

A burst of knuckles on wood made him jump.

Craig pushed in without waiting. His tie was crooked, jaw working a mint. "You good?"

David straightened up. "Yeah. Long couple days."

Craig looked at the screen, then at David's face. "You fell asleep."

David didn't answer. The pause hung between them. He didn't deny it but wasn't certain how Craig could've known.

"You know you can't do that, Dr. McCall. It's bad for business, lethal for patients."

David nodded once. "It's Addison. Things have been uphill. Tough on all of us." He felt dirty, blaming his daughter for his ineptitude. But he fell on that sword anyway.

Craig studied him. "Sure. But this isn't like you. You've been off."

David looked down at the scope. "It won't happen again."

Craig didn't say anything at first. Then: "Two frozens came in. You're up."

He left the door open behind him.

David's slumber was proof that parenthood was bad for careers. Raising a child was a tenured job with no overtime wages. Without Addison, David could've been a better pathologist. He could've done more research into soft tissue or been more involved in the local division of the American Pathological Association. He could've volunteered for more committees or marketed to secure more drug labs. Kids were an efficiency killer, anyone who said otherwise wasn't parenting right.

Fatherhood wasn't an accident, but it wasn't romantic either. David didn't dream of bedtime stories or coaching Little League. He just knew what he didn't want to be.

His old man had been the strictest there ever was—hard lines, harder consequences. David had no interest in playing the hard-ass.

Still, he had rules. Knowledge is power. Study hard, do well. Hope for the best, prepare for the worst. Be good or be good at it.

Those weren't the mantras found in baby books, but it didn't mean they weren't words to live by.

David was surprised by how naturally fatherhood came to him. Addison's affection was contagious, and he found himself overwhelmed by a love he hadn't expected. It wasn't warm or easy. It was raw, as vast and unpredictable as the ocean.

He would look at Addison, at her soft hair and those tiny milk teeth, and think, *You're the most important thing in my life.* That's why *Where the Wild Things Are* got it so right. That line, *I could eat you up, I love you so,* rang so familiar.

Love like that doesn't let you go. It grows roots, burrowing deep. You don't notice until it's too late. You're not the same after. It changes you without your permission.

David tried to find a balance between the John Wayne and Atticus Finch versions of fatherhood. A man's man with an intellectual heart. He'd watch old cowboy movies with her on Tuesdays while he coded pathology billing. By the time she was four, she had already seen classics like *The Man Who Shot Liberty Valance* ("Whoa, take it easy there, Pilgrim") and *True Grit* ("Well, if I had a big horse pistol like that, I wouldn't be scared of no boogeyman"). She wanted a Dad like that, and he wanted a girl like Maddie Ross and Scout, girls with bravery and fire.

Being a doctor didn't mesh perfectly with the cowboy lifestyle, but David wore his boots anyway, paying homage to all his heroes. They made him walk a little taller, like the world would take him seriously just because he dressed the part.

They had to put the westerns on pause when she started using words like "muttonhead."

"You're making her weird," Mary complained. "Tune down the westerns, David. She's just a little girl."

David figured they were making her tough, but he agreed to

hold off for a while, until she could appreciate the greats like *Unforgiven.*

David wasn't born to be a protector. It didn't come naturally, not like it did for other fathers. He had to force it. He learned it from novels, from cowboys who made it look easy, to take up the label and make it his job.

His day job as a pathologist slipped into the background, suffocating under the weight of fatherhood. He found himself rushing through autopsies, the scalpel's precision lost as he tried to finish faster, his mind drifting to Addison's late-night homework or the arguments over whether she could go out with her friends. The bodies on his table no longer seemed urgent, replaced by hormones and homecoming dances. The microscopic slides that once demanded his undivided attention sat untouched longer than they should, the chemical stains drying before he could finish his analysis. Reports piled up, half-filled, waiting for completion between rounds. His life, once defined by the cold precision of a lab, shifted when she called him Dad.

Another day done, and with no further naps. David's hand found the door, his leather briefcase swinging across his shoulder. He flicked the light off.

Footsteps clunked behind him, followed by a fast, "Hey, wait up." He turned to see Craig, walking briskly toward him, his tie still crooked and his jacket sleeves rolled up.

"I'll walk you out," Craig said, falling into step beside him, his voice low. The parking lot was nearly empty, though it was past 5 p.m. David matched Craig's pace, uncertain what to say. The tension between them was still palpable, like something unsaid hanging in the air.

Craig glanced at him, his eyes narrowing slightly. "You know, you seem like a good dad. From what I can tell, you're doing right by her." He paused, giving David a long look. "I'll keep it between us. You're good at what you do, Dr. McCall. Just keep at it."

David's fingers tightened on the car door, the weight of the words settling in. Craig didn't wait for him to answer, just kept walking beside him.

"Balance, man. It's a fine line. Don't be the guy who wakes up one day and wonders where it all went."

David said nothing, but the weight of Craig's words settled on him, solid and hard. He got in the car, slammed the door, and started the engine, its hum filling the space as he pulled out of the lot. Craig's advice lingered in the back of his mind as he drove, trailing him all the way home.

Chapter 23

A Backup Plan

David never remembered the fourth rule, to his detriment. Cormac, with his ROTC edge, caught it every time.

Rule number four: Always have an escape plan.

Cormac said it like gospel. Eyes always sweeping for exits, scanning doors, watching the room like it might turn on him. Even after rotations ended, he barked at David, ever the drill sergeant. He made him say it out loud until he slumped into the leather seat, half-annoyed, half-aware it might just save his ass one day.

They never mapped out a real exit. No plan for what came after if things went south. But Cormac talked like he already knew. Said he'd go back to the foothills of West Virginia. Back to the hollers where a rifle on your back didn't mean trouble—it just meant you were local. Cormac said those mountains didn't take kindly to outsiders. Didn't ask questions. Didn't answer them either.

In his part of town, everybody knew how to keep their mouth shut. A hometown where American flags hung high as did neighborly values, shouting God Bless the USA in the same breath as Remember Ruby Ridge.

In addition to his weekly drives to watch Josh, David had started taking out cash. Fifty bucks at the gas station. Another fifty at Wal-Mart when he grabbed razors. Every errand came with a withdrawal. Small. Steady. Forgettable.

He had been building the stash since the day Addison asked, and by now, he had close to twelve grand in getaway money.

That wasn't all he had. His retirement account held thirty-five-grand at BB&T. Hit-the-road savings. Just in case the cash under the floorboards wasn't enough.

Not enough for a new life. But enough to start one.

He'd vanish before seeing the inside of a prison cell. If the police came knocking, asking questions with smiles that didn't reach their eyes, he knew how he'd vanish. After the holidays, he'd start planting the seeds—casual talk about needing a break, maybe joining the snowbirds on their winter cruises. It wouldn't seem odd. Doctors burned out all the time.

Miami was a straight shot down I-95. He'd pick a cruise with a port in the Bahamas. The carnival lines had plenty of options. All he needed was one that docked for the day. He'd leave his luggage in the cabin, maybe a book open on the bed, give the illusion he planned to return.

But he wouldn't.

While the rest of the passengers posed by waterfalls and drank rum out of pineapples, David would be haggling with a local on the far end of the marina. He'd barter for passage to another island, one less frequented, with no cameras and no questions. The kind of place where cash still bought silence and nobody cared about who you were before you showed up.

He'd take only the necessities, what he could carry on his back.

The rest—his wallet, passport, digital footprint—he'd leave behind. No alert, no clear goodbye. Just a room that looked paused, mid-vacation. Maybe he missed the boat. Maybe he went for a swim and didn't come back. Maybe. Whoever came looking would leave with more questions than answers.

If the police put him on notice, planes were out. One flagged license and he'd be grounded before he made it to the gate. Buying a cruise ship ticket might get him flagged as a runner.

But the ferries? Those cheap Florida-to-Bahamas runs flew under the radar. He figured he could blend in, slip past the lazier end of American customs. The college spring breakers made that voyage every year, peeling off winter layers and returning sunburned to frozen ground. They boarded the party boats out of Fort Lauderdale, drunk before they cleared the port. Three margaritas deep by the time they hit shore. Addison's friends once bragged they barely flashed a passport. They just moseyed up to the front of the boat, letting the music and the good times roll for the flat fee of three hundred dollars.

Either way, the islands were the goal. From there, he'd play hopscotch across the archipelago, paying cash, switching clothes, blending in. He'd dye his hair fully grey, shop local, and disappear into the slow drip of island time. He'd rent a modest bungalow, live on island time. Nothing flashy, just enough to sleep, shower, and stay unnoticed.

While he bided his time, he'd work on an alternate ID. Maybe tend bar somewhere, pour drinks and nod along to stories. When the salt air wore thin, he'd find a way to Mexico. He had enough cash for a small boat, enough to drift between docks until no one remembered his name—just a missing man with no trail to follow. David possessed enough cash for a small boat, allowing him to be a drifter until they all stopped looking for his body.

He'd leave a note for Addison at home, something vague and hidden, hinting at European destinations. A Paris ex-pat, there were worse ways to live, drinking bowls full of coffee and practicing his dwindling French. Anything to throw the Feds off the scent.

His story wouldn't end behind bars, with men with tougher lives and thicker skin. He wasn't built for the inked-up, iron-barred world. He'd last a week, two if they thought he was useful. David didn't believe in luck. He believed in contingencies. His plan would get him out of the country fast if things went sideways.

The pull of the Caribbean made him feel claustrophobic. He would need to make himself small, untethered to the world he knew. There would be national news, a tourist who never came back, and his picture flashing on the screen, but there would be nothing to link his disappearance to an escape plan. The money was drawn so sporadically it did not feel like a heist. Even with his disappearance, it was unlikely anyone would connect the dots between his getaway and Josh's absence, especially if he left before the questions became station visits.

He searched his closet for short-sleeve shirts. He had none. The Boone winters could freeze his face off, and the summers still held a chill after sundown. It was time to buy one and try it on for size.

He thought of ships at sea, of getaway backpacks, of life on the lam. Of islands laid out like scattered coins. The lure of it felt almost otherworldly, like giving up his MD to become a pirate. Reckless but free. And it would cost him everything.

Saying goodbye to Addison would break him, but staying was worse. Moving between places, changing locations, would keep the trail cold. The police would never know his name. There was no such thing as too much prep. No such thing as too careful. If everything went according to plan, the sirens would never come. No cuffs and no arrest. Just distance and disappearance.

It wasn't a fantasy. It was a fallback. A way to step off the ledge he'd been living on. If he left it all behind—Addison, the morgue, the wreckage—maybe he could start over. Wipe the slate. Scrub his soul clean. Leave Josh, and every dark thought, behind for softer shores.

Chapter 24

Journey to The Dark Side

David had been watching Josh for weeks, tracing his patterns, confirming the gaps. His schedule rarely changed. Classes at Caldwell Community. Lunch with a couple of buddies. Home by mid-afternoon. Not much studying. Sometimes a nap. Sometimes a quick joint.

It seemed lonely. Still too good for the likes of this bastard.

David stood at the kitchen counter, eyes on the microwave clock. 9:30 a.m. Josh's first class started at 10. That left a solid three-hour window before he came back.

The rain didn't fall so much as needle him, cold enough to lock his jaw. It soaked through his coat in minutes, settled in his bones like a grudge.

Every step felt earned, as he locked his car door behind him. Cars passed without slowing, tires hissing like they knew better than to stop.

He'd been watching Josh for weeks, checking the times, confirming the gaps. His schedule was predictable: class at Caldwell Community, lunch with his buddies, back by mid-afternoon. Josh was still gone, would be for the next few hours. It was as good a time as any. He trudged up the hill, through the park, the freezing rain making things slick and slow. David didn't make good time. His coat clung to him, heavy and useless. Josh's red pickup wasn't in the driveway. Good. No cars lingered by the road. Just the hiss of rain and the drag of his breath.

His eyes flicked to the window above the kitchen sink. It didn't face the street, and the blinds were half-drawn, just enough to slip through unnoticed. He circled the house, careful not to make a sound. The gravel crunched beneath his boots, but the rain softened it.

He reached the kitchen window, checking for any sign of life inside before he approached it. The old sash window wasn't locked. It hadn't been the last time he checked, but he had to be sure. David grabbed the handle, his fingers stiff from the cold, and twisted. The wood groaned, reluctant to move, and he twisted harder. The damn thing fought him, rusted and worn, but it gave way with a loud crack. A few more twists and the bottom half of the window was open just wide enough.

David hopped up onto the sill, bracing himself against the counter, feeling the jagged edges of the frame against his palms. The window creaked a protest, as he yanked himself through. He had to throw his weight into it, catching the edge of the counter with his elbow and slamming down hard on the floor when he landed. The old linoleum gave a soft thud beneath him.

David's eyes swept the room, taking in the mess with a practiced glance. The furniture was a haphazard collection of old junk, most of it from Goodwill or yard sales. The couch sagged, its floral pattern faded with brown spots intermingled with the roses. A chipped wooden table sat beside it, the varnish long gone, exposing the raw wood underneath.

The kitchen wasn't much better. The cabinets were crooked, one door barely hanging on. A walk-in pantry contained chips, microwaveable meals, and boxes of stale cereal. Beneath the sink, a stack of mismatched plastic containers, lids missing or cracked, was shoved into a corner. The sink itself was half-full of dishes, soap scum clinging to the sides.

More Sunny D bottles, turned sideways like forgotten soldiers, littered the counter. Every single one of them drained dry. A few of them still had the sticky residue of the sugary drink clinging to their sides, a streaked film that caught the dim light filtering through the window.

Josh's crash pad, small, cramped, and forgotten. A tomb of neglected things, left to rot.

This was the man he was going to kill. David went to the doorway, taking in more than he wanted to. He pictured Josh there, flipping through channels, wearing an Appalachian sweatshirt like Addison's, same gold thread, same tattered logo. He stepped into the bathroom. Beard clippings speckled the sink. A toothbrush lay flat, still wet. No washer, no dryer, but a half-empty bottle of Gain sat tipped on the shelf, like even the laundry told a story.

David hadn't come to understand him. But now he'd have to live with knowing.

David's heart started to race. It felt real then, like he'd already done it. His palms sweated while he watched, thinking of Josh off-color, imagining chapped red cheeks turning grey and blue. He'd agreed to it, planned it, but here was the solution to his daughter's unhappiness, full of flesh and bone, of thoughts and favorite songs, every inch of him someone's son. A person spending a lazy day full of junk TV, drinking his daily dose of Vitamin C, keeping his door locked and his head full of previews for movies and the day's weather. The remote balanced on the arm of the couch, almost falling, not quite. A space heater clicked in the corner. Fast food wrappers bunched on the coffee table. One sneaker lay on its side near the door.

He looked for the GHB vial. Nothing on the counters. Not in the sink. Josh must keep that on his person.

David's eyes flicked back to the hallway. One last room, the most personal. He hesitated, then turned the knob to Josh's bedroom. The room smelled faintly of cologne, sharp and familiar, mixed with stale sheets. He peered inside. The bed was unmade; blankets tangled in a heap. A stack of dirty laundry sat in the corner, half-folded shirts spilling out of a basket. No pictures on stands, no posters on the walls. A dresser sat against the far wall, one drawer slightly ajar. His eyes swept over the clutter, and a pinch of guilt tightened in his chest. It felt too damn close. David didn't belong here. He needed to get out.

He checked his watch. Time to go. He turned away from the bedroom, the weight of the room following him. His socks squelched in his shoes as he moved down the hall. Wet footprints tracked behind him, dark smudges on the tile. He wiped one with his sleeve, which only made it worse. The drip of his coat echoed too loud in Josh's home. Each second stretched. He hadn't touched much, but now it felt like everything in here had his fingerprints on it.

He grabbed a dish towel from the oven handle and dropped it to the floor, stepping on it, dragging it back over the smudges. Not perfect, but better. The worst of it blurred. He wiped the doorknob, the sink edge, anything he might've brushed. One last scan. Nothing obvious. He peeled off the soaked towel and tossed it back where he found it, folded just enough to pass a glance.

Then he slipped out the window, the sash dragging with a squeak as it stuck halfway up. The frame rattled—old, rickety—but it held.

The cool air hit him as he stepped into the yard, the streetlights low in the distance. One last look at the house, and he was gone.

He'd become a hundred percent a murderer later, but for now, he took the steps there. He looked at Josh with new eyes, ones that would take this man's life without hesitation. He hadn't pulled the trigger yet, but he didn't need to. He'd already looked at someone and wanted them truly dead. If Jimmy Carter was right and lust resided in a man's thoughts, then Josh had already died, many times over.

David edged away from the tree line, taking another route down the hill instead of toward the park. It added time to his walk, and he hated it. The rain had soaked through his coat, and the cold gnawed at him, but he kept his pace steady, unwilling to rush. The extra time gave his thoughts a place to land. A plan formed, wicked and lethal. He'd seen his enemy and escaped unscathed, but something in him had already broken

David was glad to be home. Grateful for heat, for a locked door, for the dull hum of ordinary things. He'd become a murderer another day, but he'd learn to embrace the title. Etch it next to the MD on his nameplate. Let it hang around his neck, a second credential. He didn't flinch from it. He welcomed it. Not with pride, but without apology. Marked in blood, a label he claimed as his own.

Chapter 25

Driving Ms. Addison

David slipped back into the habit of driving Addison around, just like he did before she got her license. They'd been cruising together since pre-K, and it felt almost natural, like a time loop. Back then, it was unspoken: the driver of the Cadillac El Dorado called the shots on their rides to school. David perked up straighter, proud of driving something so pretty. The leather was buttery, and the music was kickin,' with the best of his brethren riding shotgun.

He was quick to shrug off his lab coat and play chauffeur. His fingers would slide through her sun-bleached hair as she rested her head against the seat, the wind picking at it. She didn't mind. He'd think of Scout from *To Kill a Mockingbird*, remembering how Jim wouldn't let Boo touch him if he were awake. Their lives felt like literature, a family tree of just two. The years passed, and Addison grew. Once, he swore she grew an inch overnight, like a chrysalis hatching fast. Addison had those natural arched eyebrows, made for '80s supermodels. But what they kept were those drives in the Caddy.

Transportation was one thing. The topics, another. They talked about everything—her day, her worries, the minute details that made life feel like it was constantly spinning. David tried not to be too strict, giving Addison room to breathe, but there were always two or three non-negotiable rules. The number one rule, of course, was the one she broke first, true to form in never doing anything halfway.

That rule? Blue-eyed girls had no business being in the sun. David told her often enough. He diagnosed skin cancer for a living. Sunscreen wasn't a suggestion; it was doctrine. She only broke it once but once was enough. Senior prom. Some half-baked idea about "getting a little color." She snuck into a tanning bed and thought she'd covered her tracks, but David noticed. Her skin was darker than it should've been in the middle of a rainy May.

Two weeks grounded, a record for both of them. He smiled, appreciating the ease of the parenthood afforded him. No sneaking out, no drugs, just an easy back and forth, without tanning beds, without lies.

The other rules were standard: don't drink and drive. Don't lie.

The Caddy belonged to another life. What he had now was ice, slope, and a Jeep that could take a hit. Boone wasn't built for sports cars, and his Grand Cherokee, with its bulk and four-wheel drive, was a far cry from that slick red coupe. Snowfall turned drivers cautious, mountain roads unforgiving. He'd chosen function over flash, comforted by the fact he was carrying precious cargo.

He'd added some flair with bigger tires, convinced they'd be useful against the December chill. They wouldn't be blowing snow at Sugar Mountain this year; it was already coming down hard, coating everything and everyone with an icy blast.

But as opposed to days past, David worried about being Addison's chauffer. As he picked her up from her British Literature class, they stopped at the stoplight, across the street from Klondike Cafe.

Her peers were spilling into the parking lot, toboggan dotted and cradling cold beers like recently hatched eggs. It was a mix and match Guess Who version of modern college kids, with dreadlocks peeking from beanies, and Greek letters emblazoned on muscled chests.

The college crowd was out in droves for the polar bear plunge. At App State, when the temperatures dropped, the boldest or most foolish dove into the Duck Pond, a manmade lake near the student union. They risked hypothermia for bragging rights and attention, and the bar crowd was set to follow, eager to observe the cold-weather tradition. Through the rolled-up windows, David could hear them hollering and taunting each other, smiles abundant.

A wave of anger surged through David, fast enough to catch him off guard, like rage was grabbing him by the collar. Idling at the light, he tried to find the root of it, searching his mind until something clicked. The college kids looked carefree- joking, and laughing, enjoying the snow and draft beer. If Addison were there, she'd be bundled up on the sidelines, solemn, far from their frivolity. She wasn't tempted to join the ranks of the college thrill seekers shivering in low-rise jeans and painted black-and-gold faces. That was all taken from her the moment Josh remembered her name.

David looked once more at the bar scene before turning left, wishing for once that Addison wasn't with him. He glanced at her, worried she was also thinking about everything she was missing. Instead, her eyes were glazed, unfocused.

David turned his attention back to the young adults, dangling off a rickety porch, their laughter cutting through the air, even with the windows up. It taunted him, their good moods, earning him another quick frown. He drove slowly, pulling into the Red Onion parking lot, known for its French onion soup being the only edible thing on the menu. He shifted the car into park, keeping the heat blasting.

"Did you see that?" David asked, angling toward her.

"What? Why are we parked here?" Addison pulled closer to the window. "I just want to go home. It was a long class."

She yawned, overly loud. It made David irrationally angry, a symbol perhaps of her newfound apathy.

"I get it. I know it's hard to engage. Hard to want anything. But sometimes it feels like your life is slipping away." He kept his voice steady, measured. Her moods had been brittle lately, her thoughts darting off before he could catch them. "I was thinking that when I saw those kids outside the bar. All that noise and warmth and living."

"I don't know what you mean, Dad." She stared at her hands. "There's no rule book for this."

"I know. But you've got oceans of years ahead. And I worry." He let the words hang for a second. "It's easier to sink than fight the pull. You don't have to drown."

Tears welled up in her eyes, blurring her gaze, the thin glassy film spreading fast.

"When's the last time you talked to Katie or Stephanie? I never hear you speak anymore. You only answer when someone asks. This isn't how it's supposed to be." David fought the urge to grab her, to shake her out of her stupor.

"I don't know. It's hard, talking to people. I don't want to explain… I don't know what to do with any of this." Her words landed flat, a wall between them. Apathy was Addison's closest companion now, keeping her cocooned and blunted, distant from everything and everyone.

David realized he didn't know how to fix it either—and now he'd dragged the spotlight to the one thing neither of them could solve.

He reached for her hand, but she didn't move.

"Then let's go. Pick a dot on the map. Somewhere warm and easy, where your biggest concern is passing Psych 101 and finding your damn sandals. This freeze-your-face-off cold isn't worth what it costs to be here. We'll start over. Your mom will blow a gasket, but I'll give her a run for her money if that's what you need."

"You don't get it, Dad," she muttered, still facing the window.

"Then help me get it."

"I'm different now. Not marked, not branded. Just... not the same. Moving would be a Band-Aid. I'd still be stuck with myself, sorting through all this. I can do that here just as well as there."

He tried again, desperate for a remedy she hadn't already swatted away.

"Honey, I know this isn't something you just shelve. I'm not naive enough to think you can brush it off."

"Good," she said, sharp. "Because that's pretty naive, Dad."

Her eyes met his, full of knives.

"It's just that... how do we find a way through this? I'm not in therapy. I don't have the answers. But I see you so far from what freshman year should look like—all the things I had—and I want to make it better."

"I told you..." She sighed, like he was a toddler and she was the tired mother, reaching for a lifeline she'd already dropped. "There's only one way to fix it. One way out I've seen, from the moment I woke up to now, sitting in this car. That's the only future that makes sense to me."

He held in his next thought, tucked it deep

What if that doesn't fix what's been broken here?

Instead, he eased out of the lot, focused on the road as the snow wiped everything white. Addison leaned her head against the window, trusting him to take her home. Trusting him to take a life to fix one.

That night, he didn't read up on murder weapons. He didn't dig through old forensic texts or wrack his brain for clues. David read about trauma instead, folded away in one of his untouched psychiatric volumes.

It told him what *not* to say, like this too shall pass, or I understand. The word encouraged him to query, and to avoid the tropes, the urge to bury sadness under silence or shame.

But there was no roadmap. No dummy's guide. No step-by-step toward redemption.

He felt a chill that had nothing to do with the snow outside.

There wasn't a cure listed. Because there wasn't one.

The author discussed how a person changed, how what happened to them tainted their view of themselves, others, and the world. The newly subdued Addison might be the only one left, a shadow of herself, who curled up in couch corners and watched with wooden eyes as the world spun around her. His daughter had become a sad changeling, one who could never fully heal, even if her medical chart said she was perfectly healthy. These wounds ran deep, no salve to make her new, no treatment to make her smile again. It hit in all the deepest places, the way a person, no their soul, could not be made new.

His spitfire had morphed into melancholy, with nothing of her former self left to remember. David was left to carry the memory for her. He could hold on to the mental picture of her crooked smile when she lost her two front teeth and couldn't eat apples for a month. He would keep the image of the goals she scored with her triumphant team whooping, her trying to be a good sport but blushing at her fast feet. The Christmas mornings when she was too old to believe in Santa but kept the dream alive for him, her sweet eight-year-old self wise enough not to ask too many questions. For the graduations, the proms, and all the highlights of her young life.

He would keep them all for her, until the end had been written and they could begin again.

David shoved the book away like it could bite him. He pitched it across the room, feeling silly for throwing it but also desperate to banish its grim future from his home. He didn't want a sad ending. He wanted to write a different one, where she got everything she wanted and life gave her back what she deserved.

Chapter 26

House Red

Living in the same town as his ex-wife meant that David was ambushed with glimpses of Mary. While Don was more of the country club type, and they claimed everything north of the Deerfield country club, sometimes a trip to Blackcat Burrito or grabbing coffee at Conrad's meant running into Mary, blissfully unaware of David's presence. He'd watch her from a distance, letting her smile linger, knowing that if she saw him, it would sink and drown her face. Like today, when he spotted her at the pharmacy, her hair hidden under a Burberry newsboy cap.

He enjoyed seeing her happy, showing all her teeth, her body long and lean. David never spoke to her if he could help it, preferring to watch from afar rather than ruin both of their moods by talking. He'd pick a disappearing act over a verbal shootout every time. But knew that's why he got the distant label, more ghost than man.

A soundtrack played when he saw Mary, all "Desperado" crooner, warning about drawing the queen of diamonds over the queen of hearts. When the Eagles sang about discontentment, they had Mary in mind. She'd always been that way, never satisfied, still the same old girl she used to be. Diamond eyes focused on bigger carats, never pausing until she got what she wanted, then moving on to the next, always searching for the biggest and brightest.

David had been warned, knowing she was born with a silver spoon and bourgeois dreams, the only daughter ripened and sweet, if only to cover a daily dose of poison. *There's a reason antifreeze tastes sweet,* he reminded himself, watching Mary elongate her neck.

Living a life less than what she wanted made Mary churn with a mean undercurrent, easily rattled and swerving his way. Seeing her was never pleasant, always full of things left unsaid, tainted by the danger of underestimating her. David left the pharmacy before he could be spotted, keeping a wide distance from his ex-wife's wake.

The Christmas spirit put him in the mood for grilling. The holiday, and subsequent time off, meant he needed to fill his days, and keep his hands busy. December also meant a break from watching Josh. Holidays brought loose structure and too many eyes. He didn't want to get caught. Or worse, recognize the boy with his family. The less personal, the better.

Harris Teeter had gone all in on the holiday décor. Red and gold tinsel hung from every aisle sign. Plastic poinsettias sagged by the registers. A blow-up Santa slouched in the corner, wheezing cold air from a loose seam.

David filled a cart. Steaks. Charcoal. The kind of lighter fluid that reeked of July. He was almost out the door when she walked in.

Mary.

Draped in something too sleek for a grocery run. Fur at her collar, lipstick too red for a Wednesday. Maybe it was in his head, the way everything slowed. But Mary had that pull. Even here, between cold cuts and discount hams. She'd never touched a coupon in her life, but she knew how to stop a room.

Two run-ins in one week. He was due for a third, or a stroke. David attempted to make a run for it, not in the mood for a confrontation, his stomach already telling him to get a move on. But she'd locked in on David, and zeroed out the rest of the store, heading straight toward him. No hesitation and no mercy. They'd be forced to do the divorced parent waltz in a public forum. He scanned his brain for an out. Fire, flood, flat tire—any excuse. Nothing came to mind.

"Well. Speak of the devil. I've been meaning to talk to you." Mary never bothered with warmups.

"Lucky for you, I was in a red meat mood." He eyed the merlot in her cart. "Looks like you were too." David shot her a smile, a weak attempt to ease the tension.

Mary glanced at his steak, then turned her nose up, not one to linger among the peasants and ground chuck.

"I'm not here to swap recipes. And this isn't the place. Peppers is three doors down, next to Conrad's. The wine's barely drinkable, but it's quiet. I don't need the whole town watching me talk to you."

"Are you asking me to join you for a holiday aperitif?" He smiled bigger, egging her on. "Gosh Mary, if I'd known I would've dressed for the occasion," he said, motioning to his jeans and collared shirt. "Let's not tell Don, okay?"

Her face flashed curse words she wanted to say, but instead she ate them, settling on, "My ex, the jokester. Thanks, but I've already had all you can offer, and I passed on it." She cut her eyes, concluding, "I'll meet you there, just one glass, your meat will be fine. No need to parlay it into a date, no matter how much you wish that could be the case." She sauntered off before he could retort.

David was pissed at her cockiness. Because he never remarried, Mary assumed he was still waiting for her return. He'd had enough of her for five lifetimes, content in the bachelorhood that gave him room to breathe. No one to impress, no demands to drain him dry. He enjoyed his evenings with detective novels and westerns, where the lines between good and bad were never blurred. His single life, a slow release from all that clutter.

He wasn't some damn eunuch. He could still be bowled over with desire. Loneliness could do that to a man. A quick whiff of floral perfume, the brush of a nurse's hand near his. He considered taking another turn on the dating wheel, taking one of the flirty shift nurses up on their offer. But the spark never caught enough to warrant a chase. Instead, he kept his dirty thoughts to himself and his hand for quick comfort. Most days, that was enough. But some nights, when the house felt too still, he wondered if he'd forgotten how to want someone.

The heavy weight of starting over, and weaving through someone else's family tree, was exhausting. Dating was a game in which every gesture and word was measured. David valued his solitude, living his life without fitting into someone's ready-made template. Compromise, and introducing Addison to a paramour, felt like a slow erosion of every comfort he'd fought for. It was hard enough juggling Mary and their run-ins. No need to complicate the plot.

David settled with the cashier and made his way toward the restaurant, part curious, part certain he was in for a lecture on his latest wrongs. Mary spoke to him in capital letters; arms crossed; a sneer waiting to be played like a King of Spades. She'd categorized David somewhere between village idiot and evil emperor, unless on the rare occasion, he was useful. For most the holiday offered good cheer and a reprieve, but Mary took no time off.

He'd learned the best way to navigate her tedious waters was to stay out of them, but no divorced parent is lucky enough to wade too far from the shore.

David ordered a glass of the house red for himself, picking

out something higher end for Mary. The waiter hesitated when he asked for it, probably uncertain if they carried it. He could almost hear the collective calculations of the staff, their eyes darting to the price tag, since her drink cost more than most meals. He glanced at his watch, the second hand ticking louder than usual. Mary had checked out before him but had yet to arrive. She liked to make an entrance, to make him sit in her absence. His stomach rumbled, a reminder that he hadn't eaten all day.

Then the door opened. The wind rushed in behind her. Her blond hair swirled around her face, mussed in the best way. For just a moment, it wasn't now. It was then. After dinner drinks, the two of them laughing, too much wine, his hand encircling her wrist. All those alternate lives, full of could haves and would haves, lay dead before them. Instead, she scurried over to the high top, dumping her black Chanel bag next to her wine.

"So, Mary, I'm guessing you have better dinner plans, with your blonde squad or husband number two. Inquiring minds want to know what's so important." He directed her to sit with his eyes.

She sipped her wine first, and he wondered if it was a drink for courage. She removed her coat, face a flush.

"I'm thinking about following up with the police. It's been months without any sort of news. Addison is annoyingly against the subject, and honestly, what kind of person doesn't want a righting of wrongs? She says I shouldn't dredge it up again, but I'm fed up with the Boone precinct."

David began to protest, but she ran right over him, her thoughts flowing fast.

"Don knows the chief, they're old golf buddies," she said, voice clipped. "No leads, none. Thank God Don's at least trying." Her eyes cut into David's, clocking the imbalance. "I told him we should have the chief over for dinner first. Open a bottle of Dom, act nice as pie before I go nuclear. This is our daughter we're talking about. Someone needs to be held accountable."

David kept his voice even. "Going to the police now only adds fuel. That's not what Addison wants." He paused, careful. "I'm angry too. But she told you no. She's not a kid anymore. If we want to help, we start by listening. I'm not trying to be lazy, I'm trying to honor what she asked."

Mary shot him a withering look.

"Yes, because letting a nineteen-year-old lead an important investigation is the wise thing to do. Listen, I thought you'd be on board, you with your cowboy vigilantism. That's what this is, a meeting of allies, or did all this Boone pacifism turn you into a hippie too?"

She loved emasculating him, making him smaller, softer, less of a man than her. Once, with that horsey laugh, she joked she had the bigger balls. David hadn't cackled back. Mary didn't notice.

"Oh, knock it off, Mary. If the police can't find anything, what's all your barking gonna do besides piss everyone off?" He nearly added *like always,* knowing just how thin the line was between her being assertive and losing her grip. She liked to raise hell in a board-room voice but still played the homemaker when it fit the moment. Mary wanted to call the shots and be praised for restraint, like she'd been handed the reins instead of yanking them out of someone else's grip.

She softened a bit, took more sips of wine.

"I just want to help, you know. I see something, I say it." Her voice dipped, softer now.

David strained to hear her amongst the dinner crowd. It wasn't regret, but it was close. The sad side of Mary always did him in. She led with her teeth, but when the girl behind the bite showed, he capitulated. It reminded him of Addison. The same cracked edges beneath all that fire.

He shifted, his voice dropping to meet hers. Steady, less combative. "I know you do. That's what makes you good. But rushing this will backfire. Addison's not some kid who'll just bend. She'll go frosty if you don't listen to her. Let's take her lead, allow her to be in charge of her own case."

David paused, watching Mary for a reaction, then added, a bit more pointed, "I know you're keen to do things your way. But the police have protocols. We shouldn't push for answers if they aren't there yet."

Mary frowned, always ready for a comeback. She would've made a ferocious attorney. He'd told her that back in her paralegal days, but she laughed it off, saying lawyers worked twice as hard as she ever wanted to. Now, he could see her reviewing his words, looking for a way to object, to cut in and make her case.

"That's strangely magnanimous of you, David," she said, her tone a thread pulled too tight. "You? Letting things be? That's a shift, for sure. Normally you'd be there, making sure everyone knew you were involved. What's with the reticence?" She gulped her wine, then cocked her head.

He needed her to listen. He couldn't afford the police poking around, not when his plan was picking up speed. Addison's case had to disappear, swallowed by red tape and unsolved threads. He took a beat, aiming straight for her Achilles' heel—pride.

"Plus, you know, Mary, the publicity of it all. Small towns, small minds. So far, no papers, no press, as a favor to you, I'd assume, by that very same chief of police. But dig around, ask questions, and suddenly, me, you, Addison and everyone else knows all that business. Not sure that's the way to go. But if you suddenly have an urge for us to be the topic of conversation, well then by all means…"

Her eyes widened, and David hated himself for playing the shame card. He had to hit Mary in her cavalier crosshairs. Her landscaped mansion, the monograms on everything, the flower beds trimmed to Edward Scissorhands' perfection, Mary's whole world revolved around keeping up with appearances.

She ironed her tennis clothes, wore mascara to the gym. That life couldn't include Addison being fractured by something she couldn't fix. For now, Addison's rape remained a secret, buried beneath layers of pristine, heavily curated perfection. It was David's best chance to keep Mary from blowing it all open.

"Maybe." Mary demurred. "That works for now. Keep tabs, watch it play out."

Mary downed the rest of her drink. She bestowed him a stiff smile, eyes avoiding his as she buttoned up her coat.

"David, a pleasure as always," she enunciated. "Should I leave some money to cover it?"

Another side swipe. Crises averted for now, she was back to her familiar vitriol.

"I think I can cover cost, but just barely, Mary. Let's not make this a habit."

She pivoted in her kitten heels, none the wiser. But David knew Mary wouldn't be held off for long, and his timeline had just gotten sped up by a month.

Chapter 27

Pick Your Poison

Time was a tickin', and David was ready to pull the proverbial trigger. He'd narrowed it down to two ways to kill the bastard, an overdose or a suicide, weighing each with a heavy hand. On the decision tree, suicide had many branches, each spikey with complications. He went down the list: slit wrist, hanging, asphyxiation, accidental drowning, gunshot wound—a list of lethality in five acts. The OD thought bubble was simple: injectables, mix and match with booze or something spiked. Combining them felt like kismet, drugs offering a quick ending to a short life. He buckled down, ready to review his options.

It was a Sunday, Christmas Eve, and David's mind wouldn't settle. Snow dusted the front yard, guaranteeing another white Christmas. The backyard looked like something off a postcard. Mary had claimed Christmas Eve, leaving David to wrap presents and finalize his plans. He'd see Addison tomorrow. His gift to her: a reckoning. The end of Josh. Her wish. His vow. While the high country dreamed of Santa, David was missing the cheer. Darker thoughts took the place of festive spirit, no visions of sugarplums here.

Cutting Josh's wrists was out. No hesitation wounds meant no practice runs. Those small, scattered nicks—just enough to test the blade, feel the skin before committing—were the mark of a real suicide. Every case David had seen had them. It was a preparation, a warm-up. David wondered if he'd be any different. For him, slicing and dicing was second nature, done without thought. But normal people? They needed to practice, and that couldn't be faked. Plus, getting Josh still enough to cut would mean a fight, which David couldn't risk.

Hanging worked fast if the person did it themselves. A scarf left no marks, just a clean exit. An electrical cord or noose would leave a furrow in the neck. Unmistakable. But David didn't have the stomach for it. Tightening the rope, watching Josh flail and kick, feeling that raw panic in real time. Too personal. Too much contact. Too human. He'd have to watch the fight drain out of him, each twitch weaker than the last, until there was nothing left but dead weight.

If he choked Josh, let his fingers find the soft give of his windpipe, David knew he wouldn't feel hospitable. But the body kept score. Pathologists could tell the difference between ligature and manual strangulation. Hands left their own signature—crescent-shaped nail imprints, uneven bruising from grip shifts, faint abrasions if the skin fought back. Fingertip hemorrhages laced just beneath the surface like bruised fruit.

They were both right-handed, which helped. A right-handed killer left deeper contusions on the left side of the neck, where the stronger grip landed. That made the scene cleaner. Easier to map. But too much pressure and the hyoid bone could snap. In a man Josh's age, that fracture would be hard to ignore.

Then came the petechiae. Pinprick dots, bright red in the

whites of the eyes, sometimes spreading to the eyelids and the inner lips. Capillaries ruptured from pressure. David had seen them often enough on his slab. A blood-flecked Morse code the coroner could read without blinking. No suicide ever left that kind of trail.

He could go softer. Find a tool to blur the line between murder and self-harm. But hands-on meant risk. Sweat. Struggle. DNA under the fingernails.

There'd be a moment of recognition in Josh before the end. David could picture it. The flash of knowing. He thought back to his own nightmares, the way violence always gutted him, even in sleep. The closeness. Skin to skin. It wouldn't work. Only distance would do.

Environmental suffocation was rare. It took an airtight enclosure—an old fridge, a locked trunk, some crawlspace no one checked. That worked on bombing ranges or abandoned warehouses. Not in Josh's prefab shack, where every square inch served a purpose. There was nowhere to wedge a body without it looking staged. Strangling brought its own problems. Sometimes it leaned sexual, twisted up in autoerotic theories. David wanted no part of that. No fingerprints near the neck, no rumors of kink. Clean. Distant. Nothing to confuse the cause or drag the motive through filth and newspapers.

A cousin to asphyxia was smothering—plastic bag over the head, pillow pressed tight to the face. David remembered the old stories, whispered over bad coffee in the morgue. Smothering bandits. Victims suffocated under a body's weight, nose pinched shut until the flailing stopped. But that method came with struggle. A lot of it. Josh was solid, the kind of man who could toss him off easy. Strangulation had too many variables and took too much time. Then there were the bruises, faint circular ones on the survivor's fingertips, reminders of the fight he didn't win. David didn't need that kind of signature. He needed a death that whispered, not screamed.

There was a case in Boone where carbon monoxide caused death from a faulty heater. It would work well in Josh's house, except suffocating gases were hard to control and there was no guarantee he wouldn't try to flee. Plus, the gas could travel and cause collateral damage, which was not David's intent. This was a one-bullet job, reserved, party of one, no need to burn down a town to take a life.

Drowning reminded him of a tongue twister Addison used to rehearse in second grade speech therapy. D's were her downfall back then. She'd skip through the house chanting, "Dizzy ducks dive deep down and drown," proud of every syllable. Hair damp from the bath, she'd plant herself in front of the mirror like it was a stage. David used to smile at the sound of it, but now, the words crawled back with a chill. Hell of a rhyme to teach a kid.

Drowned bodies typically take more than an hour to surface. They sink first, weighed down by waterlogged tissue, but after a while, gases form as decomposition sets in, pushing them to the surface. The police, of course, had a name for them: floaters. David always hated that term. It wasn't just the casual tone, but the way it stripped death of any weight, turning a person into something disposable. Less of a life, more of a discarded object—like a deflated life vest tossed aside.

Most rock stars were known to drown in the bathtub, with substance abuse always listed as the official cause of death. Accidental drowning, like Natalie Wood's, was another possibility—an ill-timed bath after too much fun. The struggle to breathe, the coughing, and then death came quickly, written off as a hazard of drinking and bathing. If Josh turned up dead in the water, it would be the next logical leap, a victim of careless drinking or a boating accident. A body found in water was almost always presumed accidental. If submerged long enough, the lungs filled with water, leaving the appearance of suffocation or drowning, regardless of whether the victim had been alive before hitting the water.

While theoretically it would be possible to gain blood clues from those who drowned, research showed that DNA was rapidly reduced in the setting of prolonged submersion and decomposition. David's commitment to leaving no trace at the crime scene would be doable if Josh drowned.

But a good medical examiner would know to look for adipocere. In bodies left in damp water, the process usually started between 8 to 24 weeks after death. The body fat would break down, turning into a waxy, soap-like substance that helped preserve the remains. This process, known as hydrolysis, slowed the decay and could mummify a body. Adipocere wasn't just a preservation method, though—it provided crucial clues. The chemical changes it caused could be detected, giving forensic experts a timeline of death, even after months submerged. It was like nature's way of offering up a perfectly preserved crime scene for anyone paying close attention.

Drowning was often portrayed as peaceful, a quiet slip beneath the surface, bodies disappearing as effortlessly as if they'd been invited. But in truth, it wasn't so clean. Holding someone under-water long enough to drown left bruising—hematomas where the skin was compressed. The closest lake was a 45-minute drive from Boone. Someone like Josh, with his build and strength, would fight, making it nearly impossible to subdue him without signs of strug-gle. The image of him sinking into the depths, tangled in rocks and debris, might seem poetic, but real life didn't offer clean endings.

David recalled his friend's bubble-wrapped words of caution. Suicide without a note always raised eyebrows. Forcing someone to write a goodbye note was a fool's errand, a scene full of false sincer-ity. It would be hard enough to get Josh's compliance. David didn't want to talk to him at all. He wanted this clean—no conversation, no noise. Without an admission, though, the scene could easily look staged, a messy illusion with too many holes.

David rubbed his eyes, trying to wrap the same present for the third time. The bow was crooked, the tag a mess of scrawl, like the work of a deranged elf. Sleep clung to the corners of his vision, insomnia his constant companion. Most nights, he turned the dusty pages of books from the Reagan era, pages that felt older than he was. When Addison was there, they'd have a quiet dinner, with half-sentences hanging between them and food pushed around on plates. Afterward, he'd retreat to his research, and she'd disappear into her room, both of them wondering if life was meant for more. Grief didn't hit like a crash; it crept in, a knife, always twisting. Only death was quick.

He decided to grab a proper glass for an aperitif. The thick, heavy ones meant for serious beer boozing were shoved in the corner of the pantry, covered with dust. They weren't dishwasher safe, and his bachelor efficiency didn't have room for long sink soaks when he was on his own. As he opened the cabinet, his eyes caught something unexpected, a full pill bottle, winking at him in the light.

Addison never touched the pain pills. Thirty days of three 10/325s a day sat there, mocking him from the cupboard—ninety pills, full to the brim. His first thought was guilt. He hadn't offered them to her. Maybe she didn't even know they were there. Those early days were a blur. He'd tucked the pills away, focused on keeping her calm, then blanked on them entirely.

He stared at the pills, letting them sink in for a second time. David saw them for what they were—a gift. Opiates, just as deadly as they were a favorite of the Wicked Witch of the West. He felt the weight of the moment, like the universe had finally given him something to work with. A house left untouched, pills sitting there, easy to crush, with plenty left over. He could leave the evidence in plain sight, just out of reach, like a puzzle piece dropped from the table. A tox screen would show everything. Presence of the drugs, confirmed. Add in a CBC, creatine kinase levels, arterial blood gas determinations. The OD package would be wrapped up tight, no questions left to ask.

It wouldn't be a painful death for Josh. It was all pinpoint pupils, respiratory depression, then unconsciousness. Good and dead was the goal anyway, no need to be all histrionic about it.

Twenty-five pills deposited into a single Sunny D. That was 8,125 mg of Tylenol—enough to start causing irreversible liver damage, but not quite a guaranteed kill. The real guarantee was in the 250g of opiates, a lethal horse dose that would shut down the respiratory system within minutes. David would grind it down, all mortar and pestle crushed. He'd add in the four leftover Valium tablets from his vasectomy two years ago, the pills contributing a sedative effect that would deepen the overdose.

Crushing those would only help the absorption rate, increasing the chances that the victim wouldn't survive the night. Josh's favorite drink, Sunny D, would make the ingestion easier and potentially mask the bitterness of the crushed pills. No signs of struggle, just a person who'd taken too much.

David could leave the bottle where it was, pills still in the container but out of immediate sight, just enough to make it look like a careless overdose. The tox screen would confirm it, opiates and acetaminophen, a CBC, creatine kinase levels, arterial blood gases. Each test would come back showing the cause: respiratory failure, organ collapse, all tied together neatly by the drugs. A home left unattended, pills here for the taking. The perfect recipe for a death that looked like an accident.

Benzos and opiates—the second half of the overdose, provided by Addison herself. The whole plan felt circular, an ugly, perfect symmetry. It wasn't without flaws. Moonlighting as an old-time apothecary might not kill the taste. There'd be a medical tang, with that much dope. The aftertaste would linger on the back of Josh's throat, a hint of decay. If his mouth registered something was off, his brain might catch up. He could spit it out or pour the rest of the concoction down the drain. Throwing up, rinsing it out—those were real possibilities. All that precision, all that planning, gone in an instant.

And then there was the timing. Overdose wasn't a quick kill. The opiates would take their time, slow his breathing, but if Josh didn't succumb fast enough, the pills could lose their grip. He'd be left in a haze, drowsy, nauseous, but still breathing. The whole thing might turn into a grotesque sideshow, one where Josh wasn't dead, just mostly dead.

David could make him drink it, threaten him—or worse. David could summon enough malice in his fifty-year-old voice to rattle a nineteen-year-old, especially with the surprise factor and the weight of a good backstory. He could be there, calm and reassuring, telling Josh it would be okay, just comply, and the world would keep spinning as it always had. If Josh thought he might make it out alive, he'd be less likely to try a fast one, to escape or throw a punch. It was human nature to follow the line when it didn't look like the end of the road. If David could sell him on the idea that the drink was just to subdue, not to kill, Josh would be more likely to follow through.

David's eyes flicked back to the pills, his mind a hurling tornado of thoughts falling into place. A Christmas miracle, after all.

Chapter 28

Happy Holidays

With the pills tucked safely in his bedroom drawer, David was ready to greet Addison with a boatload of forced Christmas cheer. The house smelled of peppermint coffee, both fragrant and delicious. He knew because he'd already downed three cups, a temporary fix to cover last night's late bedtime.

"Merry Christmas, Dad!" When she walked in, she was wearing an ugly Christmas sweater that clung to her thin frame, bright red with reindeer prancing across it. A dusting of snow clung to her shoulder blades.

"I left all my presents at Mom's. Good God, what a stack. But these here are for you."

She offered two gifts. One broad and blunt. The other tidy and bound. Her smile outshone them both. He hadn't decorated much, just a fake three-foot tree in the corner, its plastic needles angled helter-skelter. She was standing on her tiptoes before she even fully entered, peering at the ornaments she'd gifted him on the branches.

Diet Coke, Guinness, a cowboy hat and boots. A hodgepodge of his favorite things, by the girl who knew him best.

"Come in, it's freezing. Coffee's hot. Gifts are under the tree. I'll put these with the others." David kept talking, filling the space with chatter, glad she was here.

He set her boxes beside the ones already waiting. One envelope held her car insurance, paid in full. She only drove between her mom's place, his house, and the dorms, but he didn't want her thinking about bills. Her focus should be on therapy, grades, and building back a life. Not dodging past due notices. The sweater came next. Cashmere. Soft, neutral, made for late mornings and lounging. A couple of books—paperbacks, dog-ear ready.

Nothing flashy. Nothing that would glitter in a holiday ad. Just things to keep her from floating too far. Mary would've bought out half of Kohl's and wrapped it in red ribbon. David kept to what counted.

"I think you should open the big one first," Addison said, dropping onto the couch with a thud of overstuffed cushions and a burst of energy he hadn't seen in weeks.

David smirked, reaching for a croissant, its flaky crust scattering crumbs onto the worn coffee table.

"Come on, old man. You're taking forever." She grinned. "This one's important," she said, her voice leveling out. "Just… something to say thanks. For showing up. For keeping the promises you made."

"Alright, don't rush me," he muttered, fake grumbling, but riding the lift in her voice, the uptick not forced. She seemed happy, and that was gift enough. He hefted it onto his lap. More weight than expected, for a gift dressed in gold ribbon. He peeled at the paper, careful and slow. Never one to rip through the work someone else had done. A broad strip came free, revealing the clean, black stamp of Wilson's Leather, the logo of his favorite boot store.

When Addison was younger, and he still held parental projections of who she might become, he imagined her in ostrich leather boots, rocking real money on her small feet. A watered-down version of him, same spine, same kick ass footwear.

They were too good for the cheap commercial pairs sold at Belk's, embossed with gems and made in Mexico. Those knock-offs would never grace their feet, with soles that would sluff off in a month, held together by bonded leather and glue. The only place to shop for boots was at Wilson's, with the boots lined up atop their boxes, reeking of unspent money.

David pulled out a pair of size 11 Lucchese cowboy boots, harder to obtain, even harder to afford. Made of alligator leather, with a ten-year stonewash finish. A true sight to behold. These weren't just boots. These were luxury. His vision blurred, a swath of tears catching on his lashes. He aimed a quick swipe to hide them but missed.

"Addison!" he tried, his voice warbling. "This is too much, Spitfire. These set you back a bunch."

"It was easy. You trained me well. I was the youngest one there," Addison said, pride etched in her dimples.

David had always joked that no one went to Wilson's except boot connoisseurs, who chewed on the ends of their cigars and scowled, annoyed by the minimum 500-dollar price tags. But nothing could compete with hand-embroidered distressed snakeskin. It pays to love something well crafted.

"You know anvil-tanned steer hide makes me cry," David said, letting the humor do the heavy lifting.

Addison had never been drawn to fancy boots. She was more of a Levi's and V-neck kind of girl, that waifish look with the bob cut, a nod to Kate Moss, but with better teeth. But she understood what these boots meant, and so did he. It wasn't just leather and thread;

it was a reminder of how closely she'd paid attention, how she knew exactly what mattered to her Dad.

"Well, you don't have to worry much, because the next thing is just something small," Addison continued.

"Good thing," David replied. "Cause you spent all your cash on the first one."

She smiled, rolling her eyes. "Just open it," she laughed.

David tore into the smaller package, and there it was: *A Prayer for Owen Meany.* John Irving could wax political, but that was hardly a flaw. Of all the books they'd read and loved, this one stood apart. A story about boys who became brothers. About a friendship so deep it blurred the line between blood and bond. A life worth living, even when the ending was written from the start. One boy who believed in miracles. Another who bore witness. And when the time came, it was about doing the right thing, even if it meant dying for it. That wasn't lost on either of them. Not now.

"Oh, Addison," David said, stroking the cover. He thought of the story of his daughter—of the girl who believed the world was good. Even when the world devoured her tears, it was good. When her trauma shaved her into smaller bits, it was good. When all seemed lost, she looked over the last hill, searching for the lost battalion. Her optimism never wavered. She was the one who, despite it all, kept her eye on the horizon, waiting for the reinforcements to come. And when they did, she smiled. The same smile, year after year. This Christmas, every Christmas. The kind that rises after doubt is spent, and all that's left is hard-won survival.

David forced a tight smile, pushing back the rush of emotions. "Well, now my gifts will look paltry compared to yours. Thank you, I mean it. This is great."

He turned toward the kitchen, needing space to recalibrate. He grabbed the nearest snack—peanut brittle, half-gone and sticky from the jar. He could hear the sound of paper crinkling behind him, the soft rustle of unwrapping.

He stood by the counter, eyes focused on the window, but his thoughts were fixed on her. After everything this year, the way she held both sorrow and hope in her hands without letting them break apart was transcendent. All that was missing was her halo.

Addison peeled the paper from the books, never one to wreck the wrapping. She glanced at each cover, gave a single nod. "Thanks."

Next came the sweater. She ran her fingers through the stitching, then held it to her chest. "This is so soft." She folded it once and set it aside.

The last package was thin, flat, sealed in an envelope. She tore it open, scanned the single sheet inside.

Her mouth curved, subtle but sure. "Now it's my turn to be surprised."

David leaned back in his chair. "It's been... a helluva year. You've earned some downtime. No bills. Just focus on your studies."

She stood and stepped toward him. Wrapped her arms around his shoulders, chin tucked in close, like she used to in pre-K.

They stayed there, surrounded by blinking lights and torn paper, the wind pressing at the windows, the fire steady in the hearth. For a moment, all was right with the world.

That halting, stammering drawl of Jimmy Stewart drifted in from the TV. It was their family tradition to have an annual viewing of *It's a Wonderful Life*. The black-and-white film flickered softly in the background, accompanied by the nostalgic, scratchy sound of old-time cinema. George Bailey, the world's most polite former cowboy, did good showing the world his vulnerability and his shame.

Addison curled up under her favorite threadbare blanket while David sipped Mammy's Milk from his icy mug. His eyes always pricked at the same part—the pharmacist striking the boy, knuckles landing hard against the side of his head. The kid holds his ground, even with his bloody ear, certain he's right but scared to defy his boss. A good man cracking under grief. A kid refusing to back down.

David used to hide his tears. Blame allergies. Fake a sneeze. This year, he let them fall. No excuses, no cover. Just salt slipping down his face in the low flicker of the screen. She'd seen him cry more in the past few months than in all the nineteen years she'd known him. Addison shot him a small smile, no jokes this time, and turned back to the TV.

After the movie ended, neither of them moved. The snow outside picked up, tapping softly against the window, steady and cold. The credits rolled. The tree lights blinked. Everything in the room felt still. Presents were opened. Stockings tossed aside. But David had one more thing to give.

"I know this isn't the time. Not really," he began. "But I figured out how to do what you asked me to do."

Addison didn't speak. She just nodded, eyes fixed, offering the moment her full attention.

"Near Josh's kitchen, there's a window. No alarm wired to it." His voice didn't rise or fall. Just facts, laid out plain. "I'll go in there, make it look like an overdose. In and out. No one the wiser."

He glanced at her. She didn't look away.

"There's no one here to notice I'm gone. I'll keep the VCR recording. Watch it all later so I can talk about the plot. Laugh at the right parts. Pretend I was right here the whole night."

He hesitated, just long enough for it to matter.

"You're the backup, Spitfire."

Her jaw tightened, but she said nothing.

Outside, the snow kept falling. Inside, something else settled between them. Something heavier than the holiday should carry.

"Okay," she said, her voice lowered. "I'm with you so far."

"Two weeks from today," David said, eyes steady. "Go for a walk near my house. I'll give you my phone ahead of time. At exactly nine, call your cell from mine. Let it ring, pick up, stay on five minutes. Hang up mine first, then yours. Keep it near your ear. Walk slow. Make it look like you're catching up with your dad."

He scratched at the side of his jaw.

"I checked into it. The towers don't give exact locations. Just a general area—miles, not feet. Both phones pinging the same tower around the same time? That's enough to say we talked."

She didn't say anything, just watched him.

"You'll say you were out walking and called. Small talk. I was home in bed. You remember because we spoke. So does the phone."

He leaned back, folding his arms.

"Got it?"

He knew using a family member as an alibi wasn't airtight. But it gave him cover. More than that, it gave him leverage if things went sideways. He would tape the shows, watch them through, then toss the cassette. The police could ask whatever they wanted. Phone records, alarm log, TV schedule. Everything would tell the same clean story. David walked through it again in his head, rewinding each move, watching for cracks. He didn't see any.

He wanted to ask again. Hear the words. Make sure it was still green-lit. But every time he'd pushed for confirmation, she'd gotten mad. A taller version of Audrey Hepburn with her mean reds. He didn't have the stomach to challenge her again. Didn't want the Christmas light drained out of her and replaced with ire. So he kept his mouth shut. Let her lead. And hunkered down, feet dragging toward the finish line.

She didn't offer advice, didn't confirm, didn't deny.

"We should get back to our Christmas movie marathon, if there's nothing more to discuss."

She turned, rested her elbow on the armrest. Conversation closed.

David found a run of *Rudolph* in Claymation. While the misfit toys sang, he imagined the ending to Addison's big ask. No phone calls, no flashing lights. Just more of this, coffee brewing, snow curling against the patio door.

It took him a minute to realize Addison had fallen asleep, her head near his shoulder. Rest easy, he thought. Sleep well. Put all that evilness behind you, for auld lang syne, and for your dear old man. Life is about to get easier, sweetheart. Rest your pretty head.

Chapter 29

The Summer of Autopsies

There was death on his brain, and in the lab. A deluge of autopsies awaited him in the week between Christmas and New Year's, the modern scythe working overtime. Death didn't recognize holidays.

His slides flashed the big C for cancer, bright and neon, announcing their course of terror in purple whorls. David was glad to speak doctor to doctor; happy he didn't have to be the one to give patients the death sentence. It still made him queasy at times to see a blinking stage III or IV on the slide, his head thinking "goner" with his heart much more somber. Another stillborn awaited him in the lab, wrecking what was left of his afternoon. David geared up to force himself not to see all the parts, delicate and still fresh, soaking in formalin instead of breast milk.

Sometimes, David wished he could be one of the other doctors, the normal brigade. He'd thought about dermatology, of being limited to moles and skin. No rotting flesh, no mortality. Being a pathologist made it hard to switch gears. Surgeons, they got to save lives, stitch up wounds and walk out at the end of the day, heroes with their scars and sutures. David didn't get to leave the lab behind. The slides held their finality, each one waiting for his final look, the end already written before he even touched the microscope.

David's mind was heavy with dark thoughts, caught between the lab and the spiked Sunny D waiting at home. The weight of it took him back to those summer autopsies, 1977 and 1978. The sun never really touched him then, replaced by the cold, sterile morgue. His inauguration into the reality of death.

Dr. Checker, an elderly pathologist, needed a summer hand. David's summers had been spent pulling weeds for neighbors or donating blood for beer money. He jumped at the chance to make three bucks an hour. Dr. Checker taught him how to make Y incisions on the first day, something he hadn't yet learned in medical school. It was a stark reminder of death—once you prosected a body, there was no going back. All cuts, bones, and cartilage. The gristle and sinew stood in sharp contrast to the silver table. During his first autopsy, David gagged, then double checked to make sure the patient was dead.

The doc paid time and a half on weekends, so David started hoping for Friday deaths. He wanted the world to save its ills for a long weekend, the blood money hitting his pocket with more to burn. He got familiar with death that summer, on a first-name basis.

His only gripe with Dr. Checker was the Vicks vapor rub. He should've covered it, given David a bonus for the stink. If David had run the show, there'd be tubes everywhere, keeping the smell of death at bay. Making David pay to keep rot at bay felt cheap, but he kept his complaints to himself.

And the stench could be eye-wateringly horrible, full of obese patients half-rotten or decay done by nature. Granny dies at home, kids find her, no biggie. Boy dies out in the sunny fields, and soon

you must fire up the freezer to stop the maggots. But as soon as the
body thaws, the maggots come back. They were the true
cockroaches of death, coming back to feast, never picky eaters. The
job was a morbid one, but it paid well for David when his needs
were light and easy.

Forgetting to bring the rub left David with a sour stomach and
a workday spent trying not to hurl. Dr. Checker took it all in stride,
fast as a fiddle with his cuts and no-nonsense approach. He'd get the
legion of the dead in and out before the smell could touch him,
flash and gleaming knives lined up like soldiers. A house of horrors
with the speed of a drive-thru, he'd slice and dice faster than seemed
possible, drinking down all the unsavory parts on his way to the
bank. By contrast, David felt clumsy, his nerves shot but steady
fingers, shadowing and learning from one of the brightest in the
business. He had nightmares the first week, all Frankenstein fresh,
arms and legs shuffling around a locked office. But it surprised him
how quickly he acclimated to the bodies, taking in the day's work
and letting it rest on him from 8 to 5 with no breaks. It was a heavy
load to carry, but he wore it well.

All that practice paid off—David was A-plus material that first
year in residency. The class spent two months on autopsies, and
while most took 2-3 hours, he'd cut and run in 1.5, much to the
frustration of his green-eyed peers. For a semester, he was the
morgue star, sick with pride over the accolades. He would've worn a
medal if they'd offered it, ready to see his name in morbid lights.

The template for an autopsy was easy; David had been doing it
since before Addison was born. Name, age, sex, race, time of death,
location, appearance, skin abnormalities, tattoos, scars, birthmarks,
then head, neck, body, cardio, respiratory, GI, liver, kidneys,
endocrine, skeleton, CNS, summary—done. Say that three times
fast. Soon, everyone found their rhythm, a smooth flow of scalpels
and death. Who better than the morgue star to leave no trace?

David knew the body inside and out, nothing surprising left to find.

Now that his murder method was complete, David could focus on executing his plan without mistakes. Josh's autopsy would never be ordered, given his history of drug use—it was easy math. Even if it was, it would read as cardiac arrest, exsanguination, cerebral contusions. All big words for a quick death.

David knew gloves were a must, though getting a clean finger-print was harder than people thought. The Manson murders showed that—clear prints were rare, even without gloves. Most prints on fabric were just fragments, smudges, or too faint to make out. Latent prints had to be matched, one finger at a time, to a suspect's records. Some people left clearer prints than others, a genetic lottery. He'd be careful, but fingerprints were not his biggest concern.

David would bring Mary's gun but hoped not to use it. He wasn't a sharpshooter, just someone who could pull a trigger if needed. A bloody crime scene meant DNA, but dried blood left only partial samples. He wasn't planning on getting hurt. He and Josh wouldn't touch. The directions would be given and followed, no fight in between. David had picked cheap clothes from Walmart, something common, mass-produced. He considered burning them, but the smell of plastic might give him away, and burning it all would take time.

He scouted a couple of burn barrels people used for excess fire-wood at the Greenway; he may have more luck burning it there. However, a curious bystander could come and query, asking him what needed charring in such a public place. David decided it was overkill; he'd wash the clothes, store them under trash and old food, and let the dump carry them to a future full of landfills.

Tires and bullets left behind clues as well, which was why he'd walk and take only what was necessary with him.

He felt ready, but the timing sat wrong. The decorations were still up, lights blinking on porches, plastic reindeer tipped in yards. It felt colder somehow to kill a man with the holidays still hanging in the air. He pushed the plan to early January. Let the season pass. Let the cheer die down. A new year, clean on the calendar, was better suited for something this dark.

Back at work, the bodies kept coming. Real ones. Cold ones. David logged the details, made his cuts, wrote up the cause. January was full of the usual—drunks in ditches, strokes alone at home, one teen who'd been missing since Christmas and turned up frozen in a ravine. No one looked too closely at their deaths. Just transcriptions and ICD codes. The routine steadied him. Blood, bone, paperwork. Death by the book. Just like he planned.

David stepped out of the cold room, peeled off his gloves, and found Craig. "Hey, thinking of taking a couple days off in January —the 7th and 10th. Sound good?"

Craig blinked. He'd never asked for time off before. "Going somewhere warm?"

"Nah, just following your advice. Resting up for the new year."

Craig nodded. "You got it, Doc. Glad you're taking the time. We've got a locum tenens lined up. Have yourself a bit of a breather."

He'd use the extra day to clear his head. Buy Addison a sweater at Libba's in Blowing Rock. Pick out a stack of novels to help her hit her yearly count before her birthday rolled around. He'd wrap it all tight and clean, one last show of effort before darker deeds demanded all of him. Just in time to welcome 2005 in full.

Chapter 30

New Year, New Girl

The stage was set. A lethal dose of opiates dissolved in the Sunny D, waiting in its plastic shell. The trick was resealing the cap without breaking the security ring. Josh would know the feel—thumb under the blue tab, twist, pop. Muscle memory didn't lie. David had boiled the tampered bottle just long enough to slip the shrink band back over the cap, sealed tight again once it cooled. Low-tech, but it held. And Josh had a litany of half-finished bottles littering the apartment—desk, couch, floor. He never looked twice at any of them.

The spiked drink looked untouched. No sign of tampering. Josh would take it from the fridge without thinking. David placed it apart from the others. Josh would grab it, chug it, and head for the couch. David had watched him do it ten times, maybe more. This time would be the last.

His mind wasn't on his work that Friday. He didn't trust himself to sign out anything complex. David split the cases into two piles and left the harder ones untouched. His insides buzzed. He kept a bottle of Tums at his desk, chewed through them like chaw, but the burn wouldn't let up. His stomach coiled tighter with each hour. He made too many trips to the bathroom. Washed his face. Gripped the sink. Anything to get through the day. The worst would be over soon.

He hadn't been this jittery since his wedding day. Despite marrying for love, David almost passed out waiting for Mary to walk down the aisle. His thoughts flashed a warning billboard. He was headed to Big Mistake City, but all he felt was happy. Something kicked in while he was waiting, a seed of doubt growing into a beanstalk. As the bridesmaids filed in one by one, his brain kept whispering he could never be truly sure of anything. It was as if all the pre-wedding jitters hit him at once, making his knees buckle. He didn't remember falling, just that when he came to, Ricky was staring at him with creased brows.

"You okay there, bud?" he whispered, eyes asking without words. *Are we doing this or do I have to stall?* David nodded, grateful for a friend who could ask questions with his eyes.

David felt more embarrassed than nervous, all wobbly on his feet. He announced loudly that he was dehydrated and shot encouraging smiles toward Mary's parents. They blinked back at him, like possums caught in headlights. He saw Mary pacing at the rear of the church, back and forth, before the doors swung open.

Her impatience, in the end, steadied him. He blocked out the crying baby, told his doubts to shove off, and said yes in his head before he said it to the preacher. He blushed and stood tall, ready to say his vows and mean them. Sometimes a freak-out can change the tide. Mary approached him in layers of white, his own personal knockout. All the butterflies had already passed, and his head and heart reconciled. She kissed him hard, like the kiss was a vow too, sealing their future with a firm smooch because something soft was for suckers.

Today, that same sense of unease arose, an old friend who shouldn't have made the guest list. His thoughts ping-ponged, hardly making sense. He ruminated on jail time and homemade shivs. Addison and her shrinking waistline circled in his mind, as did anorexia, with a side helping of PTSD. He circled back to his soul—what taking a life could do to a beating heart. But he'd already flayed bodies and cadavers without blinking. Someone breathing wouldn't be different. Just a bloodier version of work he'd already done.

He focused on the promise he'd made, the one he'd keep. Addison's happiness was all that mattered. He'd kill for it, die for it, lie for it, steal for it. All the sins in the world couldn't compare to the pull of her smile. An eye for an eye. A life for a life. Addison for Josh. It was a simple price to pay.

He worked his way back to the complicated slides, momentary mental breakdown averted. David found a place for his thoughts to land, somewhere beyond the fear and the doubt, and his brain kept time until the day was done and ready for the main show.

January 7th, 2005, the deadline had arrived. The university was out until the next week, the college scene empty, the town a bunker. His motive was everything he'd lost, everything Addison had to endure. His mission was pure, if cold-blooded. His daughter deserved a second chance at life.

He left work, parking his Jeep securely right in the middle of the driveway. No garage today, take a gander one and all. He was staying home all night, bathroom light on, alarm set, his alibi ready to shine. Addison held both phones, her part secured and tucked in tight.

It was a Friday, so despite the holiday season, Josh wouldn't be home until later. Fridays were his apartment days, visiting the locals, peddling more than just friendship and goodwill. David would be there waiting for him when he came home, somewhere around nine p.m. He'd sneak in around eight, leaving a full hour of keeping his head down in the pantry, waiting for Josh to emerge.

He changed into the clothes he planned to wear, the cheap fabric scratching against his skin. Walmart special, cheap and necessary. And bought by the masses. Gloves in his pocket, a hat pulled low, dark clothes from head to toe. He grabbed the balaclava, a hat/face cover hard to pronounce, and even harder to wear. He looked like bad casting in an action movie. But it fit the part. Hair completely covered, face concealed. Black on black on black. Try identifying that, he told the would-be investigators in his head, his version of the devil on his shoulder.

His hands clutched the gun in his pocket. Mary and her hand me down weapon had come in handy, suitable that she'd played a part, however unknown, in helping her damaged daughter be repaired. It was loaded, he'd checked it twice, his nerves feeding him nonsense about bullets slipping out or walking away. But the full caliber remained, his *just in case* ending secured.

David had gotten a haircut, made sure they took it down to the bone. No stray hairs would be left behind. He'd showered twice, lathered up too much shampoo, still not used to the military cut. He checked again for the latex gloves, then his snow gloves. Still secured. He grabbed his fleece, armed the house, and slipped out the back window, grateful for the big yard and thick tree cover.

The next-door neighbors weren't the curious type, just English professors always at the university, never ones to press their noses against windows and wonder about his life. The sky was dark at 6:58 p.m., winter sucking out the color, repainting Boone in monochrome. Luckily, no fresh snow. The December flurries had sluffed off, leaving only cold clumps here and there. He walked toward the hill, feet driving him forward, secure in the knowledge that he'd check his own footprints by Josh's window.

David's mind was on his daughter. On the friends who'd turned into acquaintances, on the way she'd flinch with every sound of a siren. She was the same girl, with identical clothes, and matching perfume. But she was less exuberant, leaving questions unanswered, no longer able to walk alone from her science building to her dorm.

Tonight would set the stage for better days. His thoughts kept him warm as he moved through Horn in the West, then past the playground. He imagined a quaint ceremony in the backyard, a white tent draped under the stars. Day lilies bloomed in the yard, bright and full of promise, the whole scene alive with wonder. The kind of day that couldn't be spoiled. Not even Don and Mary could ruin it. Addison would stand beneath the dogwoods, grown and strong, every inch the woman who'd face her future head-on and claim it as her own.

If the night didn't go as planned, that image would stay fantasy, reserved for someone else. She'd just be subdued, all shruggy shoulders, no big plans. Content to let the world wash over her and thank it for the scraps it left behind. Scraps that would never be enough. "Proud of you, Spitfire" was what he'd offer, and she'd lean into him. They'd stand like that a long time. Him watching the dreams he'd carried for her slip away. Her accepting a life that had already passed her by.

To hell with that, he thought, still moving down the road, a pep talk at the ready.

"For Texas and Miss Lily," he said aloud—a line he loved from *The Life and Times of Judge Roy Bean*. The judge says it, with Paul Newman catching every outlaw in the Lonestar State and making them pay.

For Addison, he thought. *For the part of her who was a Lozen, first of her name. For his daughter, the tree climber. The one who shone the brightest. Here comes your rescue.*

And with that battle cry ringing in his head, he found himself beneath Josh's window, the house still, holding its breath. He reached out, laying a gloved hand on the siding, rough and cold beneath his palm. His fingers found the sill, each second louder than the last, the glass and darkness daring him to cross.

Chapter 31

It's Killing Time

B gun thoughts peppered through his mind, surrounding reasonable doubt and the gazillion ways he could get caught. David tried counting to keep his hands steady, but it didn't work. Neither did naming state capitals. All he could do was squat behind the pantry door, knees screaming under the strain. The house sat dark beneath a cloudless sky, the silence noose-like and waiting.

The lone Sunny D sat in the fridge, the star of the show, front and center. The others were off to the side, no easy access. The trap was set, just waiting for the prey to come knocking.

David assessed the pantry items, forcing his mind to focus on JIF and canned corn instead of the flash floods of doubt. He thought of Elizabeth Loftus and her research on eyewitness testimony, how memories could be unreliable and how different people could recall the same event in wildly varied ways. The truth was never fixed; it shifted with perspective, each version equally valid.

Alone with his thoughts, the details crept up again. A drugged, unreliable narrator was a risk, even if she shared his last name. Vigilante justice, in a world where words carried the same weight as a bullet, could be its own kind of peril. He remembered a story where a wife named her rapist, and the husband killed him. The next day, she repeated the information, but with a different man. In the end, the truth was as fragile as the lies that held it together. That couldn't be his fate.

He forced his mind still. The murder was the medicine. Josh was the dose. His humanity wasn't on trial, and David wasn't there to prove anything. It was all about setting Addison free.

Keep it simple, he scolded himself. *Save judgment for a rainy day.*

David reviewed his goal. Occam's razor, famous for its simplicity. Sometimes the simplest explanation is the likeliest.

Stick to the facts, and you'll come out aces, he thought. He resumed talking to himself to keep him contained, ever the consummate bachelor, alone with this thoughts, and in his head. He'd just changed locations, traded the hospital and home for this pantry. *Nothing to it.*

Josh had drug charges on the books. Easy to label, documented, and seedy. He could be the kind who sold a little extra to make rent, who sampled the goods. It was a short slide from seller to user. Most dealers wanted a taste eventually, to make sure their product held weight. Temptation was part of the job.

An OD made sense in a town that signed death certificates with head shakes. Boone and its leadership knew they were losing the war on drugs. Most college kids flirted with recklessness. It's part of the timeline, believing they're immortal until they learn they're not. Luck doesn't always bend their way. A little more here, a touch more there, until Josh's future was coffin heavy. David thumbed the pill bottle in his pocket, his own personal talisman. This would work, it had to.

There were so many things that could go wrong. Despite the stakeouts where no friend was present, Josh could bring someone into the house, like his hat wearing brethren from the apartments. He could throw up the mixture of medication. He could dump it down the sink. He could be wise to it even before he drank it.

The top could slip, and Josh might feel eyes on him, ready to pounce. Or he could drink it, but then they scuffle, a gun goes off, and everything spirals. All kinds of messed up. There's no guidebook for this, murder the same no man's land as parenting.

David heard every car roll by from the pantry cage. His breathing came hard. He glanced through the slats every few minutes. Every stray sound felt amplified. So much so that he jolted when Josh's truck barreled into the driveway.

David couldn't see his watch and had lost track of time as he tried to keep his feet from falling asleep. Josh's keys jingled. The door heaved open. David realized he wasn't breathing.

Be alone, be alone, he begged. He drew one last heavy inhale, told himself this was the moment. Now it counted. Be still. Be quiet.

Like hide and seek, he reasoned, keeping his body low and crouched.

Josh stumbled inside, not bothering to turn on the light. No one followed him. His shoes made clomping sounds as he headed toward the fridge. David heard the crunk of plastic bags by the sink. Josh turned, grabbing the closest Sunny D, none the wiser, leaving the fridge door open.

Drink, you son of a bitch. Drink.

David's thoughts barked, pleading as he watched without moving.

Drink it all. Down to the bottom. The same words he'd said to Addison that night. There was poetic justice in that.

His brain flashed a picture of the "drink me" labels from *Alice in Wonderland,* and for a second, he wondered if he was hallucinating.

David was so damn nervous, full of fast heartbeats and time that ticked like a bomb.

First, a cough. Then a sniffle. The sound of congestion as Josh threw his head back, lifted the drink to his lips, and gulped. He had a cold, which would help mask the taste. Lady Luck had finally shown up. David needed Josh to drink half for this to work.

Josh kept drinking, the slurps echoing through the kitchen, each one a little too loud. He made it more than halfway before he stopped. He stared at the bottle inquisitively and turned around.

David's heart stopped. Too soon. He couldn't be found just yet. Something had tipped Josh off. He knew it. The best laid plans undone by chaos.

He kept still, a watchful waiting. Josh paused. Then coughed again.

"Damn it, I should find some Sudafed," he muttered. "Mom said this was getting worse."

David prayed the medication wasn't in the pantry. His eyes darted around, frantic, searching for any sign of blister packs or OTC boxes. Nothing.

Josh swerved, moving to the pantry. He was so close David could hear him breathing, the ragged wheeze of a cold. Just a step away. David saw his Nike shoes through the slats, on the left toe, a smudge of mud.

David's pulse raced. He grabbed the gun, prepared to barrel out with surprise on his side. But then, at the last second, Josh veered off, searching the cabinets instead. Nothing. He shrugged, then downed the rest of the Sunny D.

David exhaled, certain he'd just survived being suffocated. He watched the wind-down begin. Josh swayed, blinking slowly, reaching for something to steady himself.

Time for act two.

David's pulse quickened, but not from fear. The shift was

unmistakable. Josh's eyes fluttered, heavy, as though the weight of sleep was pulling him under. His legs wobbled, hardly holding him upright, before they gave way, sending him staggering into the counter.

He tilted off balance, just on the edge of collapse, before his knees buckled. Josh hit the floor with a dull thud, his hand slapping weakly at the ground, searching for something to grab. His fingers grazed nothing, then went limp.

His breath was slow and shallow. Each exhale seemed like it might be the last. His face went white, then drained of color entirely. David watched the tremor in Josh's hand, the way it trembled as if caught between two worlds, the drug's grip tightening around him. The faint rattle of his breath was the only sound, like a storm waiting to break.

Josh's hands shook, spasming with involuntary tremors, his body jerking with the telltale movements of a postural collapse. The muscles in his face twitched, spasms firing beneath his skin. His lips parted, but there was no sound. David observed, counting it in his mind: 10 seconds between each breath. 12. 15. The intervals lengthened, the gaps growing more pronounced, each inhale a struggle, a desperate reflex rather than a true breath.

Josh's chest rose, then fell too slowly.

The cold knowledge of death was easy to track, but hard to witness. David's pulse spiked, his stomach knotting as he watched it unfold in real time. Josh wasn't slipping into sleep; he was drowning in it, his chest barely rising with each labored gasp. The shallow gulps were the body's final plea, a warning no one could answer. The time to intervene had passed. Hypoventilation. Death's slow, suffocating grip, heralding in the final scene. The systems shutting down one by one, the way the body folded in on itself—spasming muscles, the shallow rattling in his throat, the faint tremor in his legs. It wasn't pretty. No death ever was. A tumbling house of cards, fragile and inevitable. David looked away, unsettled, the taste of bile rising in his throat. Even with all his training, the helplessness burned through him. He felt sick.

David's pulse quickened, but his mind stayed focused. A slick sheen of sweat beaded across Josh's forehead. His lips and fingers turned mottled blue, like bruises, the progress of hypoxia. Peripheral cyanosis was settling in, a hallmark of the body's inability to oxygenate itself. David stomach churned, threatening a revolt. He held firm, watching the last act from behind the pantry door.

David willed himself to be patient. It was a slow process, waiting for a man to die, never as fast as it appeared on TV. The gurgles came and went. David occupied himself with thoughts of Addison.

A hit reel played in his mind as he waited for Josh to die. Addison, standing proud on the podium after winning the third-grade science fair medal, their volcano the biggest and messiest the gymnasium had ever seen. Still, she giggled and added more baking soda as the makeshift lava poured and poured.

He thought of Christmases long past, when she'd laugh as he handed her a mug of hot chocolate, ice cubes clinking to cool it down so her tongue wouldn't burn. He remembered holding her close during those early days, the blur of exhaustion and love, the colic and spit-up, the bone tiredness that never really left.

He didn't want to think about Josh, wanted to honor the moment with Addison. Every parent knows they're only as happy as their unhappiest child. Now, they could both live a honeysuckle life, sunny side of the street secured 'cause evil had left the building.

The gasps of Josh's inhale were shallow, between wanting to live and letting go. His fingers froze, forgetting their purpose. A jagged inhale cut through the silence, the sound of a body resigning. Then nothing, no more struggling. His body was crumpled on the floor, in the final brutal choreography for which nothing followed.

David's mouth was dry. A tremor ran through him that was not clinical detachment.

The murder was complete. Josh wasn't a perpetrator; he was just a body. And now he was gone.

David had drafted the last lines, his perfect cowboy sendoff.

"Dying ain't much of a living, boy," said with a sneer, was one of the front-runners. He'd thought it would land sharp, an homage to the western way. He'd pictured himself saying it, looking Josh in the eye. Letting the line do what the courts never did.

But now, standing in Josh's home, the words felt hollow. Too clean, and too rehearsed. The air was thick with rot and bleach, heavy with everything lost and stolen.

In the end, he said nothing. Not because he forgave him. Because Josh didn't deserve it.

Silence is violence, David thought. *You don't get my words. You don't even get my face.*

The smell of feces permeated the air, involuntary and vile. It made David happy that Josh died in his own filth. That was more meaningful than any soliloquy. And his death was enough. More than enough. It was everything.

David stepped out of the pantry, the covering still pulled tight across his face, the stink of the scene clinging to him. He kept his disguise, saw no use to slip out of his coverings. His old med school instincts whispered to call time of death, like he was standing over a gurney in a trauma bay. Instead, he listened—really listened—for the telltale rise and fall, for breath that never came.

He crouched low, keeping his elbows in, and leaned closer. Nothing. Not a flicker of air. No heartbeat thudding beneath Josh's ribs. Just skin gone slack with no soul left inside. He almost reached for the pulse point out of habit, the way he'd done a thousand times before. But this wasn't medicine. This wasn't saving. David held back. There was no need. The room had already answered.

Then David focused on not making any mistakes. His mantra bubbled up, steady and sharp. *Perfection. In this one thing, be perfect. No slips, no second chances.*

He rubbed the medicine bottle across Josh's fingertips, then tucked it into the kitchen drawer. Not hidden, just waiting to be found.

He'd already stripped the label, letting Addison's bottle tell a different story. No need to spell it out. Any decent investigator would connect the dots. The leftover pills would speak for themselves.

He rinsed the Sunny D again and left it by the sink with the others from breakfast. Nothing out of place. Like prepping a slide under his microscope, he tackled each task methodically. He wiped down surfaces and double-checked for prints. Even with gloves, no harm in being thorough. He wiped the pantry twice. Good as new. David scanned for footprints and cleaned as he backed out. He glanced at Josh. Still there. Still gone.

The words from *The Outlaw Josey Wales* came back to David, a script running through his mind.

"Now remember, when things look bad and it looks like you're not gonna make it, then you gotta get mean. I mean plumb, mad-dog mean. 'Cause if you lose your head and you give up then you neither live nor win. That's just the way it is."

He felt that way. Mean, with vengeance secured.

His checklist complete, David glanced down at Josh.

"You deserve this," he said aloud. Not for Josh. Just for himself. To mark the end of the line.

Then David hoisted himself through the wide-set window, the kind meant to bring in sunlight, not murderers. He didn't feel different, though he guessed that label applied to him now. His feet hit the ground softly. He shut the window behind him, wiped down the latch and the sill with practiced care. Then he grabbed a stick and raked it through the soft mud beneath, stirring it until his footprints disappeared into the mess. He straightened, scanning the yard. No headlights. No silhouettes. Just wind in the trees and the hush of a neighborhood fast asleep.

David moved with purpose, measured and unremarkable. Eyes ahead, pace forgettable. It felt like 3:45 a.m., but his watch blinked 10:25 p.m. He was back in his neighborhood by 11:01. The whole murder had taken a shade over four hours.

David crawled through the window of his house, slow and deliberate, same way in, same way out. No porch lights flicked on. No blinds shifted. The neighborhood, and his next-door professors, stayed still.

He poured himself a strong scotch, two fingers, breaking from his usual Mammy's Milk and bourbon habit. He didn't know when the weight of this would hit, only that it would, and when it did, he wanted something in his hand.

He left the lights off, drinking in the dark, a man hiding from himself. No glow for a neighbor to clock, no shadow to place at the wrong time. Just David and the quiet and the burn down his throat. The show had recorded. And Addison would've held up her end.

The deed was done.

David had seen cadavers before, but the freshly dead stuck different. He carried his drink to the worn leather couch, the cushion groaning beneath him like it knew what he'd done. Only a few months had passed since that postmortem talk with Addison, but it felt longer, lifetimes stacked between September and January. Whole forests could've grown and withered in the time it took to get here.

He swirled the scotch, watching the liquid catch the faint light from the streetlamp outside. Inside, he was tangled, no clean edges.

Just a mass of emotions too murky to name. Relief? Guilt? Maybe both, maybe neither. He didn't have it in him to dig deep.

David threw back the rest of his drink and stood. The weight in his limbs reminded him he hadn't slept, not really, in days. His shower would rinse the night away. His bed would catch him before his thoughts did.

The reckoning could wait.

Chapter 32

Aftermath

David slept in, his mind sluggish, dragging itself out of the weekend fog. The sunny Saturday morning felt off, his body and mind no longer in tandem. He tried to gauge the time by how heavy his eyes felt, wondering if it was already afternoon, but the bedside clock read 9:00 a.m. David dragged his feet to the side of the bed. He tested his legs, rolling his toes on the floor. The weight of last night didn't leave a physical mark, but something in his gut still felt stretched and uneasy.

He picked up his clothes from the floor, holding them at arm's length as though they were contaminated. He washed them twice, feeling the need to scrub off the majority of last night. *Out, out, damned spot,* indeed. He knew no trace of Josh would be left behind, but he still inspected every inch of fabric. Murder is for the meticulous.

Once satisfied, he shoved the clothes under old takeout containers, a stack of expired newspapers, and whatever other trash he could find. His movements were automatic, mixing the refuse together with mechanical precision. He dragged the bag to the curb, eager for the trashman to take it all away—his last connection to the night, buried in the anonymity of someone else's routine.

David expected some jitteriness, but as he dressed in his favorite pair of Levi's jeans and slid into a pullover, he felt nothing but the calm weight of the day. He tried to convince himself to wait, to sit down, eat toast, take a beat. It'd be wise to let Addison rest. An image of the last time he saw her projected in his brain. She looked drained, eyes hollow, withered from within. *College student hours*, he thought. But even so, a pinch of worry flickered in his gut. Maybe one day, he'd see her and not recognize her.

He checked the clock and made himself stall another thirty minutes. The car keys felt heavier than usual in his hand when he grabbed them. He shut down the litany of anxious thoughts. It was just a ride to Addison's dorm to grab his phone, tell her it was done, maybe cobble some breakfast together. Nothing to it.

His heart kicked, like a boot against his ribcage when he spied the cop in his neighbor's driveway, the engine already running. The black and white Ford Crown Vic pulled out behind him, tracking his slow descent. The headlights climbed up his rearview and held.

David didn't turn his head. He forced his eyes forward, both hands locked at ten and two. His knuckles bleached out. He eased off the gas until he crawled. Slower than slow, true granny speed, slower even than suspicion.

The cruiser kept its distance. No siren. No lights. Just there, a shadow that didn't flinch.

Sweat broke across his ribs. David's thoughts fractured, loud and fast. One hissed, *You're caught.* Another muttered, *Idiot.* The rest lined up like jurors, each with a sentence to hand down. He hadn't even been a criminal for twenty-four hours before getting busted.

He took the next turn at a crawl. The cruiser followed.

His throat closed. His vision tunneled. David couldn't

remember how to blink. He couldn't think past the roar in his ears, every inch of him braced for red and blue to explode behind him. For the voice to crackle through the speaker, signaling the bitter end.

The street narrowed. Houses passed in a blur. Mailboxes, fences, trees; none of them registered. He sucked in air, preparing for the worst. Then the cop turned left.

The Crown Vic disappeared behind a rusted chain-link fence and a hedge overgrown enough to swallow it whole.

David kept straight. Hands still at ten and two. Still crawling, with tears in his eyes.

It took another full block before he remembered how to breathe.

He wondered if his future would play out that way. A glitch in his wiring every time red and blue lights flashed or a siren cracked the air. He told himself it would fade. That nerves settled, that people moved on.

But David knew better.

Once those wires snapped taut, they stayed that way. Logic didn't loosen them, and excuses didn't slow the pulse. Once you'd been set off, your body didn't forget.

This was his new normal.

Raw, rattled, and ready to break at the next squawk of the radio. David would need Xanax the next time he heard the crunch of tires rolling slow over gravel. His peace was traded for his promise.

The Jeep crawled toward Addison's dorm, never inching over the speed limit. He kept his hands on the wheel, and his posture upright.

No action settled him.

At stoplights, he rehearsed what to say, trying different angles. He could start with small talk, ease Addison in. Or he could give it to her straight. Maybe she would already see it—etched in his face, curled into a new wrinkle, a fresh streak of gray at his temple. He checked the mirror like it could confirm the collateral damage. His palms slicked the wheel, the weight of last night relentless.

It was what she wanted, but that didn't make it any easier.

Addison had taken a single room over winter break, a quiet surrender after whatever burned down between her and Lisa. David didn't know the details, only that they'd transformed from inseparable to strangers. Maybe Addison never told Lisa how deep the cracks ran. Or maybe she had, and Lisa walked. Either way, the friendship didn't survive her rape. When David showed up, Addison stepped aside without a word. Her face held a sea of questions.

"Hey, Addison," he started, watching her close the door with slow hands. The room was stripped down, her bed made with a plain duvet; her books stacked like inventory on the bare desk. Just a placeholder space, to sleep and study, all warmth removed.

"Do you want any water?" she asked, already reaching into the mini fridge for an Evian.

"Sure," he said, watching her grab both waters and play hostess.

Her sweatshirt was speckled with ink; her brown hair jutting from her bun like snapped twigs. They sat on the futon, cramped and stiff.

"I did what you said. No issues with the phone," she murmured.

She slid the phone his way. David nodded, returning it to his pocket.

His mind churned with lines he couldn't say, too grim and sharp-edged for her dorm room. She didn't speak either, arms wrapped around her knees, chin resting on her sweatpants. When she finally met his eyes, she held the stare. No blink, no shift. Just giving him space to catch up.

"It's done," David began. "All over."

"Hmm," she replied.

"That's about right too."

Her brow twitched, a flicker of worry.

"You okay though?" she asked.

"Yeah. I'm okay. Just glad it's over."

"Right," she said. "Guess it's a relief."

Their conversation could've passed for anything, a bad grade, a shift in the weather. David was struck by the ease of it, how she let his answer stand without pressing. The act dangled between them, nameless and too new to be real.

He wanted to ask her a syllabus worth of questions. If she felt different. If she slept better. If she wished it had gone another way. He needed a tangible attaboy, a sign it meant something. A promise she'd heal, that he hadn't traded silence for more silence.

She looked at him, waiting.

"Well... okay then."

But it didn't feel finished.

"Alright, Addison. You okay?"

A sigh. A sip of water.

"I guess I am." Her voice was flat. Unreadable. No real clarity, and no real thank you.

David's anger flared quickly, from a spark to a forest fire. He wanted to rail at her, make her feel what it took to do what she asked. To get down and dirty with it, until her hands were as sin stained as his.

David nodded instead. His job was to protect her, keep her clear of the grime. She'd never know the months he spent planning, the nights spent watching, the lengths he went to. Keeping her sheltered was the whole point.

When nothing else came, he swallowed his questions, trimmed his thoughts down to nothing.

"Thanks for the water," he said.

She nodded. No touch. No pause. Just a glance at the door.

He was being dismissed.

Back in the car, David hesitated. He was tempted to circle back, maybe bring her breakfast, give her more time to feel. But Addison hadn't asked, and the line at Boone Bagelry would be out the door by now. So he drove home, turned on the TV, and waited for the Sunday paper to tell him his fate.

Chapter 33

Bad Boys, Bad Boys

The Sunday paper was normal. No headlines. No whispers of death. Just the usual crosswords and predictions of winter snow. The day moved on, steady and uneventful. David paced the kitchen twice before realizing he hadn't made coffee. He started the pot, poured a mug, then spilled half of it across the counter.

"Damn it," he said under his breath, grabbing a towel to sop up the mess. He'd given himself the weekend. Hell, he even took Monday off. Three days to recover, to recalibrate, to feel like himself again. By Monday night, he still felt like a crime scene in a lab coat.

At first, each day was like the last. The roads were slick with sleet, the hospital halls long and deserted. Craig loaded him up with surgical margins and fine-needle aspirations, the kind of cases that demanded detail and discipline.

The routine should have kept him contained. But his body moved while his thoughts raced. Every door slam cracked like a gunshot. His heart kicked hard even on the stairs. Once, winded at the top step, he caught himself pressing on his left arm, checking for something he already knew wasn't there.

Being a doctor didn't stop the panic. It gave it vocabulary.

He clocked in, reviewed slides, logged findings, signed out. Then he sat with the *Watauga Journal* like always, part of the routine. To anyone passing by, he looked like a man catching up on the news. But he wasn't reading. He was scouring. Squinting at every article, every police brief, every obit. Searching for fallout.

Without evidence to the contrary, unease crept in. David checked his rearview mirror at every stoplight, always looked twice at the joggers passing his house. Every doorbell chime next door triggered another round of panic. He pictured a SWAT team crouched behind his hydrangeas, radios crackling. He braced for the moment that would split his life in two.

His subconscious woke him in the dead hours with dreams he couldn't shake. In them, his license was gone, his name smeared, the sentence harsh and public. Not some white-collar scheme tucked away in court documents, but a full-blown murder charge, the kind that made headlines. *Doctor Death kills young adult. Boone Menace slays boy.* All caps, all condemnation. The world would know exactly what he was and what he'd done.

Despite all the planning, he was sure a mistake was coming. Johnny Law would show up, drag him in for questioning. At night, he replayed the crime scene in his head, eyes wide, searching for anything he'd missed, looking for a slip-up. By Thursday, his nerves were shot, every little detail gnawing at him, a steady drumbeat of worry that wouldn't quit. He opened the daily *Citizen-Times* out of Asheville, skimming through articles on politics, zoning, new football recruits, and the Polar Bear 5K race, along with the measures taken to clear the traffic jams. Just when he thought he'd drown in his own guilt, a blurb appeared on the second page of the *Watauga Journal.* Josh's demise wasn't even front-page news.

An investigation began in a suspected overdose death at 154 Oak Street in Boone. According to preliminary results, police suspect no foul play. Deputies arrived on scene Tuesday, January 13th at 2:04 p.m. after the deceased did not respond to any phone calls. Anyone with details regarding the incident is encouraged to contact the sheriff's department at 828-283-2434. The death is currently being treated as non-suspicious, but the investigation is ongoing.

David read it twice before the words sank in. He stared at the acquittal in Poynter font, then tossed the paper and took out the trash. Lid shut, job done. He was ready to close the lid on it all, let the coffin tell no tales. After all, there it was. Freedom, spelled out in cheap soy ink.

He ran through a mental checklist, the same steps he'd followed for every autopsy call.

The cold kept the worst of it at bay, but Josh had been dead for several days, and the decomposition would've already set in. David thought about rigor mortis, livor mortis, body temperature, and the other telltale signs. He considered the possibility of drug residue, the bags on hands and feet, the routine photographs, and the necessary identification of next of kin.

The overdose would likely be obvious—a prescription bottle found nearby, a common story of addiction, one that would fit neatly into the narrative. The police would breathe a sigh of relief, happy to avoid the complications of a homicide investigation.

David felt a brief pang for Josh's mother, mourning the loss of a son who never got the chance to be better. David meant no ill will, had spared her the details of her son's last moments, those last jerks of consciousness, the pants filled with feces. She saw him cleaned up and peaceful, pure under death's unyielding mask. That was the best lie David could give her.

He was home free, no flashing police vests, no red and blue

lights. Just coffee, tennis shoes, his wood burning fire. Time saved for secondhand novels, flannel sheets, and moments with Addison.

David dressed for work, dialing Addison's number as he left the house. When she answered, her voice was scratchy. He hesitated, not wanting to say too much over the airwaves.

"Hey, Addison. Just wanted to check in..."

There was a slight pause on the other end. "Hey, uh, can you hear me?"

"Oh yeah, sure, Dad. Just woke up. Sorry."

David tried to push the unease back down. "Okay, well. Good news to share. I'll see you Wednesday night, right? Joe's Kitchen, standing order—fettuccine, like always." He hated the uptick, the hope in his voice.

"Yeah, it's on. Gotta bounce," Addison replied, hanging up quickly.

David stared at the phone, confusion settling in. Something was off. He had been granted a pardon, but Addison treated him like a criminal already caught. He reached the door, his mind still tangled in the conversation. He fumbled for his keys, cursing when he realized he'd left them on the counter. He returned to grab them, flustered, and forced himself to shake it off.

David arrived at work, the cool, sterile scent of the lab welcomed him back. He grabbed his lab coat, adjusted his gloves, and sank into the rhythm of the day. His tasks involved reviewing case files, prepping slides, and dictating his surgical write-ups. Before he realized it, most of the morning had passed.

He was in the middle of detailing a report when his office phone rang.

The familiar voice of Dr. Carhartt, the surgeon he'd worked alongside for years, filled the line.

"Hey, David, it's Carhartt. Got a quick question about the biopsy you processed earlier. Specifically the margins on the OR 3 case. We're looking at it, and it seems a little wider than what your report said."

"Uh, sure," David said, forcing his voice to stay even. "I'll take another look."

He froze, glasses half removed, when Carhartt mentioned the margin had been off by a fraction of a millimeter. No hint of anger. No accusation. Just fact.

Carhartt wasn't trying to corner him. The margin was off. David had missed it.

A clean mistake, but a mistake all the same. Carhartt wouldn't make him sweat. David did that all on his own.

Maybe Springsteen had it right. He was in the clear. No charges. No convictions. But it still felt like a brilliant disguise. David buried himself in work, double-checking every slide, afraid of what his own hands had missed. Now was not the time to act out of character, to cause his colleagues to notice something amiss. He needed to be steady, to be boring. And most of all, he needed to be consistent. No mistakes.

That night he cracked open four Guinness even though it was Thursday. He usually saved beer for the weekend but it felt necessary. He needed to wind down, to let the day settle. To put Addison, and work, and all his worries to rest. By the third bottle his head spun. By the fourth he was drinking to forget.

He tumbled into a restless sleep and dreamed of Josh. He saw him in fragments. Mouth open in a gurgle. Swatches of motion. Fingers frozen, a chest turned to marble. He was back there, catching slivers through the pantry doors. Then looking down at him, studying his wet hair across his forehead. Then Josh's eyes snapped open and David jolted upright, drenched in sweat. His house answered with the ticking of the clock and the low hum of the air conditioner. He lay back, heart hammering, unable to chase sleep again.

He sat on the small balcony, watching the town wake, replaying Addison's clipped words in his mind. He'd expected angst, a wail at the world, emotions all mixed up and ready to fight. Instead she spoke like Mary, clipped and controlled, every sentence a period. No tremor in her tone, no regret in her voice. It spooked him, her absence of emotion after months of drowning in it. Now she was collected, all loose ends tied tight. It was David who was still digging through the thick of it, and he wondered what she was hiding behind that calm exterior.

The sun rose anyway, but David stayed cold, the truth still tucked away.

Chapter 34

The Times They Are a-Changin'

Friday at work rounded out another day. David's mind whirled, but his hands were cautious. He couldn't afford another mistake. At lunch, he stopped by the doctor's lounge to grab a quick coffee but didn't linger. It reminded David of all those months of planning, a history he'd rather not revisit.

The day closed out with a breast cancer case, tricky enough with its mixed features to call it malignant or not. David sent it down to Baptist Hospital in Winston for a second read. Normally, he was the call-it-like-he-saw-it type, confident in his differential diagnosis. But with his head a mess, he didn't want to over-call something, leading slice happy surgeons to remove something that wasn't there. Another set of eyes was the right move.

The diagnosis was out of his hands now, riding on someone else's certainty. That did little to ease his mind. He capped his pen, then uncapped it.

His eyes burned from lack of sleep. A fog moved through his head, slow and stubborn, like it meant to set up shop and stay.

Uncertainty in life, in murder, and now in work moved through his day, an unsteady pulse. It wasn't venial, not just wrinkles or grey hairs. It was doubt, and it kept him frayed. He longed for a mentor, someone to call, but this was a line he had to walk alone.

He winced at his own melodrama.

Hell, he thought. *Cue the Johnny Cash soundtrack, you sad sack.*

Insulting himself was the surest way to rustle up confidence. He didn't care to dwell on what that said about his psyche. He kept ticking off the cytology boxes, managing his workload and his self-criticism in equal parts.

After work, he called Addison. Straight to voicemail. He didn't bother with a message. *Gotta bounce* still rang in his head—casual, careless. Like what he'd done didn't matter. A disposable deed. For her, a footnote. For him, a haunting.

The evening dragged. He flipped through channels, but nothing kept his attention. Just CSI reruns, which wouldn't help him wind down before bed. David picked up a John Connolly novel, flipped through a few pages, but couldn't focus. By 9, he could no longer sugarcoat his boredom. He grabbed a Tylenol PM, hoping it might force his body into sleep.

The over-the-counter drug didn't touch his REM. It was an ant-sized dose, and he needed something stronger—Trazodone, maybe Ambien. The hours slipped by, his mind too loud, searching for rest but finding only static. His body was exhausted, but sleep came in fragments. His thoughts spun in manic circles, winding him up instead of down.

He finally gave up the ghost of sleep, flicking the bedroom light on at 5 a.m., the harsh glow stinging his eyes. He stared at the ceiling, eyes raw, counting the minutes until six, wishing he could bend his body to his will.

Then, a rat-tat-tat, hard and booming downstairs. The sound of a thick fist, nothing dainty, banging with enough force to pound his skull. The sound echoed through the house, sharp and insistent. His body jerked in response, heart leaping through his throat. He stood frozen for a moment, disoriented and drowsy.

Another knock, louder this time. David covered his ears, trying to drown it out. Panic spread like wildfire down his veins. He staggered toward the door, but his legs felt heavy, like they didn't belong to him. He hesitated, then glanced over the balcony. Two Boone police officers stood at his doorstep, their figures imposing in the gray light of dawn.

David took the stairs two at a time, then paused at the landing.

He crept to the door, raking his fingers through his damp hair, the strands clinging to his scalp. The scent of stale sleep rose from his armpits, the acrid smell of body odor mixing with his breath, which still carried the remnants of old coffee. His pajama bottoms, damp from sweat, clung uncomfortably to his legs. He wasn't put together. Not even close.

He took a minute, calling out an "I'm coming!" to give himself a second to regroup. His mind raced, thoughts piling up, searching for a way out.

He prepared himself for the sight of their holstered weapons, the gleam of their badges, the weight of their utility belts sagging with handcuffs, flashlights, and radios. David's hand lingered on the door handle. He had to open the door, though his body tensed, not wanting to give a warm welcome. He braced himself and turned the handle.

The door opened slowly, revealing two officers frowning on his front stoop. A man and a woman in dark navy-blue uniforms, their patches gleaming like they'd just been spit-shined. The woman's jaw was tight, her eyes scanning him with unflinching sharpness. The man, bulkier, stood with his arms loose but ready, the stance of a boxer. They took in David's appearance while he clocked the make and model of their guns. The holsters at their sides held identical Glock 19s, winking at him from their confinement.

"Hello, are you David McCall?" the woman asked, her voice all no-nonsense. David froze. The words hit him like ice water, his heart kicking into overdrive. His arrest was right here, face to face. Seven days and then one more. That's all he got before they found him. Not a mastermind. Not a monster. Just a pajama-clad fool, sweating and slumped, dripping to death on his own hearth.

He scanned their faces, their stance. The man's eyebrows shot upward, letting his expression do the talking. The woman was all sharp angles, nothing soft in her posture. "Are you David McCall?" she repeated, slower this time, like she was waiting for him to crack.

David didn't speak. He glanced over his shoulder, desperate for a distraction.

Then he saw it. Big white plastic buckets, the kind used for police fundraisers.

They weren't here for him. They were here to beg for change.

David pivoted fast, his body jerking with mechanical urgency.

The enthusiasm hit all at once, a wave crashing through drywall.

"Hi! Oh, hey! You're here about the donations!" The words tumbled out, quick and clumsy. "Let me grab my checkbook, just hang on a sec."

He turned too fast and caught his foot on the small wooden stool by the door. It rocked, tipped, then hit the floor with a dull thud.

"Whoops," he said, too bright. His cheeks flushed. The officers exchanged a glance.

He bent to pick it up. One hand hit the wall. The other missed. The stool slid again, legs scraping the tile.

He froze. Then stood upright and left it there.

The cops said nothing. Just watched.

David didn't want them stepping inside. Not even one foot.

His eyes flicked to the doorframe, and for a second, *stay there* nearly slipped out.

Instead, he forced a smile that didn't fit and blurted, "Be right back!"

David left the door cracked behind him. Too late, he realized that was a mistake. Still, he kept up the caffeinated chatter, his voice bouncing from the kitchen.

"Just gotta find a pen that works! You know how it is. Three drawers and not a decent one in the bunch."

The clatter of open drawers echoed through the house, sharp and frantic, a hundred metal mouths gnashing at once. He rummaged harder, gravity bending strangely beneath him.

"You okay in there?" came the call from the doorway, the woman's voice on edge. David gripped the counter hard, afraid that without it he'd fall.

The blue of his checkbook emerged from the mess of papers in the junk drawer, a flash of color amidst the clutter. Relief slinked down his body, covering him with calm. A guillotine malfunction at the last possible second. His head still intact, heart still pumping, but the blade had dropped close enough to kiss.

He ran back, holding the checkbook aloft like a game-winning trophy, chest high and grinning, caught in the high of his own survival. Then the words hit.

"That's a squirrely one."

His relief cracked, dead on arrival. David slowed, tiptoeing closer, his eyes narrowed into slits. The male officer mumbled something else, the woman laughed, easy breezy.

"WHAT did you say?" The words shot out, sharper than he intended, a blush of a threat inside them.

The officer blinked, confused for half a second, then smiled like he'd mis-stepped onto a rattlesnake.

"Your yard's got a lot of squirrels. Must be the birdfeeders. They love that stuff." The officer motioned beside him to the bird feeder, half full, with runoffs dotting the pavement.

David nodded, the motion jerky, like his body hadn't gotten the memo to relax. His fingers clutched the check too tightly, like he wasn't sure if he meant to give it or eat it. When he finally let go, the male officer gave him a slow blink and a half-cocked head tilt. That was police speak for wondering if David was high or just strange.

The woman started to thank him, stopped mid-sentence, then tried again.

"Well… thank you… uh, we appreciate it." Her voice tripped over itself, caught between duty and discomfort. She put him out of his misery with a brittle smile.

David shut the door and slid down with it, his back dragging against the wood until he hit the floor. Knees bent, arms limp, he slumped, leaning against the door's heavy weight. That was so much harder than he thought it would be. A laugh bubbled up, but nothing was funny. He let it out anyway, the sound dry and off-key, a cough released at a funeral.

§

HE PREPARED THE SPAGHETTI HIMSELF, DECIDING AGAINST takeout. It stilled David's mind to follow the directions, boiling and salting, making the sauce from scratch. His kitchen was warm, even a bit stuffy, so he opened the window to let the cool air in. He was looking forward to greeting Addison, sure that a tight hug and a warm smile would shake off any awkwardness between them. Wednesday was their special time, and he meant to make it count.

He heard a knock on the door just after setting the table. He paused, praying the police weren't back again. It wasn't like Addison to knock. Typically, she barreled in, quick to sluff off the cold. His feet pattered quickly to the door, so fast he could fall, hands smoothing his hair. He stood straighter, his eyes adjusting to the peep hole.

Instead of the police, with their badges and blunt force, he saw his daughter. Addison was dressed in jeans and a peacoat, swaying back and forth on his stoop. She wore makeup that was smudged around her eyes.

"Addison," he chided, before even letting her in, "why did you knock on the door? You have a key!" His voice reeked with irritation, wondering if he should disclose his previous police altercation.

She followed him inside, shrugging off her error. She laid her purse down on the counter, eyeing the dinner offerings.

"Why all the fanciness? There's no way I can eat all of this. Where's Joe's?"

He took in the scene, the prepared bowls, the garlic bread, the lone candle. It looked all wrong, set for a date not his daughter. In his effort to make it special, he'd curated it all wrong.

"Just wanted to do something nice. Should be good, I made it from scratch."

She mumbled, 'Lots of effort, could've just picked something up.' David couldn't read her, unsure if his harsh tone turned her haughty.

Addison pulled out the chair, no words, and dug into her food. David grabbed the Parmesan, noticing she'd started without him. He sat down, eyes on her, watching her eat.

Her words were sparse, just yes or no, no details. Since Josh, she'd shut down in every way she could. Even here, where she could speak freely, she chose not to.

David tried to push it aside. The stillness was familiar, a rhythm they'd settled into. At least she was eating. He latched onto that, unwilling to let anything else unsettle him.

He took the dishes to the sink, hands moving through the motions, ready to fill it with water and finish their Wednesday routine, the muscle memory of passing and washing. He turned to make room, then froze when he saw she'd slipped on her coat. David gaped, not fast enough to cover his reaction.

"Sorry, Dad, gotta get going. I have a big final tomorrow in Advanced Statistics."

"Oh, hey, wait a minute. I have dessert—one I didn't make, and I wanted to talk to you about…"

She cut him off, fumbling for her purse, already swinging it toward the door.

"Thanks for the food, but I really gotta run," her voice short and less sweet.

"Oh," he slumped, directing his voice to the running water, listening to it soak the sink. He kept his hands under the burning water, letting it hurt him. The water wasn't comfortable, a shade below scalding, but he couldn't make himself stop.

The lifeline between them felt shattered, Addison annexing him like he'd gone to seed. He left the dishes to dry and picked up the phone. The phone rang once before the voicemail kicked in. So much to say. Once he started, he wasn't sure he could stop.

The beep came too soon.

"Hey Addison, It's me, again. Hey, I just wanted to make sure everything's okay. I don't want to be needy, or… whatever, but things seemed weird tonight and I just, I don't know, feel like something is wrong. Can you call your old man back when you get this?" He chuckled, attempting to ease the tension. "I'm just paranoid, but I'm trying here. Give me a call."

He shoved the phone back into its cradle and packed up the pasta in silence. Upstairs, the water ran hot. Good, he liked it that way now. He stayed in the bath until his skin pruned, then dried off and opened the book he'd been pretending to read all week. The phone lit up just as he was slipping under the covers.

Hey. I'm fine.

She didn't offer more, and he didn't ask.

A two-minute text, maybe less. Just long enough to say nothing at all.

Chapter 35

The Distance Between

The days passed with no calls, no visits. Addison was gone in every way that counted.

Don't overthink it, he repeated. But David's chest thudded, a Morse code no one could crack. He imagined her leaning against the couch, her ghost drifting up the stairs. Everywhere in his home her reflection lingered, but always through a mirror that was cracked. The warmth of her smile lived only in memory.

In his more generous moments, he blamed college. Late nights. Strict professors. The kind of grind that turned schedules to mush. Maybe she was buried in the library, chasing grades, too busy to bother with his theatrics.

His subconscious spotted every lie, calling his bluff.

At least she kept their Wednesday routine.

David moved through the kitchen with practiced ease. He had picked up Addison's usual from Joe's: fettuccine and garlic bread. While the distance between them remained, she hadn't missed a single Wednesday dinner at Dad's.

He smiled as he set out the half-flat soda she preferred. Rituals mattered. That was how a family held itself together.

He checked the clock. Five minutes to seven.

She was never early. He knew that. Still, he paced the living room, his steps uneven, his pulse out of sync. Every sound made him glance at the door.

The doorbell rang.

David flinched, then smiled.

Not this again.

Addison, ringing the bell like a stranger in her own home. The same house that held the inch marks from her childhood, the curve of her bedroom walls, and a beach-themed shower curtain she had picked out last spring.

He moved to answer it, already picturing her face.

But it wasn't Addison at the door.

It was Professor Halterman, the male half of the Literature PhDs next door. He was semi-retired now and had been David's neighbor since the day Addison came home from the hospital.

His glasses were, as always, slightly smudged, and he wore the perpetual scowl of a curmudgeon. Tonight was no different. He stood with his arms already crossed, the posture of the grievously annoyed.

This, David thought, *was exactly why they didn't socialize.*

He held a small manila envelope like it might contain state secrets.

"Evening, David. I hope I'm not interrupting."

David shook his head, already hoping the conversation would be short.

"Just noticed your porch light's been flickering a bit," Halterman said. "Thought you might want to check the wiring. These old homes can be temperamental. Sometimes a fire hazard, even."

David fought an eye roll. "Thanks, Professor. I'll take a look."

But Halterman lingered. His eyes drifted past David, toward the table.

"You expecting someone?"

David felt the shift. The question didn't belong. It was a thread stitched too neatly onto the rest.

"Just dinner."

"Routine's important," Halterman added, still peering into the house. "Keeps us old guys young."

He guffawed at his own joke. David didn't laugh. He wasn't *that* much younger, but the line still rubbed.

"Anyway," Halterman said, holding up the envelope, "this came to my mailbox by mistake. I think it's yours. I tried to bring it by weeks ago, but no one was home. Then my better half tossed it under *The New Yorker* and a stack of *McSweeney's*."

He gave a short laugh. "Probably just spam, but figured it was the neighborly thing to do."

David reached for the envelope, his fingers slower than they should have been.

"When exactly did you come by?" David asked. His voice snagged at the edges.

Halterman scratched his head. "After New Year's, that's for sure. One of those bone-deep cold nights we always get around here. I slipped on your walkway, actually. There was ice under the leaves. Nearly went down flat."

He gave a slow glance toward the porch.

"Surprised you haven't had someone break a hip out there. Bit hazardous, all things considered."

David's stomach turned. The walkway had been iced over for weeks. But on that night, when he returned, there was no snow and no footprints. He exhaled, his secret safe.

David forced a smile and stepped back. "Appreciate you bringing it by. Have a good night."

He went to shut the door, a curt dismissal, maybe a touch too rude. But the old geezer was interrupting Addison's time, and he still needed to check why she hadn't shown.

Halterman hesitated. "Sure. No trouble."

He paused at the top of the steps, then turned halfway, voice casual but carrying.

"Oh, and David? Our literature department's got some writer coming next week. A book's just hit the shelves, *The Silent Scalpel.* One of those thrillers where the surgeon takes it upon himself to... well, start cleaning house. Says it's justice, or something close enough. Not exactly highbrow, but it's got people talking."

He gave a thin smile.

"Figured it might be your kind of thing."

He turned with care, one hand on the rail, and hobbled down the walkway.

David shut the door and locked it, this time with a tremor in his hand.

"Your kind of thing?" What did that mean? His breath hitched. Maybe it was nothing. But maybe it wasn't. He peered through the blinds, watching his neighbor trudge home, wondering what he suspected.

David spied the garlic bread, long cooled, and the fettuccine congealed at the edges. He moved back toward the table and pulled out his chair.

That was when he saw his phone.

One message.

> Can't make it

He stared at it for a long moment. Then typed back, his fingers clumsy on the screen.

> Come on, Spitfire.

The reply came fast.

> Pls don't call me that

He didn't move.

The message stayed on the screen, a final reminder of all he'd lost. He stared at the table, the ghost of Addison in every detail, marked with all her favorites.

Then it hit. The kind of grief that held no dignity. His chair scraped backward, and his hands found his face. He crumpled, the first sob silent, the second too loud. He cried until his chest hurt.

Until the plate blurred and the pasta found the trashcan.

Until the name *Spitfire* became a curse word in his mouth.

By morning, the trash had been taken out, the counters wiped clean. No trace of dinner, or the man who had wept beside it.

David sat at the desk, writing out a check for Addison's therapist. The envelope was already addressed. He sealed it, pressed it flat, and set it by the door.

Maybe that was all he was good for now. Send the checks. Keep the engine running. Pay for the healing he couldn't give her, while no longer tagging along.

His daughter, replaced with a doppelganger, all clipped tones, leaving him less and less to hold on to.

He began calling Addison every day after work, just to hear her voice. She didn't answer, but rather than alter his protocol, he kept at it, an addict, hungry for an explanation.

The voicemails piled up, unreturned. Addison was stubborn,

but she couldn't keep this stalemate forever. He'd done all she asked, took every hard thing and made it his own.

David knew he was still her backup. He might've been riding the bench, but he knew she'd come around when she needed something. She was in the frenzy of tests, the constant grind of papers, the chaos of quizzes that hit unexpected. In college, the bills stacked up fast—groceries, clothes, unexpected expenses. It was an unpredictable rhythm, and it could overwhelm even the most contentious freshmen. Her first flush of independence, and here he was, trying to wreck it.

Maybe her own guilt had crawled under her skin, a tick that grew, no matter how many showers she took. Addison was complicit. The whole plan had been her idea. She'd need space to process, to recalibrate, to find a way through the growing gap. He tapered down the calls, not wanting to overwhelm her.

With Addison, he knew how to take what she gave. To trust that their bond was too big to break. His brain smoothed the worry out, buying in to every excuse. His heart tracked every unreturned call, plunging down like a cardiac trace when he was ignored.

But something shifted as the snow let up, melted into puddles, and splashed against the cars. David feared the closeness wasn't snapping back into place. The silences stretched, a patchwork of hurt and sadness settling over him like cement. He felt like he'd traded places with Josh, like whatever bond he'd once had with his daughter had been severed that night in January. The phone calls never came. The visits were fewer. The dial tone came too soon.

David kept offering, even when her excuses felt flat, even when the calls stopped altogether.

If there was an activity in Boone, he suggested it. Fettuccine nights, beer in the fridge, a movie he knew they'd both like. Each time, she turned him down, no explanation, no call-back. But David still fixed the food, set the table for two, waiting for the doorbell, her face pale from the cold. He kept waiting for the prodigal to return, holding out a plate, keeping the space warm for her. Sometimes, he listened for the drop of her bookbag by the front door, the sound she used to make when she came home from school. That thud had once meant she was back, safe, his.

Now he waited for it again, foolish or not.

What was lost hadn't been found. Not for lack of trying. The weather was bleak, and the house felt colder, with not-quite-spring ennui staring him down and holding him in place.

Chapter 36

A Little Hope

"Dr. McCall, line one, Dr. McCall, line one."

The intercom blasted his name. David paused, listening hard to make sure he heard it right. He wasn't the one who got paged. As a pathologist, he got it easy, no emergencies, no color-coded chaos. He liked it that way, buried behind his microscope with no drop-ins, no need for social graces. Some people would call it lonely. He called it peace. Keeping each day contained, doing what needed doing and nothing more. Just a man, a microscope, and a carefully curated Pandora mix playing only for him.

The day was already a flood of new surgicals. He'd just settled in, first rack lined up beside him, scope humming, phone screen blank. The office line rang, unexpected. He picked it up, forehead already creased. The old worry returned, uninvited but familiar, the kind that had come since Josh's death. He ignored the shake in his hand as he answered.

Addison's voice rushed through the line.

"Hey Dad, I'm really sorry. I remembered the hospital number and knew you'd be there. My car just died in the Harris Teeter lot. I think it's the battery. And my phone is dead too. I know I should have charged it. I tried your cell first but it went straight to voicemail. I'm calling from the store phone. Can you come get me? It's freezing out here and I didn't know who else to call."

He promised he'd leave right away, his heart lifting at how good it felt to be needed. A soft spot opened inside him, like the first riff of a song you never skip. Her voice had returned to its old rhythm, not the recent slow, flat version that dragged like cold molasses.

David didn't hesitate. He left the stack of slides behind, grabbed his keys, and headed for the door. The Jeep groaned to life. He didn't speed, but his hands were anxious on the wheel. She had called him, chosen him, asked him for help. He grinned, canyon-wide, ready to play the hero. The standstill between them had ended. He even thought about swinging by AutoZone for a battery, but the temperature read in the teens so he drove straight there.

But when he pulled up ready to rescue her, Addison was already being helped by a local do-gooder. The stranger's head was under the hood of her car, all cheerful and helpful, full of mechanic-laden advice. The top of his head was covered with a hat, his hands around the battery, and Addison chattering beside him. David got out of the car, zeroing in on his daughter. He wanted to urge the man to move along, now that David was there to give it a go.

Addison registered his presence. "Oh sorry, thanks for coming, Dad. Guess I don't need you anymore." She turned her attention back to the middle-aged man.

"You ever try tapping the terminal with a wrench? That'll wake it up if it's just stuck corrosion," the man said. He knocked on the post for good measure, proud of himself.

David frowned. That wasn't how it worked. If the contact was bad, sure, a jiggle might buy time, but tapping battery terminals like it was a vending machine didn't fix the issue. It just made people *feel* useful.

"I'd bet it's just low juice. You don't need a new battery yet," the man added. "These things run forever. My Civic's still on the original."

David clenched his jaw. That kind of logic is why people ended up stranded again the next week. Addison nodded anyway, polite and locked in on the man's directions to the nearest shop, like she was hearing gospel. She didn't explain that she was a Boone goon, born and raised. Just leaned in, listening. David hemmed and hawed beside her car, not sure of the protocol.

He decided to stay put. He'd outlast this charlatan and make her laugh. Two points for the price of one.

The lid closed, her car started, and she flashed a smile at both of them. It was an equal dismissal, a disposing of guests.

"Thanks!" she intoned to the helpful assistant before putting her foot on the brake.

David realized he also was getting the boot and turned to go back to the Jeep, calling the whole thing a wash. She didn't wave goodbye to him, just turned onto the highway, a mix of breaks and cranks.

He thought about what she'd said. *I guess I don't need you anymore.*

Just words. Just filler. Except to him, they weren't.

He'd always known she'd grow up, take off running, move into a life that didn't include him. All parents feel that countdown— every report card, every birthday candle, every summer slipping through their fingers. The sentimental ones always said you only get eighteen. There's a shelf life to being needed. You love them anyway.

But David believed their relationship would be different.

He pictured the sweet spot. The reward years. No curfews, no punishments. Just mutual respect and easy company. He'd retire early. Spoil the grandkids. Teach them to fish, make pancakes in shapes that made no sense, then let them eat ice cream for breakfast when Addison wasn't looking.

He imagined her coming home often, rolling her eyes at his bad jokes, pulling in the driveway with the kids in tow, grateful for all the ways he had stayed solid.

He'd built up equity in being predictable. That's what he worked toward when she was eight and cried over multiplication. She couldn't remember seven times three and got so frustrated she chewed up the flashcard, jaw working hard to swallow the thing whole.

That's what he worked toward when he talked her through every lost friendship, every unfair teacher, every teenage betrayal. Every time he waited up for her to make curfew, forcing himself not to think of car wrecks or strangers in the dark.

It was all for the golden years. For the finish line where they'd meet not as parent and child but as equals. As adults, and as friends. David didn't raise her to lose her. He raised her to keep her in a different way. He never thought he'd be the one left behind.

If anyone was going to be edged out, it would've been Mary. His ex-wife had always tried to sand down Addison's edges. Always coaching, always correcting, with words that sounded helpful but landed harsh. If any grandparent would be relegated to cards with crisp bills inside, it would be Mary. Not him.

But now, even the givens felt negotiable.

He drove home clammy, hands cold, stomach twisting. He made it to the bathroom just in time to throw up. His body said shock, his brain called it melodrama. His soul called it loss.

David curled on the cool tile, breath shallow. David curled on the cool tile, breath shallow. He offered no call, no cover, no care.

The slides waited for him, and he let them, content to sluff off responsibility for the rest of the day.

Eventually, he dragged himself to bed. He put his phone on silent, changed into twice-worn sweats. He didn't notice the tears until the pillow soaked through. Sleep took its time. When it came, it came hard. The sleep of the dead or the ones who wished they were. David joined those desperate ranks, all cried out and weary. Not with drama, or declarations. Just with the slow sinking, a realization of letting go.

Because sometimes when the game's over, when the board flips and the pieces scatter, it's not worth crawling around trying to collect them.

Sometimes you just stay down.

Chapter 37

Georgia on My Mind

The hum of the fluorescent lights felt sharper this morning. David stepped into the building like he hadn't missed a beat, but the tension in his shoulders told a different story. He'd skipped out yesterday. No notice or excuse, just absent. Today he'd pay the piper, but he was hoping he wouldn't get caught.

The lab was quiet as usual, empty except for a few technicians and junior staff. No one clocked his late arrival. He slipped from the specimen processing area to the hematology bench, almost making it to his office. He read his doorplate, David McCall, MD, shining in gold, but feeling as dull as unpolished granite.

He'd almost made it when a well-timed cough stole his entry.

"Dr. McCall?"

David froze. His mentor, Dr. Gill, stared him down. The one person he didn't want to disappoint.

"You didn't call yesterday. What happened?"

David forced his back to straighten, a fleeting moment of panic turning into sharp, practiced composure. "Had some personal matters to attend to," he murmured, knowing better than to lie.

"Right. The staff said you took off. That's fine, but the not coming back part. That's not." Dr. Gill looked stern, so far from his typical grandfather mode.

"I meant to come back, it just took longer than I thought." David knew the excuse was flimsy, but he said it anyway, hoping to earn a touch of sympathy in the process.

"The slides didn't get read," Dr. Gill said, his voice cutting sideways. "I've talked to Craig, and to Dr. Rudger. They say your work is slipping."

He paused, his gaze steady, measuring.

"I know all you've gone through." Dr. Gill sighed. "And I don't want to be harsh. But I have a hospital to run."

David hung his head, feeling lower than low. "I understand."

Dr. Gill's eyes softened, just for a moment, but his tone remained firm.

"We think it's best if you take some time off. Clear your head. Have a little vacation. Let's say, a week. Come back refreshed, and it's water under the bridge."

"Starting when?" David asked, the words coming out flat.

"Tomorrow's best."

"Am I going to be fired?"

David kept the wail out of his voice, or most of it. He'd been a pathologist his whole career. He'd never learned how to be anything else.

"That's not on the table. Not for now. Just take the time. Use it wisely. The rest will sort itself out."

Dr. Gill gave him a tight grin, the kind generals give soldiers in a war—steely, hard, and a little too knowing.

"Thank you, Sir." David's voice was tight, the words scraping out. "I hate letting you down. It won't happen again."

Dr. Gill nodded, content with the verdict he'd delivered.

David spent the rest of the day hangdog tired, weary from all the people he'd disappointed. He wanted to say to hell with Boone, and the snow that dragged its way into May. Might as well head to Georgia with his time, to drum up some brotherly love with his older brother Mitch. He could soak up some sunshine, in a place build for people, not snowmen.

He called Addison and Mary, checking in lightly, letting them both know he didn't do a runner.

Just a quick "Hey there, going to see Mitch. You need me, you know my number."

He hoped that would drum up some curiosity from them, seeing as he wasn't one to take vacations. Neither returned his call, not so much as a "Let me call you back."

He was used to the silence, had taken in enough to drown.

It'd be good to vacate his old haunts. These days, they made him twitchy. Grabbing a beer at Macadoos used to help him think. Now it just left him bracing for impact. He pictured running into Addison, her back turned, offering only her profile. Saving her smile for strangers and secondhand friends.

"Hey Mitch, mind if I come lick my wounds at your place? Got some ideas to bounce around?" David made the call a bit too late at night. He figured Mitch would be up. His two boys were teenagers, who kept night owl hours.

"Come on in, the water's fine," his brother joked in his drawn-out Southern accent. "It'll be good to see you. It's been years, Davie."

His voice held in a reproach, and David chose to ignore it.

David booked a last-minute flight to Georgia, hoping his older brother might have some generic wisdom, or at least enough famil-iarity to tide him over. David wanted someone to remind him of his place in the world, hoping Mitch had a good locker room speech prepared in his back pocket.

By the time the plane touched down, David was a tangled mess of worry, certain he'd spent big bucks on a plane ticket to visit a relative in name only.

He hailed a cab and paid in cash. The taxi dropped in off in front of a non-descript house in Palmetto, Georgia. It was only 20 minutes from Hartsfield-Jackson but held no urban appeal. The setting was rural, and Mitch's house was quaint.

David lugged his suitcase up the porch, checked out his brother's modest surroundings. It was late in the evening, and he glanced at his brother's burly frame through the screen door.

"Got a cold one?" David began, uncertain how to cover all the time between them, all the holidays missed, all the phone calls never made.

"Always, man."

Mitch opened the door, enveloping David in a great bear hug, like only a brother can.

Their age difference had always caused a bit of hero worship. When he was younger, David imagining joining the army or being a detective who caught the crooks every time. To him, Mitch always stood on the right side of justice, throwing well deserved punches and basking in the glory of the town prom queen's admiration. He inspired a lot of David's vigilante justice, since he'd grown up with a brother who fought first and asked questions later.

But now, Mitch wore glasses, and his body type had widened, no longer just big boned. He'd traded a pigskin for spreadsheets, ball games for tax seasons. It was a less showy future than the name in lights story David had envisioned for him.

They moved to the porch, kicking their feet up, like no time had passed. Beer bottles sweated between their fingers. David leaned back, grateful for the Southern heat that didn't claw at his bones the way the cold back home did.

He dialed up the courage to talk to Mitch, brother to brother, since his two teenagers were nowhere to be found.

"Where are Brian and Miles?"

"At Lisa's, or at their friends. It's hard to keep track anymore. Soon as I say hey, they are out the door. I'm in the ATM season man, where the only thing I'm good for is dollar bills."

"I hear ya. It's strange. Now there's all these video games and iPods. It's like the world changed and I haven't caught up yet."

They sat backed and sipped. A melancholy took hold, kept in time with their rocking chairs.

They weren't the tell-it-all type. Both had banked on different futures—Mitch on sports, David on facts. Neither rose to the heights they'd expected. Both were divorced, living in small towns, earning a good wage but nothing to brag about at a high school reunion.

"Glad you came down," Mitch remarked, a subtle way of asking why David decided to visit when he hadn't called in a month of Sundays.

David took a pull from his bottle. "Hell, I was just thinking, looking at your backyard. This beats the way we were raised."

Both of their parents were long gone. Their father had passed with an aggressive form of prostate cancer, barely a shade over 60. All cancer will take a person's pride, but their father and all his machismo seeped out of him in what seemed like a month. At the end, his skin looked like moths' wings, cracking and dry, his mind not much better, a whisper of the formidable figure they'd known and feared.

David paused, eyes on the dark line where the porch ended and the yard began.

"You ever think of Mom and Pop?"

"Every now and then," Mitch said. "Not the way we left them, though."

David nodded. "Yeah. Not those last days."

"Remember when he tried to show me his underwear?" David said, voice low.

The porch provided cover, the dark rising, covering them with a privacy that felt right and true.

Mitch exhaled through his nose. "Yeah. That was rough."

David gave a dry laugh. "Of all the things to remember."

"Not exactly the legacy he had in mind," Mitch replied, "but he wasn't in his right mind."

David laughed again, this time bitterly. "That's the one I'll never forget."

It had happened while Mitch was out for coffee. Their father, frail and bedridden, lifted his gown and tugged at his waistband. It still made David sick to remember.

"Come here, look. Come closer, it's all right here," his father wheezed, hands fumbling, tugging the fabric with urgency. David barely made it out of the room before breaking down in the rental car.

David couldn't handle the awkwardness of watching a proud man's dignity shatter. He let Mitch take point, told himself that was the natural order. Big brother handles the hard stuff. But now, years later, he wondered about the cost.

"Do you think we handled it right? With Dad?"

Mitch took a long swig. "I think about it. But I don't blame us. It was too much."

David stared at the table. "Still feels off."

"Most things do," Mitch said.

At the end, he couldn't bear to look his father in the eye. The man who had once been larger than life, with his methods and his Motown, was reduced to skin and bones. David couldn't bring himself to hold his father's clammy hand, much less sit by his bedside.

Mitch held it together better, letting his hand rest near their father's, speaking to him as though he still understood. David wished he'd done the same.

"Sometimes I think I should've helped more. I was weighed down by it all. It wasn't right to let you carry everything."

It was shame, David wore on that porch, covering him like a coat. When his father finally passed, David felt a twisted relief.

The funeral was a blur, with Mitch handling the details, shielding his sadness behind logic and numbers.

"That's what I remember from the funeral. That I never figured you for a numbers guy," David said.

Mitch smirked. "Didn't figure you'd end up cutting up bodies for a living, either."

David chuckled. "Touché."

He was surprised that Mitch had chosen such a structured profession, so far removed from the rough-and-tumble guy David remembered. The one quick to shut shit down with his fists.

David shifted in his seat, half a bottle of beer in his hand, the cold neck against his palm. "You needed a change of scenery, I guess. This place suits you."

Mitch raised an eyebrow. "Uh-huh. So, what's really going on? Last time we talked, you sounded... off."

David let out a breath, avoiding his brother's gaze. "Just... a lot of things, Mitch. Stuff with Addison, Mary... I don't know anymore. Everything feels tangled."

Mitch gave a slow nod, lifting the bottle again. "That's one way to put it." He leaned forward. "You still thinking about what happened? With Mary?"

Mitch was twice divorced and knew a thing or two about ex-wives.

David's throat tightened. "Mary's remarried, and out of my hair. It's Addison I worry about. She's in college now and finding her way. I thought I could just let it go, give her space, but it's like I can't. She's not even talking to me much anymore."

Mitch sat with it, bottle balanced on his knee.

"She's grown. You can't force her to care. If she wants distance, she'll take it."

David's jaw tightened.

"You think I haven't tried?"

Mitch's brow ticked up, a quiet check.

"Easy! I'm not saying you didn't. Just saying maybe she needs space. Let her figure it out on her own time."

Mitch leaned back in the chair, exhaled slow.

"It's like Mom at Dad's funeral, remember? We got it all wrong, imagining that she wanted a life without Dad, like she'd been waiting for her time in the sun. You can't predict how things will play out."

Their mother had spent her life in service to their father, mouse-quiet, appearing only when summoned. A shadow figure, blending into loud wallpaper, content with second fiddle and fading edges.

"We assumed she'd hightail it to Florida, and dye her hair pink," David chuckled.

There was no fanfare. After he died, their mother wandered the house, pausing at photographs like they might answer back. She sat in the living room without turning on the lights. Ate crackers for dinner. Spoke only when asked a question. Freed from his iron grip, she didn't come alive. She withered. Pneumonia took her a year later, sneaking up like a thief, filling her lungs with toxins. She lived quietly and went out with a whisper.

David's jaw tightened, angry at all the unfairness at the way life played out. For him, for Addison, for his Mom, Dad, and Mitch.

"I just get in the weeds with it, Mitch. I want to help, not control. That's my kid. But she treats me like a stranger, and I don't know what I did wrong."

Mitch leaned back, running a hand through his hair. "I get it. But, hell, Davie, I don't have the answers either. You get the job done, day after day, and hope you're doing enough. That's all parenting can be."

David looked up. "Is that what you think? I'm not doing enough?"

Mitch raised his hands, palms out, his gesture a mea culpa. "No, I didn't mean it like that. I'm saying... sometimes, you just have to let go. You can't fix everything. Hell, I can't even fix half the stuff in my life."

David laughed, a hollow sound. "You always seem to have it together, Mitch. I don't."

Mitch gave a dry chuckle. "Yeah, well, that's a whole other problem. I don't have it together, I just pretend to. You know what I mean? People think I've got it all figured out, but inside, I'm just... winging it. Same as you."

David sighed. "I don't know if I can do this anymore. I can't just keep pretending."

Mitch stood up, crossed the porch, and came back with two fresh brews. "Maybe you don't have to pretend. But you do have to figure out how to live with it. Whatever 'it' is."

David took the beer and cracked it open. The sound was too loud in the quiet night. "I don't know how."

Mitch sat down beside him. "None of us do. But you'll get through it. You're stronger than you think. You just gotta stop holding on to what's already gone."

David's throat burned. "I wish I could."

They sat in silence for a long while, the weight of the past pressing down on them like the thick Georgia air.

David remembered the night their father vomited blood. It

splattered the sheets, pooled in the creases of his neck. David stood by the bed, frozen. He knew what to do, had cleaned up worse in the morgue without blinking. But this was different. This was his Dad. Mitch had come to the rescue, rolling their father on his side, towels pressed to his mouth. David busied himself running water in the sink with shaking hands. It sat on him, a layer of rust and shame.

Mitch's voice broke the silence. "We're not our parents, David. They didn't know how to do this. But we do. We don't have to follow their path."

David looked at Mitch, feeling something stir in his chest. "Yeah. I just don't know where to start."

Mitch clapped him on the shoulder. "Take it one step at a time. And hey, if you need someone to talk to, I'm here. You don't have to go through this alone."

He kept his hand steady on David's back. "I mean it, don't be a stranger. You and me, brother. That's really all we got left."

David nodded, a heavy sigh leaving his chest. "Thanks, Mitch."

They sat there for a long while until the regret left, and in its place, an understanding, an inkling, of brotherly love.

David exhaled. This visit provided a direction, a compass built from scars.

Chapter 38

A Meeting of the Minds

David's head was renewed and refocused from his trip to Georgia, committed fully to confronting Addison and asking her what exactly she was playing at and why. He pumped himself up, full of not taking no's for answers, ever the father wielding authority.

He got up the courage to call her, voicemail stern, to say he was back in town and wanted to meet.

"Let's meet at the playground next to my house, over by the Greenway." He figured that a public place could generate goodwill. It was strategic, that had been their favorite spot when Addison was little, when all she wanted to do was swing until dusk, when the cold finally called them back home, her cheeks baby doll pink.

"Alright, Dad," she said when she called back. "I can meet later today, I'm out of class and have nothing better to do." She sounded resigned on the phone, but at least she wasn't dodging his calls. She'd made it her full-time job to duck, weave, and ignore him as of late.

David dressed nervously, feeling the body jitters and a bit of dry mouth. He had a couple more vacation days left and was thankful for them, glad to not have to pretend to focus on work. He spent the day watching the clock, counting down the minutes like a doomsday watch.

She had gotten there first, and was sitting on a swing, head resting against the links. She looked sad enough to shake the earth, in a place meant only for happiness and merry-go-rounds. She wasn't swinging, just rocking and waiting.

The park was empty. David jogged to meet her, grabbing the open swing beside her. He knew she'd speak first. It was her rodeo; he understood that now.

"It's not fair, I know," she began. "I asked you to do all this. But I thought I would feel different. Vindicated or avenged, or better than I was." Addison stopped her feet, the swing no longer moving. She turned to face him.

"But all I feel is sad. About this, about everything. I lost myself when he did this to me and now, I lost even more because of what you did. Soon I'll have nothing left."

He paused, wanting to interject but knowing her well enough to know that she wasn't done.

"I thought that's what I wanted, Dad. Him gone. But I realize now that it won't bring what I lost back. And now what I've lost is you. I feel like our closeness shriveled, and when I look at you, I see Josh and what you did."

David didn't react, but he thought, *I guess there's a difference in wanting John Wayne for a father and having him.* He'd been reduced, less paternal, more criminal. It wasn't fair, but he let her speak her peace.

"Now that I know, how can I not let it change us? There's blood on my hands and yours too. We are sick with it. And I did this, I made you a murderer, and for that I will always be sorry. You're a good man and I took that from you."

She looked at the ground, studying every pebble.

It was David's turn to assuage her.

"That's too simplistic a take, Addison. I'm still the same person, just a man that loves his daughter. What I did proves that, but it doesn't change us. Or me."

He kept to himself the troubles at work and the mandated suspension, the drinking that had up-ticked, the sleep that never fully came. Those were his secrets, not Addison's to bear.

"I just don't agree," she gulped, heavy with the truth of it all.

She couldn't look at him. She looked at her bare legs, and he saw a tear fall onto them. He wanted to hug her, but the distance between them was canyon deep. David thought he might still be able to reach her, might still connect, but was afraid she would flinch if he touched her, which would be worse than never trying at all.

All that he had done before and would do in the future was erased by a singular night in January. His emotions dialed up, threatening an explosion. This was not how the narrative should be written. He expected an ocean of thanks but got only averted eyes.

"So, what you're saying is that to you, I'm William Munny, a stone-cold killer of kids who thwarted Lady Justice." He laughed but it sounded hollow. "There's already a script for that, and it's called *Unforgiven*. Don't reduce me to that, Addison. It's not fair. Think with your head. You're better than this."

He crossed his arms, fuming, wishing he could vacate this playground and this conversation.

"It's not my head saying all this, Dad, it's my heart. When I look at you, I feel like I don't know who you are anymore. I can't see you the same, it's all messed up, and I just think I can't see you apart from what you did. I wasn't there, I don't know the details, but it's written all over your face."

So she'd stay away, to spare herself the trouble of taking ownership in this, he thought.

He didn't say a word, but in his imagination, David morphed into the Hulk, angry, green, and soaking in rage. He felt his fury could topple the playground, that he could put his fingers in the dirt and cause earthquakes.

"I think that's pretty rich, coming from you Addison. This whole thing was your idea, and now you want to let me hang for it. What you need is a mirror, Spitfire. And maybe, a better heart."

It was another one of the parental stings he'd later wish to undue. David knew as soon as he said it that turning on Addison would only make her cry, make things worse. He wanted to be mean because he was hurt. But that wouldn't change her mind.

"So, let me understand here. I did what you asked, and it didn't change a damn thing."

She nodded, chin to chest.

"Exactly," she whispered, "it only made things worse. It broke everything, completely. I feel worse, you feel worse. We're complicit."

David's body trembled with anger, and he didn't trust himself to say another word. Nothing in his life compared to this. Not Roque's sudden change of heart. Not Don holding Mary's hand at the hospital cotillion. This feeling was brand new and pure heat. Anger so volatile, if he opened his mouth at that moment, it would cause a flash flood, set to topple every good thing.

The only option he had left was to leave, and leave fast, before he started throwing punches or worse. His feet found the ground, his shoes got to walking.

"Dr. Coben says…" she started.

David froze and turned around. He looked at Addison and took a deep breath.

What came out was not pretty.

"Oh, give me a break with this surrogate parent shit, Addison. Your mother and I spent months nursing you back to health. Never mind the fact that you weren't supposed to tell your fucking dime store therapist anything about this. What I don't understand is why you'd think I care what some shrink has to say? It means nothing to me."

His words were hatred, he spat them so they were harsh. Spittle creased near his mouth.

"I DIDN'T tell her anything about this!" Her voice edged into a whine. "What I meant was, you aren't hearing me. You don't listen to me, and she said that…."

"Oh, I heard you PLENTY, Addison. I heard what you wanted, how you felt, and every other emotion for the better part of this year. In fact, I'm sick of hearing about it. I did what YOU WANTED, now you want to complain, to hang every bad thing on my head." He wanted to stop, to pump the breaks, but he couldn't. "So now, you are gonna quote some wanna be physician advice back to me, from therapy that I PAY FOR. I finance your mental health and do your dirty deeds, without so much as a thank you."

Addison shook her head, reverting to tears, which was always worse than anger. The silent treatment stayed, way past his slow counting to one thousand, past the time it took David to leave the park and climb in the Jeep. He idled the engine, still waiting to give her a ride.

She stayed on the swings.

Fine, let her stew, he spat. David turned up the heat in the car, the temperature matching his mood.

His drive home was peppered with furious thoughts. He'd expected to be a cuckold for Mary, not Addison. The person to fear here hadn't been Josh. It was his own spoiled daughter, asking for vengeance then taking none of the blame.

David felt chilled at the evidence of his daughter turned

monster, the kind of kid who could switch masks mid-sentence and make love look like weakness.

David slammed the door to the Jeep, his anger leaking through the garage, up the steps, and through the kitchen. It pooled in the living room and trickled to the bathroom. By the time he got to his bedroom, the deluge had been reduced to apologies and excuses, ways to mend things that were broken.

He lay on the bed, staring at the ceiling, trying to make sense of how it had all unraveled. No answers came. Just the low hum of the fan and the quiet scrape of old mistakes.

Chapter 39

Lost and Found

A lost daughter. He couldn't explain what Addison meant to him, to pack an entire person's life into a summation of moments. It was easier to drift into the past, reviewing those early pool-laden summers with her becoming brown as a biscuit in a way his Irish pigment never could. He thought of what was, not what is, distracting himself with a movie reel of the daughter he felt he lost.

I could start over, David reasoned. *50 is ancient, but playboys do it all the time.* Bu the idea of replacing Addison with another child just made him feel low-down. He'd had the perfect child, but that future got spoiled, left out like milk in the summer sun.

David trudged back to work, still lost in a treasure trove of memories. Last night he'd looked through photo albums, reminiscing about what he told Addison about his father. He'd turned the old man into a nicer version than he'd known, someone who died young and was worth missing.

Maybe that's what she will do to me, David thought. *Turn me into someone else, or cut me out, like forced amnesia.*

A daughter that wasn't. A father, long gone.

The lab was silent. He tossed his leather briefcase on his desk.

He peeked out the hallway, hoping for Craig.

Instead, he found Dr. Rudger, the worst one of the bunch.

"David. Welcome back. Have a seat. Let's chat." Dr. Rudger gestured to his office chair while he gathered himself behind his executive desk.

David pressed his hands together. Dr. Rudger was the kind of doctor who only liked the accolades, not the work. He was quick to author paper after paper, as evidenced by his degrees and certificates on the wall, and the magazines he'd saved with his publications. To David, he was a walking eye-roll, one best ignored. This quick chat could turn into an hour lecture since Dr. Rudger loved nothing more than having a captive audience.

"As I said, glad to have you back, David. I'll let the others know you're here. I hope your rest gave you some perspective." He smiled, but it was slimy, all used car salesman.

"Thanks. It was useful. I'm back and ready to work."

"About that," Dr. Rudger began. "The way things are structured here at the hospital, and with your contract, is that you accepted a lower base salary in exchange for performance or quality bonuses."

"Yes," David replied. He withheld the last of the sentence, which was, *I've worked here for almost twenty years so I know how my paycheck works, you cocky idiot.*

"Well, as such," Dr. Rudger continued, "you can also see our concern, since your performance has not been exemplary as of late." He frowned, clown-like, over-hyped and drawn on. "It pains me to be the one to tell you that you won't be earning a bonus this quarter. For obvious reasons." Dr. Rudger leaned back in his chair, tapping his pencil against the desk.

It took every ounce of restraint not to walk out of the building.

David inhaled and held it. He thought of the four years of

college, then medical school. Of Ricky his roommate, and all his mentors. Of Cormac, and residency, and the murder club. Of Springsteen, and cowboys, of Craig, and Dr. Gill.

And of Addison, the one he knew best. Of her ins and outs. How she laughed when David didn't realize he had his shirt on backwards, or had left his Breathe Right strip on at breakfast. The culmination of the movies and songs they shared, the books they loved, the secrets they kept. His daughter, his best friend, his only friend, the one he thought was worth fighting for.

David kept quiet, drained of all emotion and resolve.

Dr. Rudger couldn't break his heart. Money meant nothing. Everything he cared about, he'd already lost.

"Thanks for the chat," David said, standing up, signaling the end of the conversation. "I understand, and now, I have work to get back to."

"Ask Craig about taking overnight call next month!" Dr. Rudger concluded, yelling his last admonishment at David's back.

David went to his office and shut the door. It didn't have a lock, but he no longer cared. He went to his desk, held his head in his hands, and sobbed.

For all he had lost. For all he had yet to lose.

After twenty minutes, he grabbed tissues, blew his nose, and started his day in earnest.

The day trudged by and his phone remained silent, no word, no ring from Addison.

Nights haunted David, reminding him of every flaw he possessed. Nightmares of Josh's last moments ping-ponged through his brain, rounding the bases, breaking him down further. David used to love geometry, and the way you could see a shape from all angles. But he was sick and tired of himself.

The next morning, he took a good look at himself in the mirror. His hair had grown out scraggly from his buzz cut. His face was gaunt, and a quick weight check showed another twelve-pound weight loss. He looked scared and slim, a sliver of who he once was.

He realized he was a man with a choice. He stared at himself in the mirror, playing it three different ways. He could wallow and ruminate on all he lost. He could become Addison's punching bag, or go to the cops, confess it all, and take his prison sentence on the chin. Or he could quit work, as the drive had left him anyway. Most days he had to force himself to enjoy what he once adored, the temptation of unused sick days dangling, precious apple temptations, just waiting to be used. That way was to fold, to give up and shut down, to live a less than life.

Or door number four: embrace the villain Addison already believed him to be. Shrug off the wreckage, chase what he wanted, and never look back. After the months of planning, analyzing, and worrying, he deserved a break. He could take a leave of absence or go back to Georgia and drink beer with Mitch. He could curate a sabbatical fixed on his own desires, be selfish for once, or for a lifetime. He'd continue to fight with Addison and Mary, to wage war at Harris Teeter, on King Street, or wherever their paths crossed. He grumbled, noting that path led only to anger, with vengeance and regret at the wheel. He'd done enough of that.

There was only one path to take, the hardest and best of all. He would be the hero, the one that rides into the sunset. The martyr who stepped aside, giving Mary and Addison the freedom his absence allowed. He'd transfer to somewhere warmer, start living his life on his own peaceful terms. A plot of land, a fridge full of Mammy's Milk, with his westerns to keep him company. He could curate a future, one of his own making.

David grabbed a razor, ready to clean the mess he'd made of his face.

All new starts should begin with a fresh shave.

Chapter 40

A Simple Favor

Before he decided to ride off into the sunset, David reached out to Mary. He owed her a mea culpa, or at least an attempt to make things right. After sorting through his newfound feelings, he realized it wasn't fair to lump her in with their daughter. For once, Mary was innocent.

He'd drop by her place, hat in hand, and see if she could dole out any motherly wisdom. David wanted to exhaust all his options before writing himself a hero's sendoff.

David let the radio play on his drive to Banner-Elk. He took in the views as he circled Mary's driveway, the flowerbeds overflowing, the three-story porch abuzz with wind and bees. He'd miss summer in the High Country, Boone's greatest season. The town rejoiced since they only got two months' worth of shorts-wearing days. Locals came out of their hibernation, and the mood was buoyant and bright. A whole legion of people enjoying Frisbee golf in the sunshine, sleeping in hammocks, and singing Bob Marley. There were worse places to live.

David jogged to Mary's doorstep, ready for whatever lecture

she'd given him. He wondered what she made of Addison and their newfound silence. He hadn't called to let her know he was coming. Catching Mary off guard always worked in his favor. She gave more droplets of her former self if surprised. If not, the veneer of trophy wife held fast, and all he got was her distaste.

She answered the doorbell on the first ring, dressed to impress even though she was home alone. David wondered if she dressed up just for the housekeeper.

That's sad, he thought. But who was he to judge?

Mary wore cashmere and pink lipstick, bright and bubbly beneath the fluorescent lights.

"Well, well, well. Look who it is," she drawled. "Seems like you're the one at the bottom of the barrel now." She turned, inviting him in. David followed, taking in the marble staircase, the two-story gas fireplace.

"I've waited years for this to happen," Mary gloated. "Me. First-place parent." She raised her arms, clasped her hands like a champ, and gave him a smug little bow.

"And Don said something about your work not going so well?" Mary dropped herself on a stool in the kitchen. She tilted her chin, gazing at David, unpacking all she saw.

David didn't even have the energy to roll his eyes.

"Yes, that's correct."

"Cut the shit out, David. You know I don't want to win by default."

She tapped her manicured nails on the counter. He pulled up a chair. Like everything in the house, it was pretty but uncomfortable, over-stuffed and over-patterned with no give to it.

Her kitchen was decorated in gold and smelled like juniper and something sharper. She'd paired down the blonde, muting it with streaks of honey. David tried not to study her, but Mary encouraged it, puckering her lips.

Everything in her home was staged, down to the silver bracelet dangling on her wrist and sparkling white cabinets, no bright colors to compete with its shine. Tables glistened too, and Mary spun in the center, a sparkling version of the American dream.

"I don't know what you mean, Mary," he admitted, "Everything you just said is true."

Mary's posture was straight, her eyes meeting his, as if their meeting were an audition and he was to begin. David eyed the wall-papered walls, half-expecting to see Martha Stewart step out with a matching throw pillow.

He cleared his throat, wondering how to navigate the minefields of things Mary couldn't know. But she surprised him by speaking first.

"I've spent years where you are, at the low rung of the parenting ladder," she said, her voice heavy. "Addison loves to cast me into various roles for her own amusement. Mom this, and Mom that, full of ideas about things I didn't do."

"I'm sure." David didn't know how to address the distance between her and Addison, every bit a hung jury.

"No need to think I'm an enemy, David. I don't like this new distance between you two anymore than you do." That surprised David. He'd assumed Mary was always ready for easy competition.

She continued, "Usually she loved comparing us, playing one against the other. You know, typical divorced kid stuff. But this time she went quiet. That's when I knew something was off between you two. And nothing good would come of it."

Again, he struggled to hide his astonishment. He thought Mary would be gleeful about his demise, that she'd wield this victory all over town, letting the world see a rekindled mother-daughter rela-tionship, fresh and blooming. He fully expected to have to grovel for intel, to beg or bribe Mary till she took pity on him like the stray dog he was.

"You and I," she said flatly, "ended a long time ago. No point dragging through the ruins. As a husband, you were passable at best. Barely a C student. Too closed off, lackluster." She studied her manicure.

David sighed, familiar with the critiqued refrain.

But then she looked up. "As a father, though? You were aces, David. I mean that. I couldn't have done it without you. If anything, maybe you did too much. The two of you had this... thing. This bond. I was always just orbiting it, watching from the edge."

David glanced down at his hands in his lap, willing himself not to cry in front of a woman who wouldn't acknowledge his tears. He nodded, not trusting his voice, knowing any waver this way or that could be used for ammunition.

Remember that whatever you say, she will use it for her own devices, his head warned. But like Addison, he'd cast Mary too harshly, letting her play out a template he'd devised, not one of her own making.

She spoke softly, a kindness, allowing him to gather himself.

"I know you were meant to be a father. And you know that's true because that's the function of an ex-wife. They will always be around to tell you the truth. That's all I can do now."

One teardrop snaked down his cheek. He willed himself to limit it to one. One was pure, it was humbling. Any more and she'd kick him to the curb or video tape it, run it for 24 hours on his next birthday.

Mary didn't pretend not to notice, her eyes widening and her face a shade of concern.

"It can't be all that bad, David. Children go through phases; she just needs time." Mary's voice removed all emotion. She was at her best when she channeled the British, a stiff upper lip, content to sweep anything sordid under the rug.

He shook his head. He wanted to argue, to let Mary know something was broken. But he couldn't give her the truth or a confession.

"Will you put in a good word for me?" he asked. "I figure you owe me a couple favors." He shot her a smile, and she returned it.

"Sure David, it looks like you need it." Her voice was crisp, not questioning, certain as the sun would rise.

"I think I do."

There was more she could say then. Ask if he was okay, get him a coffee, a book to borrow, brew a tea. He saw those hostess mannerisms flash over her features, ways that she could comfort him, debating if she should. She settled instead on a hand pat, one a nun might give, something short and perfunctory, edging him on his way.

David wanted to hate her. Not with the anger he'd reserved for Addison and her selfishness. He couldn't produce anything that fierce. But a tiny flick of irritation bubbled up, about what he deserved, about the times he'd cared for her in sickness and in health.

He glanced her way, debated starting a fight.

She was inspecting her nails, not even glancing his way. Not a single crease touched her forehead. Botox had erased both wrinkles and emotion. She continued to search for chips in her perfect polish.

David recalled who he was speaking to. This was Mary, someone who could pick up and put down emotions so fast it'd give normal people a migraine. She was perfunctory, and impersonal, but she didn't owe him a thing.

Their lives only ran parallel, where she could witness his pain and not want to heal it. That was as it should be, Mary adhering to her side of the deal. It was David who wanted comfort but was too proud to ask. Comfort from a place no longer allowed; no bosom to burrow into, no one to ask about the status of his heart. He was the inappropriate one, set to blame Mary for her lack of affection when he'd spent years rejecting it.

As he trudged toward the door, another wave of self-deprecation caught him in a riptide. He was the one who made Addison his universe. Mary had diversified, with Don and her legion of blondes, who spent every Saturday listening to live music at Twigs in Blowing Rock.

David had allowed Addison to fill up every lonely crack in his heart, preferring the twinship of her company. Now everything was severed, and he was left reaching for someone who was long gone.

"Thanks, Mary," he mumbled, leaving her holding the front door open, watching him walk down the path to his car before shutting it tight.

He'd let her sink in Addison's newfound affections, bright like a Christmas ornament. It was only that, a shimmering falsehood. If Mary wanted that life, she could have it. A storm cloud of emotion followed him into the car, each thought sadder than the next, full of life's unfairness, reigning down atop his hang-dog head.

Chapter 41

The Good The Bad and The Ugly

Looking back, David wondered why he agreed to do it. He took on a one-sided bargain, content to take a life just because Addison dictated it.

The emotional cues factored in, her wincing, the antiseptic smell of the hospital, the too bright flickering lights. Maybe all those sensory clues collaborated to cloud his better judgment.

Dark thoughts had warned him that first night. His subconscious sent up an emergency flare that Addison might've written the summary before the prologue, knowing things would change, but focused only on her own well-being.

David had shrugged off any other explanations. He'd been the sacrificial lamb, late to the party, certain he was dining with the others until he read the menu. Addison had sent him to the slaughter.

It wasn't all her fault. His cowboy obsession had tipped his hand. David knew he always wanted to be the guns-blazing hero, the vigilante doing what any father worth his salt would do. Like Mitch, like a man, ready and willing to make things right.

But David forgot that love was a fickle mistress.

He'd woken up that morning, his face slick with sweat. His dream was a memory from way back. It was real, and he hated that his mind had saved it for this moment.

Everything would've changed it he'd remembered it months ago. A parable, right there for the taking, straight out of their shared life, only recalled too late.

Addison had been five and had come with David to do a round at the local drug lab. While he was dictating, she saw a mouse, not full grown, but big enough to make her scream.

She stood on a chair, begging him to kill it.

"It's huge, Daddy do it! It'll bite me!" He heard that hint of fear in her voice and that's all he heard. He rushed over, not thinking, and stomped it with his boot. He turned, afraid Addison would topple off the chair.

The look on her face was terror. He glanced down, seeing what she saw. The mouse was twitching, its flattened shape removed of all fullness, a stain of blood and bones. The crunch rang back in his ears, and his stomach soured. Nausea threatened to call his bluff. He covered the crime with his foot, keeping it glued to the floor.

But it was too late. Addison had seen, and she was wailing. At first he thought it was from relief, and he felt like a gladiator for a whole 60 seconds. But the tears kept coming and he realized they were from regret. She'd realized after the fact that's not what she wanted at all.

"You killed him!" she said, voice edging toward hysteria, the same one that had asked him to do the deed moments earlier.

"You killed him!" she screamed, like the mouse was her child-hood pet she'd raised from a mousling, feeding him bits of stolen cheese.

"Dad! You killed him, you killlllllled him." She wouldn't stop. She crumbled to the ground, a ball of tears and snot. David, ashamed, shuffle-footed to the door to clean up the mess. He'd thought he'd earned the champion prize only to discover he was the antihero after all.

If only he'd remembered the mouse, the symbolism, the idea that wanting something gone and doing the deed were in different leagues. But of all the memories he'd turned over the past months, that one got left out. The most important one, the best parallel, was kept out of his subconscious until now, left to torture him with regret.

And regret was what it was. Just yesterday, outside of Wilson's, he clocked Addison across the street. She'd walked alone, shoulders back, dressed in a white jumpsuit he'd never seen before. He watched her, wondering what she'd do when she saw him.

Before, she'd have crossed the street, called out a quick, "Hey Dad!" a spring in her step and her tone. Her arm would've waved high in the air, a smile perched on her lovely face, her voice carrying across the street.

But now, a pinprick hesitation. A caution in her eyes. She saw him, knew he was there, thought of calling to him, but her arm conducted a series of starts and stutters. She held it close to her chest, thinking better of it. She cocked her head, a veil of doubt covering her face. She turned around, walking against the wind, and never looked back.

Their relationship had been reduced to the once-a-week duty call. David held in his emotions, but she kept it impersonal, light on details, light on love.

She shared hastily purchased birthday gift items, things under "Good for Dads" lists instead of the homemade pictures she used to make for him. Now, gifts were formalities, like a plain tie, when she knew he wore a polo to work.

It was as if Josh had erased all the facts of David, and Addison was content to write him off with perfect penmanship and cold calligraphy.

Next Christmas he'd be lucky if she got him a candle, if she showed her face at all. He'd become a generic store-bought version, a manager's special Dad. Someone she could reference on Father's day. A last name, and nothing more.

David wrote letters upon letters in his mind, with themes of apology, anger, and regret. He sought for the best words to right old wrongs. Mostly, he just wanted to convince her everything they had was still there. He still loved Addison the same, his blood and hers still wrapped in family DNA. Because she dodged his calls, he could only create his own monologues of what to say, words to make things right.

He'd summarized all his thoughts in one last letter, short and to the point. It contained a truth, boiled down and spit out. While he didn't use the word murder, he let her know his narrative.

In the end, he killed Josh himself. He wanted the instant revenge, he longed to pull the proverbial trigger, he needed to do something for justice, that he couldn't come back from fully.

In David's life, he'd always been the good guy and he wanted to have a taste of what it felt like to be the bad one, the one who did something and didn't stare, or cry, or whine about the way the world was.

He didn't get a taste for it. Killing Josh didn't spring-load a wish to start stacking up victims or higher body counts. It didn't spark a challenge in him to become a serial killer, nor did he wonder anymore about ways to kill. Having done it, like Harper Lee writing *To Kill a Mockingbird*, he realized he only had one murder in him. As the great Josie Wales said, "There are some folks out there that just need killing," and now there was one less of that type.

David told Addison so when he decided on the words, vague

enough to plead plausible doubt, written in his chicken scratch
scrawl.

*Maybe you're right about what you said, Addison.
But for you, any ending to your pain was worth it,
no matter what the cost. As Judge Roy Bean says,
it's been my honor to adore you. You're the best
daughter I've ever had. I will always love you,
Spitfire.*

Love, Dad.

David read the words and still found them wanting, tearing up
the paper into pieces of confetti, because there was nothing left to
say. Every hand had been played out, except the final card waiting
in his sleeve.

Chapter 42

End and Begin Again

David knew he was done when he was out of words. Addison could have the freedom she wanted, and he'd sail down the open road, carried there by a modest bank account and what could fit in the trunk and back seat of the ol' Jeep.

David put his house on the market the next day, not alerting anyone, tired as he was of other people's opinions. The next week, it sold over value, the realtor pink-cheeked with such an easy commission check. He donated the furniture, ready to wash his hands of anything complicated. He'd had enough drama to last two lifetimes, and furniture was the least of his concerns.

David knew he must tell Mary now that their days of sharing a town and a daughter were done. She'd be ecstatic, given that she could now visit the gym and her favorite restaurant, Coyote Kitchen, in peace, without the threat of running into her ex-husband. Boone would officially be hers, and she'd rejoice with girl-friends at Twigs, drunk on Cosmopolitans and the assurance that David was long gone. They'd always loved Don more, pleased that he showered Mary with gifts galore, agreeing to ignore his widening midsection with every gemstone proffered. They'd all made the same deal, allowing those mediocre men to woo them with talks of built-ins and bank accounts. Each blonde was identical, thin and trim, passing their days with generous Griego, and laughing too loudly to cover up life's hard questions.

Mary would reign among them, queen of the women who settled.

So be it.

If she thought this was a hat-in-hand visit like the last one, Mary would be wrong. This was a just the facts ma'am, in and out, a signoff that hopefully never left the front stoop.

David carried a shoebox full of pictures with the unloaded gun placed on top, this time ready to cut off every protest. The would-be murder weapon needed to be reunited with its rightful owner, tying up another loose end. This time he called ahead, wanting her ready and waiting for him and the quick goodbye he'd offer.

He stood in the cold, looking at the swept sidewalk, wondering who she paid to take care of all the minute details. Probably a neighborly handyman, one easy to dismiss, the courier and intermediary to her version of keeping up with the Joneses.

Mary came to the door, all gentlemen prefer blondes, over-dressed and perfectly coiffed for a dreary stay-at-home day. He could see her now for the caricature she was, reminding him it was time to get the heck outta Dodge.

"Another visit? To what do I owe the honor, David?" she purred.

"Just came to drop off something you left behind a while back. Addressed to *Annie Get Your Gun*, I believe?" He tried for a smile.

She opened her eyes wide and ushered him inside, unwilling to do a weapons exchange on her front stoop.

"Goodness gracious, David, who brings a gun into a house like that?" she clucked at him, shooing him to the side. "What's gotten into you? I thought you'd already taken care of this."

"I wanted to return it you, Mary," his voice already sneaking toward sarcastic. "Seeing I'm leaving the state, and you are the rightful owner. You should've taken it a long time ago, if we're going to start throwing stones at each other." He crossed his arms. "But it's too early for all that. Let me return it and be on my way."

"Oh okay, so you want to go for the dramatics of it all. I see."

She eyed him up and down, until what he said registered.

"What do you mean going away?"

He wondered how much to disclose. David had been practicing his explanation, but even a devout Buddhist would struggle going even one round with his ex-wife. David aimed for an explanation that would assuage her curiosity but discourage lingering questions.

"You always said I pretended to be a cowboy. Well, Mary, I've taken your advice to heart, and I'm moving out West. I figured it's never too late to change, and that's where I'll be the happiest. Turns out you can take the man out of the western, but not the western outta the man."

He was banking that by incorporating an old joke of theirs that she'd acquiesce faster. Mary had loved to tease him about cattle drives and being long in the saddle.

She cackled, sure he was joking, until he didn't join in.

"Just something I've gotta do for me, I guess." He shrugged, hoping the nonchalance seemed authentic.

She gave him a side eye, like his story wasn't adding up right.

"Retiring. At your age, it seems a bit uncharacteristic of you. Think you better have something to drink so I can get this straight. You're just up and leaving the hospital, the town, Addison, every-thing... YOU?"

"Well, I don't know if you know me that well anymore." He said it flat, not wanting to prolong this farewell into an argument.

She gave him her best principal stare and his heart beat double time. Mary was the only one so far who had questioned his narrative.

David had given the hospital a short version of an "I'm sick of the snow, seeking employment elsewhere" speech. Dr. Rudger had frowned and talked about locum tenums before providing a stale cake send off. Craig gave him a card, and the lab girls were more concerned about how this would impact their job than his future whereabouts. Dr. Gill gave him an extra bonus for the road, confusion in his face with questions he didn't get to ask.

David ate his mediocre goodbye party cake, even though the buttercream tasted sour. The administrators had begun screening for his replacement immediately. They tried to dampen their enthusiasm, but he knew they were hoping for a younger model willing to work for less. It hurt that he was easily replaceable.

He packed up the next day, telling Addison he wasn't leaving for another week.

"It's not goodbye forever, Addison. Just for right now. Take some time in Colorado." He paused, ever hopeful. "Maybe you'll come visit and like it."

"Good for you, Dad," she'd remarked.

David decided then to head for North Carolina. All those beach dreams by her hospital bed belonged to Addison, not him. But when Wilmington flashed a want ad for a board-certified pathologist, he took it. He'd go to work, then soak in the sun and salt. Those fever dreams of waves and buckets of Corona that once felt prophetic now offered a chance at his own healing.

He ditched his cell and bought a burner phone, cutting every last thread. No forwarding number, no "just in case." There would be no search party, no police, no suspect, no crime. Just an overdose, a dad, and a daughter growing up. Now came the final severing—no breadcrumbs, no safety nets.

It was petty, not telling Addison goodbye. But David had been distraught, all these emotions weighing on his chest like a prodromal heart attack. If Addison was done having a father, she deserved to know how that felt.

He'd take off in the night, a trail of echoes and dead ends. A coward, like he always thought. But he'd been reduced to a ball of hurt, ready and willing to give anything else a shot. He'd tried to find the words to tell Addison what she meant to him, and how he'd hoped for a reconciliation. Instead, there was nothing left to say, and he was already barely keeping his head above water.

Mary poured herself a copious amount of wine in a glass that looked like a margarita bowl. Her chef's kitchen gleamed, not a dish in the sink or a crumb on the counter, but that just made it look unlived in.

"Well David," she began, settling him back in the present moment. "Just one more question remains. What about our daughter? You think up and leavin' is the best for her? I doubt that."

He noticed that Mary always slipped into an accent when he was there, never able to tame down her roots around someone who recognized them. She'd unknowingly hit the crux of the matter, the bullseye in the damned if you do, damned if you don't puzzle he was in.

He couldn't say that Addison wanted him gone without opening a whole can of nosiness for Mary to feast upon. He hadn't clarified if the request in the park was a literal one, or an exaggeration created by his brain's neurons. He'd gotten the gist of it, that what was left for them held no redemption. Addison had been clear that their closeness had ended, so David developed his own plan, a new take on the old man and the sea.

He stayed silent as Mary stared him down.

She squared her shoulders, a fighting stance, content to wait him out. When Mary's mind was set, her stubbornness was a gauntlet no one could tame. Hell, she might lock him up till he confessed. She was a patient jailer, punishing him with stillness until his thoughts gave way.

"She knows about this, Mary. I'll be around. Just a bit farther away."

Mary continued to squint at him, hesitant, then dismissing him with a quick nod and practiced shrug. She grabbed the shoebox, holding it a good ways from her body, like it might bite her.

David slinked off with a quick "I'll call you, keep in touch" aside, the lie warm on his lips, as he cranked up the Jeep, owing nothing to nobody.

For Addison, he left a cardboard box of used books and a letter in the middle of his living room floor. He'd arranged for the realtor to let her in, told her that Addison had the only lingering key.

A weak way out, swift and without messy explanations. He feared a face-to-face confrontation would rip the last thread of his resolve. Walking away from Mary all those years ago had shattered him and he did not love her half as much. Leaving Addison felt treacherous, a living, breathing termination of parental rights. It was a betrayal carved in flesh, a wound that breathed and bled. Leaving was his only choice.

He left the house keys on the counter for the realtor, thinking of how big the house looked without furniture. He turned and breathed in the air that held no goodbyes. With each step, he thought of words he could say to make it all right. If he'd wronged a lover, the template was already set: roses, chocolates, good wine, and petals on a bed.

But with a daughter, there were no Hallmark cards, no apologies easily rendered. He still didn't know what to be sorry for, only that he'd undergone a loss to save her. That was the hero's version of how the story ended.

The letter he left was tucked into their shared favorite book, *A*

Prayer for Owen Meany, his last Christmas present from Addison. He left it on top of the box, the Post-it tucked around Hester's first introduction.

> *Addison, nothing has changed for me. Having you for a daughter was my life's greatest blessing. I have, do, and will always love you. Forget the rest, remember that. A father's watch begins with love and ends with love, and all I did was for you. I hope you find what you are looking for, and when you do, I hope you let me know.*
> *Love, Dad.*

He wasn't a poet, nor was he aiming to slap her senseless with reminisces, deciding instead to keep it short and sweet. Leaving a note felt like a tenant shucking out of paying rent, a forced flight in the dead of night. This was his last bit of courage, to write the words he knew and let them be.

He added a burned CD to the offering, labeled SOS in his sloppy penmanship. It was the culmination of all their favorite playlists. Addison had been 12, on the cusp of adolescence, when he made that CD. He'd labeled it a cry for help, proffering a musical remedy when the world got to be too much.

Addison joked that it really meant "Sick Of this Shit," so he added an alternative title beneath it, deciding to play along than be offended.

The music was good for what ails ya, no matter what it was called. As music aficionados, the McCalls were making mix tapes before it was cool, and this one was the best of the bunch. A joint effort, they'd hemmed and hawed about what to include and how each song should land. It took a week before the final product was created, in all its trebles and clef glory.

They agreed on the strong start (Mama's and Papa's "California Dreaming") then onto the slow build (Dexys' "Come on Eileen" and Townsend's "Let My Love Open the Door"). Then onto the break your heart set ("Operator" by Jim Croce and "He went to Paris" for all the Parrotheads), injecting a little pain that hurt so good. They rounded out the middle by hitting the audience with a little bit of nostalgia (Warren Zevon's "Werewolves of London" and The Band's "The Weight"), nothing too serious, a light sprinkling to keep it breezy. They argued about the way to close it out, her favorite being "You Can't Always Get What You Want."

He could hear her in his head, all tween edges, trying to impress him.

"IS there a more perfect song? Isssss there???" mouthed a toothy grin.

He preferred "Take a Walk on the Wild Side," and in the end, they settled

upon both. First Mick then Lou Reed, leaving Addison to pretend to sing with her hand mic.

"Du Du Doooooo…" she sang, until the nothing was left and the notes petered out to end the song.

They must've listened to the mix more than a thousand times. As the last note concluded, he'd say the same thing.

"It's only rock n roll, Addison," he'd say with a smile, setting up the punchline.

To which she'd reply, goofy until her age told her she couldn't do it anymore, "But I like it, I like it. Yes, I DOOOOO!" She'd say it loud and empowered, in a voice that knew they were the coolest of cool.

"I like it, I like it, yes, I do," David said it aloud now, the house so still that even his echo seemed lonely.

Then he decided to write his own ending, not content with how these cards had landed. David was tired of having other people dictate the terms of his life, and, as he checked the car one last time, he wrote himself a new narrative, more *Lonesome Dove* than a father's regret.

In his mind, Addison was there, yelling like "Shane, come back Shane," but instead it was for her father.

"Dad! Dad! Please don't go!" She should beg him not to leave.

But in his story, he gave her a stalwart, "I'll be around." In the movie of his life, that's how it all ended, with him resting with watchful eyes for the next big bad thing on the horizon. He'd utter a "Take her easy, Pilgrim," letting Addison know he'd be there in a jiffy should she ever need his service again.

He closed his eyes to the should have beens. He'd said goodbye to Boone and its memories.

Then David pulled out of his driveway, not a whiff of nostalgia, ready to go where the road took him. Alone again, alligator-skinned cowboy boots on and shining, ready to tackle what sins lay ahead with open eyes and a poorly stitched heart.

His Jeep was no steed, his leather seats no saddle, but he carried with him something all good cowboys knew.

When the tough got going, and there were no happy endings to be found, just more cattle drives and fireside chats, the good ones continued on. They let the sickness of life fall on their ready shoulders, holding it up because they had to, not because they wanted to. He'd join their ranks, those lost heroes, carrying a candle aloft for those who dealt tough justice, consequences be damned.

"For Texas and Miss Lilly," he said and turned on "Spirit in the Sky," playing it loud and proud, Ray-Bans on, back in the driver's seat, ready for part two of his story. No looking back allowed.

THE END

Acknowledgments

I am thankful for my father, John Boswell, who raised me in the lab and told me dark stories to keep me company. You never got to see me in my author era, but I think you'd be proud. I'm thankful for the parts of this novel that are true: for the way you shaped my taste in music, taught me about cowboys, and always promised to be there at the end of the line if I needed help.

I miss you every day. Writing this book cost me something. But it gave me you—the literary you. You used to say stories didn't need to be the way they were, just the way they should have been.

This is mine.

For that, and for you, I'll always be thankful.

To my husband, Bruce Baker, for your encouragement, your help, and your belief. Sometimes you believe in me more than I believe in myself. I knocked it out of the park when I married you. It was the best and easiest decision I ever made.

To my children, Addy and Julian Baker. Someday, I promise I'll write a book that you can read. I love you. Thanks for your patience when this book stole me away.

To my friendship Friday home team—Hayley, Katie, Mackenzie, and Peyton. Not everyone's friendship lasts a lifetime. I am so glad ours has! I couldn't love you more.

Thanks to Heather Felder for her book memes and recommendations.

To my friend Ashley Semerenko, for her thoughtfulness, cookies, and her reviews.

To the best librarian in the world, Alicia Cavitt, and her renowned editing prowess, and to the staff at Sharon Forks library. Parts of this novel were formed in the Adult Writing group. I am so thankful for your programming.

For Uncle Mike and Aunt Denise, for being the family I can depend on.

For Gayle and Mike Baker for your love and support.

To Carol Baker, for your encouragement.

To all my own Boone Goons, at Watauga and ASU, including Regina and Virginia. This book is a love letter to 2004 and 2005, when hacky sack was played, Klondike was rocking, and the living was easy. To my KD sisters who witnessed way too much. I'm looking at you April, Chels, Katie, and Cookie. Love to you always.

And finally, I owe this book to Leya and Steven Booth. Leya, I am sorry for that epically bad first draft. Thanks for not giving up on me! You make me a better writer, and I am beyond lucky to have you for an editor. Your diligence and details remain unmatched. This journey was made possible because of you.

And Steven, I remain so thankful for your passion, your know-how, and your perseverance. You took a chance on me, twice, and for that I'll always be grateful.

Finally, to readers everywhere—I want to know what you think! Before I was a writer, I was a reader, and my first love will always be words. Thank you for your time and commitment, and for peeking inside my brain and heart. I'm so thankful you read this book.

About the Author

Ashley Baker describes herself as a clinical psychologist by day, and a writer every moment in between. When she's not seeing patients or writing, she's in her North Georgia garden or playing Switch with her family. *The Ashes of Us* is her second novel. Her first novel, *The Furious Others*, was also published by Genius Books & Media. More information can be found at www.ashleybaker.net or connect with Ashley on Instagram @bakerwordnerd and on Facebook at Author Ashley Baker Page.

Linktree (all links & platforms):
https://linktr.ee/bakerwordnerd

Instagram:
https://instagram.com/bakerwordnerd

Facebook Author Page:
https://facebook.com/bakerwordnerd

Substack:
https://bakerwordnerd.substack.com